THE GRAMMAR RULES OF AFFECTION

The Grammar Rules of Affection

Passion and Pedagogy in Sidney, Shakespeare, and Jonson

ROSS KNECHT

UNIVERSITY OF TORONTO PRESS
Toronto Buffalo London

ISBN 978-1-4875-0847-0 (cloth)   ISBN 978-1-4875-3833-0 (EPUB)
ISBN 978-1-4875-3832-3 (PDF)

Library and Archives Canada Cataloguing in Publication

Title: The grammar rules of affection : passion and pedagogy in Sidney, Shakespeare, and Jonson / Ross Knecht.
Names: Knecht, Ross, 1979– author.
Description: Includes bibliographical references and index.
Identifiers: Canadiana (print) 2020040847X | Canadiana (ebook) 20200408690 | ISBN 9781487508470 (hardcover) | ISBN 9781487538330 (EPUB) | ISBN 9781487538323 (PDF)
Subjects: LCSH: Sidney, Philip, 1554–1586 – Criticism and interpretation. | LCSH: Shakespeare, William, 1564–1616 – Criticism and interpretation. | LCSH: Jonson, Ben, 1573?–1637 – Criticism and interpretation. | LCSH: Emotions in literature. | LCSH: Education, Humanistic, in literature. | LCSH: Figures of speech in literature. | LCSH: English literature – Early modern, 1500–1700 – History and criticism.
Classification: LCC PR428.E56 K64 2021 | DDC 820.9/35309031–dc23

University of Toronto Press acknowledges the financial assistance to its publishing program of the Canada Council for the Arts and the Ontario Arts Council, an agency of the Government of Ontario.

Canada Council **Conseil des Arts**
for the Arts **du Canada**

ONTARIO ARTS COUNCIL
CONSEIL DES ARTS DE L'ONTARIO

an Ontario government agency
un organisme du gouvernement de l'Ontario

Funded by the   Financé par le
Government   gouvernement
of Canada   du Canada

Canada

Contents

Acknowledgments

This book was written at three universities over the course of a decade, and in writing it I have incurred many debts that I will never be able to fully repay. I owe first thanks to John Archer, Karen Newman, and John Guillory, who shepherded the project through its early stages at New York University. This book would not have been possible without their mentorship and the examples they set as scholars and intellectuals. I would also like to thank other faculty members at NYU for their guidance and generosity, including Haruko Momma, Elaine Freedgood, Martin Harries, Patrick Deer, Phil Harper, Dustin Griffin, Pat Crain, Ernest Gilman, and Gabrielle Starr. I am immensely grateful for the solidary and support I received from my fellow graduate students: Rachel O'Connell, Anjuli Raza Kolb, Spencer Keralis, Lenora Warren, Katie Vomero-Santos, Christian Gerszo, Albert Sergio Laguna, Roy Perez, and James Brooke-Smith, to name only a few of many.

No less essential to the completion of this book than my graduate studies was the post-doctoral fellowship I held at the University of Queensland after completing my degree. There I was privileged to work alongside Peter Holbrook and Brandon Chua, from whom I learned much about early modern literature and scholarship in general. I would also like to thank Simon During, Lisa O'Connell, Alison Scott, Ian Hunter, Peter Harrison, Peter Cryle, Elizabeth Stephens, and Richard Yeo: my research benefited immensely from their presence during my time at UQ. The fellowship I held at UQ was part of the Australian Research Council Centre of Excellence for the History of Emotions, a network of junior and senior scholars working at numerous universities across Australia. Among those I was lucky to work with are Stephanie Downes, François Soyer, Rebecca McNamara, Katie Barclay, Una McIlvenna, Erin Sullivan, Will Sharpe, Katrina O'Loughlin, Penelope Woods, Francesco Ricatti, Giovanni Tarantino, Robert White, Charles

Zika, Stephanie Trigg, Yasmin Haskell, Andrew Lynch, and Susan Broomhall. I would like to make special mention of Philippa Maddern, who directed the Centre until her untimely passing in 2014.

I am deeply grateful for the support of past and present colleagues at Emory University, including Sari Altschuler, Pat Cahill, Deepika Bahri, Paul Kelleher, Jonathan Goldberg, Rosemarie Garland-Thomson, Liz Goodstein, Laura Otis, Michelle Wright, Erwin Rosenberg, Kate Nickerson, Jim Morey, Deborah White, Ben Reiss, Walter Kalaidjian, Valerie Loichot, and Nathan Suhr-Sytsma. I am indebted to Urvashi Chakravarty for her incisive comments on this manuscript and her generosity in various conversations and collaborations, and to Leah DeVun for advice and guidance throughout my academic career.

A version of the fourth chapter of this book was published in *ELH* 82 (2015) as "Shapes of Grief: Hamlet's Grammar School Passions" and is reproduced with kind permission. I thank *ELH*'s readers, editors, and editorial assistants, whose work significantly improved the chapter. I am grateful to Jonathan Hope, Lynn Enterline, Lynne Magnusson, and Alysia Kolentsis, who all organized seminars at the meetings of Shakespeare Association of America that provided me with important feedback on work that would become part of this book. Many thanks to Suzanne Rancourt, my editor at the University of Toronto Press, and to the press's external readers, whose generous comments were of great help in the editing process. For their essential support, I would like to express my gratitude to the administrative staff at NYU, UQ, and Emory, including Alyssa Leal, Lissette Flores, Shanna Williams, Rebecca Bayliss, Meredith Blankinship, Gerri Moreland, Eric Canosa, and Alonda Sims. Though there are far too many to name, I would like to thank the graduate and undergraduate students I have had the privilege to work with over the years. Finally, I thank my family for the support they have provided for the duration of my academic career.

THE GRAMMAR RULES OF AFFECTION

Introduction

My Grammar, I define to be an Art,
Which teacheth me to write and speak my heart
                                    – Christopher Harvey, *Schola cordis*
A verb passive ... betokeneth passion.
                              – John Brinsley, *The Posing of the Parts*

William Shakespeare's *Merry Wives of Windsor* is deeply engaged with the culture of humanist pedagogy. The play features Shakespeare's most direct representation of the grammar school setting in which he himself was educated, a scene in which a parson instructs a young boy in the rudiments of Latin. A subtler but no less significant allusion to the schoolroom appears in Falstaff's description of his intent to seduce Mistress Ford: "Briefly, I do mean to make love to Ford's wife: I spy entertainment in her: she discourses, she carves, she gives the leer of invitation; I can construe the action of her familiar style, and the hardest voice of her behaviour, to be Englished rightly, is, 'I am Sir John Falstaff's'" (1.3.40–5). Falstaff uses a pedagogical idiom to describe his relationship with Mistress Ford, representing the act of courtship as a scholarly exercise and desire as a language to be translated.[1] Just as a sixteenth-century schoolboy might parse a phrase of Cicero's, identifying its formal grammatical properties and rendering it in English, so does Falstaff "construe" Mistress Ford's gestures, facial expressions, and manner of speaking, translating the "voice of her behaviour" into a simple English declarative. Falstaff's estimation of Mistress Ford is of course mistaken, and his mistranslation will ultimately lead to his humiliation. But the passage is nevertheless characteristic of a widespread tendency in Renaissance literature to unite the affective and the linguistic through the appropriation of pedagogical discourse. These borrowings from the language of the grammar school imply that passions like Mistress Ford's are not simply psychological or physiological phenomena. They are instead embodied practices, patterns of action and expression rendered coherent by a set of conventional standards, just as the speaking of a language is made intelligible by the rules of grammar.

Scholars have long recognized the crucial role that humanist education played in the development of English Renaissance literature. Humanists like Erasmus and Thomas More developed a pedagogical program in the early sixteenth century that emphasized grammar, rhetoric, moral philosophy, and other subjects conducive to eloquence and civic engagement. Shakespeare, Philip Sidney, Edmund Spenser, Christopher Marlowe, and Ben Jonson were all educated in the new grammar school curriculum, and, though spaces in the schools were reserved for boys, aristocratic women like Elizabeth I and Mary Sidney received extensive private tutoring in accordance with the humanist model.[2] In the early twentieth century, scholars such as T.W. Baldwin and Donald Lemen Clark showed how the grammar schools provided early modern writers with the exposure to classical literature and the training in rhetoric and poetry that enabled their literary achievements.[3] In Baldwin's words, the schools supplied the raw materials that writers like Shakespeare wove into "beautiful fabric" (*William Shakespere's Smal Latine* 2:664). Later criticism took a more anthropological approach to early modern education, focusing on its acculturative effects. This tradition was inaugurated by Walter Ong's provocative comparison of grammar school training and traditional male puberty rites and includes Richard Halpern's crucial work on the role of the schools in socialization and subject formation.[4] A comprehensive understanding of the grammar school's influence, however, cannot be limited either to the formal matter of its instruction or to its role in acculturation and socialization, for the two are inextricably bound up with one another, as Lynn Enterline has recently argued in *Shakespeare's Schoolroom*. It was the explicit aim of early modern schoolmasters not only to provide language instruction alongside ethical and affective education, but also to shape the characters of their students through language instruction.

It is at this intersection of affect and education that this book seeks to intervene. The process of socialization by means of linguistic and literary instruction impressed upon early modern writers the connection between the verbal arts and the world outside the schoolroom's walls. Renaissance writers routinely draw upon the idioms and images of the schoolroom in their depictions of emotional experience, recurring to a space of strict discipline and adolescent *eros*. Memorable instances of this tendency include the representation of love as a schoolroom exercise conducted under the disciplinary gaze of the mistress, melancholy as a process of gradual decline like the declension of the noun, and courtship as a practice in which the participants are arranged like the parts of speech in a sentence. I argue that this singular synthesis of affective and pedagogical discourse in Renaissance literature implies a sophisticated conception of emotion as a normative practice, an activity structured and constrained by conventional standards just as language is governed by grammatical rules.

This distinctive way of apprehending and representing affective life chimes with the philosophy of Ludwig Wittgenstein, who understood emotions as practices guided by conventional norms that he called "grammars."[5] The conditions in which Wittgenstein developed what has been called his "schoolmasterly" late philosophy are similar to those in which many Renaissance writers came of age: he taught in a provincial Austrian grammar school with a curriculum not too distant from that typical of the early modern period.[6] As in the Renaissance, the schoolroom experience seems to have emphasized the importance of habituated norms and practices in human life, leading Wittgenstein to speak frequently of action and experience in pedagogical terms.[7] His account of the "grammar" of emotion is strikingly similar to early modern formulations like the "grammar rules of affection," the line from Sidney's *Arcadia* that lends this book its title.

In this book, I read Renaissance literary texts alongside the philosophical writings of Wittgenstein and others, emphasizing their common conception of emotion as rule-guided practice. In doing so, I hope to advance a historical argument about Renaissance literature as well as a theoretical claim about emotion itself. My historical analysis seeks to show the importance of humanism to Renaissance representations of passion and interiority. Humanist pedagogy elevated linguistic usage over abstract grammatical rules and insisted that students learn Latin by engaging in practices of translation, composition, and oratory. It introduced students to the rigours of grammar and the pleasures of classical literature, joining disciplinary constraint to expressive possibility. I contend that these methods led Renaissance writers to interweave representations of affective experience with reflections on language, employing the discourse of grammar to describe the norms and conventions implicit in the expression of emotion. In addition to this historical argument, I use the combination of the pedagogical and the affective in Renaissance literature as an occasion for thinking about the nature of emotion itself. The insistent comparison of the expressions of feeling and the activities of the schoolroom is consistent with the accounts of those like Wittgenstein who conceive of emotion as an embodied social practice. It emphasizes the fact that emotion is an extended process rather than an isolated object or condition and suggests the role of habituated norms in defining the contours of emotional life.

Language, the Body, and the Affective Turn

Interest in emotions and affects has been significant enough in recent years for commentators to speak of an "affective turn" across a number of fields and disciplines, a movement that has been characterized as "a reaction against the linguistic turn or the deconstruction of the subject" and a "turn from language to the body."[8] In response to a post-structuralist criticism that seemed all too often to neglect the reality of embodied experience, the turn to affect restores us to the physical world and the domain of feeling. Affects, conceived as the pre-rational and pre-linguistic phenomena of the body, exist prior to signification and testify to the elemental materiality of our existence. In early modern studies, this move from language to the body took the form of a renewed interest in the discourse of Galenic humoralism, the medical theory formulated by the ancient physician Galen that had an unparalleled influence in Western medicine from the ancient to the early modern period.[9] Humoralism envisioned a body composed of four fluids or "humours" – blood, phlegm, yellow bile, and black bile – and posited that the excess of any single humour produced distinctive physical pathologies and affective temperaments. Should black bile, for instance, prevail within a person's physiology, she would become melancholic, disposed to sadness and disquiet. In attributing affective states to the influence of bodily fluids, humoralism represented a thoroughly materialist understanding of affect analogous to that maintained in modern theory, suggesting that "the passions or perturbations of the mind were fully embedded in the order of nature and were part of material being itself" (Paster, "The Body and Its Passions," 45).

The book that inaugurated this field of inquiry was Gail Kern Paster's brilliant and pioneering study *The Body Embarrassed*. Drawing upon the theory of Michel Foucault, Norbert Elias, and Mikhail Bakhtin, Paster's book argued that Galenic humoralism provided the framework through which early modern men and women experienced their own bodies, emphasizing "the difference humoralism, or *any other* influential account of human physiology, makes to the subjective experience of being-in-the-body."[10] The chimeric physiology envisioned by humoralism served as an internal bodily habitus, a shared picture of the body's inner world that conditioned self-understanding and social behaviour. Paster is particularly attentive to the way humoralism reinforced the period's patriarchal ideology: "humoral theory," she writes, "was instrumental in the production and maintenance of gender and class difference" (7). Humoralism pathologized the female body, conceiving of it as a "leaky vessel" prone to excesses of the "lower" humours and characterized by porosity, excretion, and disorder. In doing so, it imposed "an internal hierarchy of fluids and functions" upon "the external hierarchies of class and gender," employing shame over bodily emissions as an instrument of social control (19).

While *The Body Embarrassed* was primarily concerned with the historically specific discourses by which the body came to be "inscribed as a social text" (6), later work in the field, including Paster's own, granted a more prominent place to the material body upon which these discourses operated. We are encouraged by Douglas Trevor, for instance, not to "empty out the body of the early modern writer in the name of a 'historicized' subject" and to recognize his or her "personally felt passions" (*Poetics of Melancholy* 3–4). Carla Mazzio contends that we may find in plays such as *Hamlet* adumbrations of "exralinguistic dimensions of feeling" (*The Inarticulate Renaissance* 193). This work of recovering the body that subsists beneath the accumulated layers of discourse and ideology – of "*finding* the early modern body amidst the texts that inscribe it" – is licensed by Galenism itself, which is paradoxically upheld as a sign of the mutability and contingency of physiological understanding and as a thoroughgoing materialism instructive to us in the present day.[11] Consistent with this renewed interest in the body, Bruce Smith has proposed a mode of analysis that brings together historicism and empiricism, taking as its object "an amalgam of biological constants and cultural variables" (*The Acoustic World* 8). This method, Smith suggests, may serve to bridge the historical divide that separates us from the early modern period: through an analysis of the discourses that inform bodily experience and an appreciation of the immutable perceptions and faculties of the body itself, we may come to understand early modern affective experience.[12] Somewhat surprisingly, then, what began as a strongly culturally constructivist program of study became increasingly concerned with that which resists culture, with a material body that persists through shifting regimes of discourse and ideology.[13]

In recent years, this increased interest in the material body has led early modern scholars to adopt the methods and concerns of affect theory, an interdisciplinary program of study that draws from such fields as psychology, philosophy, sociology, and political science. Affect theorists conceive of the affective as a realm of vital forces and physiological intensities that precedes rational reflection and discursive articulation.

Affect in this sense is distinct from and prior to emotion, which exists in the social realm of expression and discourse. As Brian Massumi describes it, an affect is a "prepersonal intensity," while an emotion is a variety or instance of this intensity recognized and given a name, "the sociolinguistic fixing of the quality of an experience which is from that point onward defined as personal."[14] The model maintains the primacy of affect over the social and linguistic: as Stephanie Trigg writes, "'Affects' or 'affective' feelings are produced independently of ... the discursive mediation of language, and are accordingly often granted a form of ontological priority" ("Affect Theory" 11). By insisting on this distinction, affect theory has provided a valuable way of thinking outside the often reductive framework of rational agency, emphasizing the fact that people routinely act in ways that are not determined by conscious intention. It has facilitated innovative and important new work in Renaissance studies on such topics as the role of affect in early modern politics, the discourse on melancholy, and the affective dynamics of the Shakespearean stage.[15]

By distinguishing between undifferentiated bodily intensities and the articulation of distinct emotions, affect studies helps to account for feelings that fall below the threshold of conscious attention and escape explicit linguistic representation. This attention to that which is prior to appraisal and expression raises intriguing philosophical questions and has prompted a new interest in the ineffable. As critics of the program have frequently observed, however, the opposition of the corporeal and the rational entails certain conceptual problems. First, it threatens to remove affects entirely from the realm of language and culture, making them inaccessible to historians and critics. Second, and perhaps more significantly, it involves an untenable opposition of the mind and body.[16] By positing a field of physiological activity that precedes intentional action and verbal articulation, affect studies casts the corporeal and the rational as fundamentally different entities in a manner consistent with Cartesian dualism.

The recent work of Monique Scheer is valuable in both diagnosing and addressing the problem of dualism in contemporary discourse on emotion.[17] Scheer shows that philosophers and theorists have tended to conceive of emotions as possessing two distinct aspects or dimensions. First, there is an "inner" dimension, an involuntary experience or corporeal arousal, like the physiological intensities with which affect theory is primarily concerned. This dimension of emotion is bodily, passive, and experiential, and thus distinct from the realm of language and culture and resistant to historical change.[18] Second is emotion's "outer" dimension, the recognition and expression of feeling that follows upon the corporeal experience. Involving cognitive appraisal and verbal articulation, this aspect of emotion is active and rational, something we do rather than something we suffer.[19] While affect theorists grant primacy to the first half of this dyad, cognitivist philosophers consider the second to constitute emotion's essence. Whichever aspect is assigned priority, however, this division is essentially dualistic: emotion is conceived either as a bodily phenomenon beyond the reach of language and culture and thus inaccessible to the critic, or as a mental event somehow detached from the body with which it is so evidently involved. Both of these positions have shortcomings and fail, in my view, to provide a comprehensive picture of our emotional lives. To challenge the first, one has only to consider the clear difference in the way that emotions are not only expressed but experienced in different cultures. A person's involuntary experience of shame, for instance, depends on what she has been taught to consider shameful: the bodily reflex of blushing is contingent upon cultural habituation. The second position also comes into conflict with our everyday experience by neglecting the body's role in emotion. While appraisal and articulation may have a crucial place in the experience of emotion, it is difficult to see why they should be more fundamental than the physical phenomena being evaluated and named.

Scheer avoids this dualistic perspective by adopting a view of emotion founded in practice theory, a program that considers practice as, in the words of the philosopher Theodore Schatzki, "the principal constitutive element in social life" (Schatzki, *Social Practices* 12). Rather than seeking to isolate emotion in a mental event or bodily state, Scheer considers emotion to be coextensive with such practices as courtship, mourning, and confession. In this view, it is not that a person's inward desire motivates her to pursue a lover, or that her sorrow leads her to engage in a process of grieving, but that desire and sorrow themselves are manifest in the practices of courtship and mourning. Departing from models that distinguish between a subjective individual and an objective world, practice theory considers people as embodied actors deeply enmeshed within their environments and operating in accordance with both inculcated habit and conscious intention.[20] It emphasizes, in Scheer's words, "the infusion of the physical body with social structure, both of which participate in the production of emotional experience" ("Are Emotions a Kind of Practice?" 199). Practice itself encompasses the circuit from experience to expression, involving bodily affection, habituated reflex, and deliberate action. By locating emotions in the activity of everyday life, practice theory may help to deliver us from the dualism that has vexed recent scholarship, allowing us to navigate between the twin hazards of reductive materialism and linguistic idealism.

Wittgenstein on Emotion

Among the foremost sources for practice theory are Wittgenstein and Pierre Bourdieu, the former particularly important to the version of practice theory developed by Schatzki.[21] Scheer is primarily inspired by Bourdieu, but she concedes that he "rarely addresses emotion directly as a category of analysis" ("Are Emotions a Kind of Practice?" 204). Wittgenstein, by contrast, writes extensively on emotion, occupying himself almost exclusively with psychological questions in the final years of his life, though his remarks on the subject are characteristically elliptical.[22] In what follows, I will attempt to elucidate Wittgenstein's views on emotion, showing that he conceives of emotions as normative social practices. Wittgenstein's emphasis on the normative character of emotion, the way that emotion is defined and distinguished by social convention, is particularly crucial to this study, as it leads him to speak of the grammar of emotion in a manner that echoes the language of early modern pedagogy.

Schatzki associates Wittgenstein with the turn to process in modern philosophy, numbering him alongside thinkers like Nietzsche, Bergson, and Heidegger who opposed the Platonic tradition by granting ontological primacy to flux and change, subordinating being to becoming (*Social Practices* 26). Consistent with this movement, Wittgenstein conceives of human existence as a continuous cascade of embodied actions and experiences that he describes as the "stream of life" (*fluss des lebens*) (*Last Writings on the Philosophy of Psychology* §931). This stream is not, however, simply a succession of undifferentiated events. Repeated actions gradually acquire the force of routine and coalesce into coherent patterns. These conventionalized actions provide a framework within which subsequent actions take place and allow those actions to be recognized and evaluated. Actions thus become practices: conventionalized activities that carry social significance. Practices are guided but not determined by convention, and the framework of established conventions is constantly transformed by innovations in practice.

According to this model, what we often understand as internal objects or entities – thoughts, beliefs, feelings, and emotions – are in fact embodied practices, distinct and coherent episodes in the "stream of life." We grant these episodes names and meanings by virtue of their place within the sequence, evaluating them by their relation to existing convention. A cry or groan, considered in isolation, may be without meaning, but when voiced at the appropriate moment in a society with an established tradition of mourning, it will appear as the expression of sorrow. It might be distinguished by its unusual vehemence, signalling that the sorrow it expresses is in excess of expectations. Or it might be particularly restrained, suggesting the stoic resilience of the one who expresses it. In any case, when a pattern of such actions and expressions meets the criteria established by existing practice, we identify it as an episode of sorrow or grief and ascribe these feelings to the person who performs the actions. Emotions such as sorrow are thus modes of embodied action that are socially recognized and defined in relation to existing conventions. They are normative social practices.[23]

The process I have sketched here may recall the practice of language, in which established convention determines the use and meaning of words, and verbal innovation in turn alters established convention. Language, for Wittgenstein, is indeed the paradigmatic human practice, illustrating most clearly the fundamentally conventional and social nature of human action. His late philosophy of psychology develops from the exhaustive analysis of the nature of language in his *Philosophical Investigations*. In that work, widely considered his masterpiece, he rejects traditional theories in which language is understood primarily as a system or instrument of representation, arguing instead that language is a practice, a social activity of limitless possible variation:

> But how many kinds of sentences are there? Say assertion, question and command? – There are *countless* kinds; countless different kinds of use of all the things we call "signs," "words," "sentences." And this diversity is not something fixed, given once for all; but new types of language, new language-games, as we may say, come into existence, and others become obsolete and get forgotten ... The word "language-*game*" [*Sprachspiel*] is used here to emphasize the fact that the *speaking* of language is part of an activity, or form of life. (§23)

To speak a language is to engage in a practice, much like playing a game. And it is through their use within this practice, rather than through correspondence with some extralinguistic object, that words come to be meaningful: "the meaning of a word is its use in the language" (§43). As the analogy of the game suggests, the function of language depends upon certain rules of use that Wittgenstein calls grammar. Grammar names the flexible set of rules and conventions that direct the use of language. As Wittgenstein identifies use with meaning, the rules that guide linguistic usage similarly govern the meaning of words: as he writes in the *Philosophical Grammar*, "It is grammatical rules that determine meaning (constitute it)" (§133). Crucially, the rules of grammar are not logical or metaphysical principles, nor are they derived from the facts of the world. Instead, they are conventions implicit in linguistic use, contingent upon acculturation and subject to negotiation and change over time. They are analogous to what Bourdieu calls "the precepts of custom" and "the semi-learned grammars of practice," conventions that have nothing in common with "the transcendent rules of a juridical code" (*Outline of a Theory of Practice* 17, 20). Meaning is governed by implicit convention rather than explicit principle. It is not determined by correspondence with some external scheme or state of affairs; instead, it emerges from the linguistic and social practices of a community.

As a meaningful human practice, language takes place within the context of what Wittgenstein calls a "form of life" (*lebensform*), an often nebulous but crucial concept in his philosophy. At times, Wittgenstein speaks of a single form of life, suggesting human life in general and its distinctive characteristics (language, tool use, and so on). In other contexts, the phrase seems to suggest a specific way of life: the practices, institutions, and customs that belong to a given culture or community. Whether general or specific, a form of life is the context in which our linguistic activity takes place and the foundation upon which its meaning ultimately rests: "What has to be accepted, the given, is – one might say – *forms of life*" (*Philosophical Investigations* 238). For a word or action to have meaning, it must be situated amidst a network of practices, customs, and traditions. We ascribe meaning to an expression relative to our sense of what a person should say or how a person might act in a given situation, judging her intentions against the norms and conventions of everyday life. It is for this reason that certain words closely tied to ritual practice prove so difficult to translate, for to understand them one must be acquainted with the cultural conventions with which they are associated.[24] As Hans-Johann Glock writes, the concept of form of life "stresses the intertwining of culture, world-view and language" (*A Wittgenstein Dictionary* 124). Language is inseparable from our ways of living in the world, intimately bound up with the other practices and institutions that collectively constitute our forms of life.

Wittgenstein's philosophy of psychology, which I will now examine in greater detail, follows from this understanding of language as a social practice: just as verbal expressions derive meaning from their relation to grammatical rules and their place within a form of life, so do the verbal and physical expressions that make up emotion have meaning and value by virtue of their relation to established practice. Wittgenstein's comments on emotion are threaded throughout his late writings, with particularly important discussions appearing in *Remarks on the Philosophy of Psychology*, *Zettel*, and the second part of the *Philosophical Investigations*. In these works, Wittgenstein shows that emotions are necessarily normative: the nature of an emotion is defined by a set of rules, social conventions that lead us to identify a particular expression or feeling as "love," "anger," or "fear." We identify "love," for instance, by a set of criteria that differentiate it from such feelings as physical pain: "Love is put to the test, pain not. One does not say: 'That was not true pain, or it would not have gone off so quickly'" (*Zettel* 504). Love is distinguished from pain in that it is subject to trial and judgment. We identify a feeling as love only when it endures, when it persists in spite of obstacles, when it is borne out by devotion and fidelity. If it fails to do these things, we say that it is false, or a different thing altogether: a passing fancy or an adolescent infatuation. We have tacitly agreed to call that love which abides by certain conventions, rules and standards that Wittgenstein calls "grammar." Other remarks similarly observe characteristics that distinguish emotions from similar phenomena such as beliefs and sense perceptions. An emotion, for instance, may fluctuate over time, while knowledge and belief typically remain constant: "I may attend to the course of my pains," Wittgenstein writes, "but not in the same way to that of my believing or knowing" (*Remarks on the Philosophy of Psychology* §972). And unlike physical sensations, emotions are not localized in a particular place in the body: "we do not speak of a physical place of grief" (§439). Such conventional rules, which Francesco Bellucci calls "Wittgenstein's Grammar of Emotions," define both the nature of emotion in general and the character of particular emotions. Collectively, they form a normative framework that determines how we describe and understand emotion, defining its contours and establishing its place within the social world. They are the conditions of intelligibility within which emotions emerge as distinct and coherent phenomena.

In addition to their normative dimension, Wittgenstein emphasizes the situated nature of the emotions, arguing that the context in which they take place determines their meaning. In the second part of the *Philosophical Investigations*, he describes hope and grief as characteristic patterns of action situated within our forms of life:

> Can only those hope who can talk? Only those who have mastered the use of a language. That is to say, the manifestations of hope are modifications of this complicated form of life. (If a concept points to a characteristic of human handwriting, it has no application to beings that do not write.) …
>
> "Grief" describes a pattern which recurs, with different variations, in the tapestry of life. If a man's bodily expression of sorrow and of joy alternated, say with the ticking of a clock, here we would not have the

characteristic course of the pattern of sorrow or of the pattern of joy ...
"For a second he felt violent pain." – Why does it sound odd to say: "For
a second he felt deep grief"? Only because it so seldom happens? (175)

Hope and grief are part of the "form of life" or the "tapestry of life,"
practices situated amidst the interwoven threads of language, action,
and experience that make up the world we share with one another. They
are not isolated bodily states or mental events, but patterns of expression and experience that stand out within the course of our lives.[25] The
nature of an emotion such as grief, as Wittgenstein's comments suggest,
is defined in part by this social and cultural context. It is strange to
imagine a person suffering from a single moment of "deep grief" because we understand grief to occur for certain reasons and to entail an
enduring practice of grieving. If we see a person clutching at her heart,
we understand the gesture differently depending on what we know of
the wider situation: if we know she has been recently bereaved, we will
likely interpret the gesture as part of an extended process of mourning.
But if we know of no such reason for her to grieve, we might worry that
the gesture is a sign of some physical pain or illness. Even the sufferer
herself, finding her hand reflexively grasping at her heart, might need
a moment to reflect on her situation in order to understand the nature
of her action. Grief is a practice typically prompted by an experience
of loss and involving a protracted process of mourning: it is this characteristic arrangement of experiences and expressions by which it is
made intelligible, recognizable as the phenomenon we call "grief." This
is a radically non-reductive account of emotion: in refusing to define an
emotion such as grief as any one particular thing and insisting that it
must be understood within the context of a form of life, Wittgenstein's
account is one of the few that does justice to the richness and variety
of our affective lives. It demands that we attend to emotion through
qualitative analysis and thick description rather than attempt to fix its
nature through a universal definition.[26]

As the practices that make up our affective lives may include both
verbal expressions and physical actions such as gestures, cries, and facial expressions, Wittgenstein's account traverses the divide between
language and the body that has characterized recent approaches to the
question of emotion. Wittgenstein suggests that emotional practice may
have both a verbal and a physical dimension, incorporating words, gestures, facial expressions, and the ostensive display of objects.[27] No one
of these elements is more fundamental than another: they exist alongside one another, each occupying a particular place in our expressive
practices. Countering classic theories in which apparently natural

expressions such as an infant's cries are prior to spoken language, Wittgenstein argues that physical and verbal expressions are essentially equivalent, though the latter may be more wide-ranging and complex: "the verbal expression of pain replaces crying, it does not describe it" (*Philosophical Investigations* §244). Further comments in the second part of the *Philosophical Investigations* continue this exploration of the relationship between verbal and physical expression:

> "I must tell you: I am frightened."
> "I must tell you: it horrifies me." – Well, one can say this in a *smiling* tone of voice too.
> And do you mean to tell me that he doesn't feel it? How else does he *know* it? – But even if it is a report, he does not learn it from his feelings ...
> Suppose that the feelings are produced by *gestures* of horror: the words "it horrifies me" are themselves such a gesture; and when I hear and feel them as I utter them, this belongs among the rest of those feelings. Now, why should the wordless gesture be the ground of the verbal one? (175)

The verbal expression of fear is essentially equivalent to the other non-verbal phenomena in which we recognize fear: the shivers, blanches, and cries that may seem at first to be more fundamental than verbal expression. Like a blood-drained face or a quivering hand, the words "I am frightened" bring fear into being, manifesting one's feeling in the presence of others.[28] Both the physical and the verbal expressions have a place in our affective practices and a role within our various forms of life. The continuity between verbal and physical expressions observed by Wittgenstein suggests that there is no need to oppose language to the body. Speech, gestures, and physical affects and agitations all contribute to the ways that we express ourselves and understand one another. They help to make up the practices that precede the idealized models bequeathed to us by linguistics and medical science. The apparently foundational concepts of language and the body, which struggle for primacy in our various determinisms, are in fact belated abstractions, derived from the practices of our daily lives.

For Wittgenstein, an emotion such as hope or grief is a mode "of this complicated form of life." It is a pattern that stands out within a continuum of lived experience, an ensemble of actions and experiences that might include verbal statements, facial expressions, manners of comportment, and the involuntary reflexes of the body. It is not defined by any single essence or quality; instead, a fluid set of conventions, a grammar, determines its general shape, allowing it to be recognized amidst the other practices with which it is enmeshed. Taking this philosophical

account as a guide for understanding passion in early modern literature may seem arbitrary or anachronistic, but there are reasons why it
is useful and even necessary for approaching the subject. Grammar and
psychology have always had an intimate relation with one another: as
I will show in the next section, the earliest theoretical accounts of psychological concepts derive not from the observation of the world but
from the analysis of linguistic forms. The historical tradition on passion
thus provides evidence for Wittgenstein's claims that psychological
concepts are grammatical rather than empirical. This relation becomes
especially apparent in the early modern period because of the intense
self-consciousness about grammar cultivated by humanist pedagogy.
Because of the recursive emphasis it places on grammar and the anal-
ogies it draws between affective and pedagogical practices, early modern literature provides an ideal space for an analysis of the normative
and social dimensions of passion.

Grammar and Passion in the Philosophical Tradition

The word "passion," the foremost term in the pre-modern affective lexicon, testifies to the long-standing relationship between language and
psychology. The ancient Greek term *pathos*, from which we derive "passion," named both a psychological state and a grammatical position.
Though it may at first seem a mere accident of philological history, this
concurrence of terms reveals much about the discourse of the passions.
As I will argue, it demonstrates that passion is not named by language
but inherent in it, interwoven into the ways we speak and engage with
one another.

Pathos was a concept of central importance in a variety of ancient discourses. In its most basic sense, it was simply an instance of passive affection or suffering, a reception or experience, a state of being-acted-upon.[29]
The concept of *pathos* as passive affection had particular significance
within the discourse of psychology. In texts such as Aristotle's *De Anima*,
the *pathe* are states into which the soul enters when it is affected by some
outside influence: frightened by a fearful spectacle, angered by pain or
insult, inflamed with desire.[30] It is from this use that the familiar sense
of "passion" as a psychological state derives. More foreign to us is the
use of the term in grammatical study. In the *Art of Grammar* of Dionysios
Thrax, the first systematic grammar manual in the Western tradition,
pathos is one of the "dispositions" of the verb, a mode of inflection equivalent to the passive voice in English (*The Grammar of Dionysios Thrax* 12).
Both of these senses of "passion" persist into the Renaissance. The understanding of passion as a passive affection of the soul was axiomatic

in the period: as Juan Luis Vives writes in *De Anima et Vita*, the passions are so called "because the soul is passively submitted to their blows and buffets."[31] And passion remained a grammatical term as well, as we may see in John Brinsley's grammar manual, *The Posing of the Parts*: "A verb passive," he writes, "betokeneth passion" (16).

What are we to make of this concurrence of terms across disciplines so apparently distant as grammar and psychology? The association of passion and grammatical passivity suggests that passion is not simply a psychological or physiological fact that exists prior to the use of language. Instead, what is called passion emerges out of certain characteristic patterns and structures inherent in linguistic expression. Both Aristotle and Dionysios derive the concept of *pathos* through what is essentially an exercise in descriptive grammar: an analysis of the use and practice of language, and in particular the use of passive verbs. In the *Categories*, Aristotle outlines ten categories which are predicated of a subject through an examination of what he calls *ta legomena*, "that which is said." The last of these is *paschein* ("suffering"), a general category he abstracts from the passive verbs *temnetai* ("is cut") and *kaietai* ("is burnt") (2a). Observing that we say that a thing "is cut" or "is burnt," Aristotle derives the state of "being cut," "being burnt," or being affected more generally, a state he designates as *pathos*. Passions such as anger or fear are likewise derived from the use of passive verbs in everyday speech: when one is angry, writes Aristotle, "We say 'Such a man is affected.' Such states are affections [*pathe*]."[32] Dionysios derives the grammatical category of *pathos* from a similar study of passive verbs: his example is *tuptomai*, "I am struck" (335). In each of these analyses, *pathos* or "passion" is a name granted to certain ways of speaking, abstracted from recurring patterns and structures in language generally characterized by passivity.[33] Remarkably, similar patterns contribute to our own affective discourse, which remains punctuated by the use of passive voice expressions: "I am frightened," "I am touched," "I am moved." Despite the emergence of the discourse of emotion, which implies a distinct set of cultural assumptions based in novel vocabularies and idioms, the concept of passion as passive affection persists in such language.[34] As passion is thus inherent in language rather than existing before it, the patterns of speech that comprise the discourse of the passions are performative rather than referential.[35] They are expressive practices by which speakers manifest passion, establishing affective relations between one another, rather than referential terms used to describe some prior state of mind or condition of the body.

As we have seen, Scheer emphasizes the way that practice theory overcomes the opposition between passivity and activity. An emotion is not composed of a passive experience that is followed by an active expression of that experience: it is simultaneously experiential and expressive, the practice of an embodied actor that is deeply engaged with her environment. That the concept of passion is abstracted from the use of the passive voice provides important evidence for Scheer's argument. The passive voice grants verbal form to the union of the passive and the active: to speak in the passive voice is simultaneously to engage in a linguistic activity and to manifest a passive experience, to act in the world and to register the world's influence. As I have argued elsewhere, there is an acute awareness of the tension between active speaking and passive feeling in early modern literature.[36] The state opposed to *paschein* in Aristotle's *Categories* is *poiein*, "doing" or "making," the root of the English word "poetry." The impassioned poetry of the Renaissance thus occupies a paradoxical position, as it is both an active expression and the index of a passive experience. In his comments on Sidney's *Astrophil and Stella*, the early modern scholar and antiquarian Brian Twyne provides an impression of this paradox when he muses on the "active passion of love," which is "a passion and yet an action."[37]

The Pragmatism of Humanist Grammatical Theory

Brian Cummings's landmark study *The Literary Culture of the Reformation: Grammar and Grace* has demonstrated the central place occupied by grammar in Renaissance culture. As "the *ars* before and within every other *ars*," grammar encompassed far more in the early modern period than the rules of morphology and syntax.[38] Its subject matter, which often overlapped with that of logic and rhetoric, included the study of languages (both classical and vernacular), eloquence in writing and speaking, textual interpretation, scholarly practices like translation and commentary, and the theory of language in general. Though much of the culture of early modern letters was inherited from the medieval period, the advent of Renaissance humanism marked a major upheaval in the understanding and teaching of grammar. As I will discuss in greater detail in my first chapter, medieval grammarians saw the rules of grammar as an ideal system corresponding to the ontological structure of the world: independent of and prior to linguistic practice, the rules gave language meaning and shape. The Modist grammarians, a movement that represented the culmination of medieval grammatical theory, sought to articulate this abstract structure and establish its correspondence with the laws and properties of the world. Thus grammar, though it remained classified as one of the *artes* of the trivium, was reified as an object of study, a "thing" that fell under the purview of *scientia*. Humanist grammar, by contrast, was generally pragmatic, privileging historical linguistic usage over the *a priori* laws of the medieval grammarians. For the humanists, as for Wittgenstein, language was immeasurably various and protean, and refused to abide by the dictates of a prescriptive syntax: no one set of systematic rules could account for what John Colet described as "the varietees, and dyuersitees, and chaunges in latyn speche, whiche be innumerable." The syntactical rules delineated by ancient authorities such as Donatus and Priscian were not eternal laws, but rather accounts of the actual use and function of the Latin language. "For in the beginning," Colet writes, "men spake not latyn bycause suche rules were made but contrary wyse, bycause men spake suche latyn, vpon that folowed the rules were made. That is to saye latyn speche was before the rules, not the rules before the latyn speche" (*Aeditio* D6). As language is always changing, grammar cannot be reduced to a collection of immutable rules or laws: it must be conceived as an ongoing practice, a set of pedagogical, scholarly, and literary activities. The proper way to learn grammar, as the humanists insisted again and again, was not to memorize a detached system of rules, but to read, translate, and imitate the writings of classical Latin authors, attending to the actual practice of language and its infinite particularities and vicissitudes. In a reaction against the reification of grammar as an object of *scientia*, humanism emphasized the "artful" or pragmatic character of grammar.

The humanist reconceptualization of grammar as practice entailed a new perspective on the relationship between language and passion. In the medieval scheme, passion was a "thing," a property of the world that was reflected in the rules of grammar. The passive voice (*genus passivum*) was derived from a specific mode of being, the *modus passionis* or "mode of passivity." The passive verb was therefore *quod significat passionem*, "that which signifies passion," and to speak of something in the passive voice was to describe its passion or passive property (*propertias patientis*).[39] But with the rejection of grammar's ontological foundations and the shift to the conception of grammar as a practice, affective language could no longer be understood as a simple reflection of a worldly property or thing. Under humanism, the metaphysical apparatus thought to lie behind or beneath language falls away.[40] To speak passionately was to engage in an activity, to move others and to suffer passion oneself. It was grammar that made such affective engagement possible: as Christopher Harvey writes in the phrase I have used as this chapter's epigraph, "My grammar, I define to be an art / Which teacheth me to write and speak my heart."[41] Grammar in the early modern period was no longer a static system that reflected some prior ontological or psychological reality; it was instead a set of fluid, conventional rules that guide verbal practice. In this way, humanist pragmatism parallels contemporary practice theory by rejecting the metaphysical opposition of language and the world.

It is in this context that we find Sidney's suggestive phrase "the grammar rules of affection," a formulation that anticipates Wittgenstein's characteristic use of the term "grammar." The phrase appears in the *Arcadia*, in a scene in which the hero Pyrocles, disguised as the Amazon Zelmane, saves Philoclea from a marauding lion. Philoclea's parents, Basilius and Gynecia, who are both in love with the cross-dressed hero, praise his deeds with such vehemence that they subtly reveal their desire:

> But then [Basilius] told Pamela – not so much because she would know it, as because he would tell it – the wonderful act Zelmane had performed, which Gynecia likewise spake of, both in such extremity of praising as was easy to be seen the constructions of their speech might best be made by the grammar rules of affection. Basilius told with what a gallant grace she ran with the lion's head in her hand, like another Pallas with the spoils of Gorgon. Gynecia sware she saw the very face of the young Hercules killing the Nemean lion; and all with a grateful assent affirmed the same praises. (180)

The passage suggests that there is a manner of speaking appropriate to gratitude and a distinct way of speaking that is characteristic of love, one that follows what Sidney calls "the grammar rules of affection." In the "extremity of their praising" of Zelmane, punctuated with the classical allusions one would have learned in the grammar school, Basilius and Gynecia have exceeded the bounds of the former and moved into the latter, making their desire manifest or legible, "easy to be seen" by the assembled onlookers and by the *Arcadia*'s readership. Wittgenstein's grammatical investigation of psychological concepts sought to make explicit the social conventions governing the way we speak about and understand emotion, the rules that determine the character of individual emotions and distinguish them from similar phenomena such as sense impressions or beliefs. By emphasizing the "grammar rules" that govern the practice of love, Sidney anticipates Wittgenstein's grammatical analysis with remarkable precision. He suggests that there are rules that subtly distinguish the practice of affection from that of mere gratitude and tribute, tracing a rough outline around the constellation of actions and expressions to which we assign the name of love. Sidney's arresting phrase implies that love is a normative practice, an action defined by its adherence to social convention.

That love follows grammatical convention suggests that Sidney conceives of passion as a phenomenon native to language rather than simply reflected by it. This point is made explicit in *The Defence of Poesy*, in which Sidney advances an anti-mimetic theory of poetry that echoes the humanist critique of grammar's ontological foundations. For Sidney, poetry does not simply reflect the world. It creates its own world, one which is superior to that of nature: "Nature never set forth the earth in so rich a tapestry as divers poets have done ... Her world is brazen; the poets only deliver a golden" (216). So too is passion manifest in poetry; it is not a natural occurrence to be defined by philosophers, but an effect of the poet's art:

> Tully taketh much pains, and many times not without poetical helps, to make us know the force love of our country hath in us. Let us but hear old Anchises speaking in the midst of Troy's flames, or see Ulysses in the fullness of all Calypso's delight bewail his absence from barren and beggarly Ithaca. Anger, the Stoics say, was a short madness: let but Sophocles bring you Ajax on a stage, killing and whipping sheep and oxen, thinking them an army of Greeks, with their chieftain Agamemnon and Menelaus, and tell me if you have not a more familiar insight into anger than finding in the schoolmen his *genus* and difference ... passions [are] so in their own natural seats laid to the view. (222)

Passion, according to Sidney, cannot be understood by the technical definitions of the philosophers. Only when its causes and contexts, its place and function in a form of life, are traced in the language of the poets does passion truly come into being. By drawing our attention away from the definitions of the Stoics and the Scholastics and toward the rehearsal of passion in poetry, Sidney rejects an essentialist view of passion in favour of a performative one: passion is to be understood in its expression, its realization in the language of the poets.[42] It is in poetry that passions appear "in their own natural seats": they are not simply described by the text, but manifest within it.[43]

The Contents of This Book

In the chapters that follow, I analyse poems and plays by Sidney, Shakespeare, and Jonson, paying particular attention to the use of pedagogical language in the representation of affective experience. The discourse of the grammar school, I argue, emphasizes the normative standards implicit in the rituals of courtship, practices of mourning, and expressions of envy that these texts rehearse. To adapt Bourdieu, I consider the use of "the ambiguous vocabulary of *rules*, the language of grammar" in Renaissance literature to represent moments at which "the unconscious schemes" of emotional practice are brought to light.[44]

Chapter 1 analyses grammatical theory from the fourteenth to the sixteenth century, showing how the shift from the idealism of the late medieval period to the conventionalism and pragmatism of the humanists set the stage for Renaissance literature's reflections on the nature of grammar and affect. Medieval grammarians conceived of the rules of grammar as an ideal system corresponding to the psychological structure of the mind and ontological structure of the world. Humanist grammar, by contrast, was descriptive and pragmatic, privileging historical linguistic usage over *a priori* laws. The proper way to learn grammar under the humanist program was not to study a system of abstract rules, but to engage with the writings of classical Latin authors, attending to language as it is practised in the world. I contend that the humanist understanding of language as a fluid practice structured by convention rather than natural law suggested a comparison with other human practices, leading early modern writers to emphasize the normative and pragmatic dimensions of human life through playful and self-conscious adaptations of pedagogical language.

The second chapter analyses Philip Sidney's *Astrophil and Stella*, the most influential sonnet cycle of the Elizabethan period. *Astrophil and Stella* habitually recurs to the scene of the schoolroom, representing Astrophil as a devoted schoolboy and Stella as a schoolmistress who unites desire and discipline in a manner consistent with Petrarchan convention. At times, these representations of pedagogy seem to critique the traditions of Renaissance poetry, rejecting the dominant Italian model as insufficient to the experience of love depicted in the cycle. The celebrated words of Astrophil's muse, "looke in thy heart and write" (1.14), are often taken as evidence of a new metaphysics of interiority that privileges the natural over the conventional. Against this proto-Romantic reading of the poems, I argue that Sidney's invocation of the schoolroom experience implies a pragmatic and conventionalist understanding of affect. The imperative to look to the heart rather than the book is in fact derived from a central concern of Renaissance pedagogy: the distinction between the rote repetition of words and true understanding, the deeply inculcated knowledge that was the goal of humanist education. In adapting these pedagogical terms and themes to the portrayal of the love affair, the poems represent love as a practice one learns through instruction and experience, a phenomenon formed through acculturation and inseparable from social expression and engagement.

Chapter 3 turns to Shakespeare's *Love's Labour's Lost*, a highly self-conscious play that has long been intriguing to critics for its reflections on the nature of language. The play engages with early modern debates between naturalist and conventionalist conceptions of language and experiments with a remarkable range of linguistic styles and forms. I follow several scholars in focusing on the prominent rehearsal of what J.L. Austin calls performative speech acts, utterances such as promises and christenings that perform actions in the world. While much of the play's language descends into farcical nonsense, the oaths its characters swear in the first and last scenes have significant consequences, suggesting the play's sophisticated awareness of language's social agency. This performative understanding of language, moreover, extends to the play's representation of love, which is similarly conceived as a form of social action, as the reference to love's labour in the title indicates. This conception is most clear in the play's final scene, when the women of the French court compel their suitors to prove their love through a series of clearly defined tasks, demanding that they commit themselves to a year of ascetic isolation in order to demonstrate the sincerity of their vows. Recalling Wittgenstein's observation that "love is put to the test," this trial of the suitors' devotion shows that love is defined by such criteria as fidelity and persistence, making explicit the typically unspoken standards that determine love's nature.

Chapter 4 concerns Shakespeare's *Hamlet*, a play famous for its attempt to adumbrate an inward passion that transcends outward expression, as we see in its protagonist's insistence that he has "that within that passes show" and lacks the necessary "art to reckon [his] groans" (1.2.85; 2.2.120). I argue that the play's subtle echoes of grammar school discourse demonstrate the harmony of inward states and outward expressions, contrary to Hamlet's own protestations. Some of the most famous passages in the play, such as Hamlet's "To be or not to be" soliloquy, reveal the influence of the grammar school: that speech's basic terms – "To be," "to suffer," and "to stand against" – recall, I argue, William Lily's lesson in the infinitive: "The Infinitive signifieth to do, to suffer, or to be" (Lily, *A Short Introduction* B3). This echo of Shakespeare's grammar book suggests that the abstract terms of the soliloquy, which have led many critics to associate the speech with various metaphysical schema, are not only states of being but also ways of speaking. Hamlet is ultimately unable to sever the links that bind him to the humanist culture in which he was educated, as his very declarations of an ineffable interiority rely upon grammatical terms and concepts. By tracing the passions of its characters in the terms of the grammar school, the play reveals that passions are not inward states, but instead expressive practices that abide by social rules and conventions.

In a fifth and final chapter on Ben Jonson's comedies of humours, I hope to clarify the nature of the rules that govern the performance of passion. Jonson's *Every Man In His Humour* and *Every Man Out of His Humour* satirize the "humours" of late Elizabethan society, a term that implied both psychological temperament and prideful affectation. Jonson describes the plays as presenting his audience with "a mirror / As large as is the stage whereon we act": he confronts his spectators with representations of their own affective habits and vices to compel them to amend their conduct. Like the humanist schoolmasters who instruct their students through model texts rather than abstract rules, Jonson uses representations of humours and passions to discipline his audience's behaviour. This conception of the theatre as a mode of exemplary instruction suggests that the rules that guide and give shape to affective practice are nothing other than the artifacts of past practices, actions and behaviours that have acquired the force of example over time. That affective behaviour is judged against historical example emphasizes the necessarily situated and contextual nature of passion.

Chapter One

"Precept and Practice": Grammar and Pedagogy from the Medieval Period to the Renaissance

So that the art and practic part of life
Must be the mistress to this theoric

— Shakespeare, *Henry V*

In *On Interpretation*, Aristotle writes that "words spoken" are the "signs of the affections or impressions of the soul," which are in turn "representations or likenesses" of things.[1] The claim subordinates language to psychology: words are understood to signify or reflect the content of the soul or mind, which is itself a reflection of the things of the world. The mind is the mirror of nature, and language the mirror of the mind. This classic formulation provided the blueprint for Western thinking on language for centuries. Indeed, its influence persists into our own time, from the common understanding of language as the expression of thought to academic discourses such as Noam Chomsky's innatist theory of grammar.[2] In the sixteenth century, however, we find this hierarchy challenged and at times radically disrupted. Humanist scholarship and pedagogy constituted a reappraisal of the relationship between language, psychology, and ontology. Privileging eloquence and historical usage over the idealized structures of the previous generation of medieval grammarians, the humanists understood language as an activity and a practice bound up with our worldly existence.

In this chapter, I examine the transition from the grammatical theory of the late medieval period to that of the Renaissance, focusing in particular on the writings of the Modist grammarian Thomas of Erfurt and the humanists Lorenzo Valla and Desiderius Erasmus. The Modist position held that the principles of grammar were reflections of the ideal structures of the mind and the world: each of a word's formal grammatical properties, from tense to mood to gender, corresponded to some aspect of the world's being. The humanists rejected this theory, adopting in its place a conventional and pragmatic approach that located meaning in linguistic use. I contend that the pragmatic approach to grammar and language that obtained among the humanists emphasized connections between grammar and everyday experience, leading those writers trained in the humanist program to make novel use of the terms and concepts of grammar, employing them in a way that ranged freely across the border between word and world.

As the intellectual history of humanism has been a controversial topic over the years, a few qualifications are in order. In examining the conflicts between the late medieval period and the age of humanism, one risks being swept up in the teleological narratives of progress and revolution that figures like Burckhardt and Cassirer used to characterize the Renaissance.[3] One may also be seduced by the often-exaggerated claims of originality made by the humanists themselves. I do not intend to chart an epochal shift from the medieval to the modern in the debate between scholastic and humanist grammar or to take the metaphysical theory of the *Modistae* as a representative image of a monolithic medieval culture. I wish only to address a particular debate occurring at a particular historical juncture and to consider the impact it had on the literature produced in its wake. I also want to emphasize that the most significant implications of early modern thinking on language result from the interaction between medieval and humanist grammar, not simply the wholesale rejection of the former by the latter.

It is also worth observing that while there may not be an unbroken genealogy uniting the humanists to modern linguists and philosophers of language, the latter did at times directly engage with the debates of the medieval period and the Renaissance. Chomsky, for instance, explicitly rejects the grammatical and philological program of the humanists, which he regards as a "natural history" void of explanatory and predictive power, in favour of the universalism of the Port-Royalists and Cartesians (*Language and Mind* 15). On the other side, Heidegger, who wrote his habilation thesis on the *Modistae*, engages with the theory of the *modi significandi* in *Being and Time*, arguing that it continues to characterize our thinking on language in the modern period. Heidegger's refutation of the Modist position and his emphasis on the necessity of *"liberating grammar from logic"* echoes the humanists' disdain for a grammar encumbered by "the complexities of logic and metaphysics."[4] Ignoring these explicit connections for the sake of an unyielding historicism or an exaggerated fear of anachronism would be counterproductive.

A particular controversy over anachronism arose upon the publication of Richard Waswo's *Language and Meaning in the Renaissance*, perhaps the most sustained analysis of the relation between humanism and modern philosophy of language. Waswo makes the claim that the insights of the linguistic turn in the twentieth century were prefigured in the fifteenth by the humanist Lorenzo Valla, to whom he ascribes the remarkably modern view that "Language and the people who use it do not 'represent' a reality but constitute one" (109–10). For Waswo, this insight is scattered throughout Valla's scholarship, Martin Luther's theological writings, and Sperone Speroni's defence of vernacular literature. The lack of a fully formed linguistic vocabulary, however, made its articulations necessarily tentative, and it was quickly muted by more conventional theories of language like that of Juan Luis Vives. Thus, the Renaissance represents something of a backwater of intellectual history, its novel intuitions bypassed by the main current of learned discourse. The book staged an original and important intervention in the history of Renaissance humanism and established compelling parallels between humanism and the philosophy of Wittgenstein and other modern theorists of language. But it attracted charges of anachronism and selective readings of the humanist texts it celebrated. A particularly strong critique came from John Monfasani, who argued in "Was Lorenzo Valla an Ordinary Language Philosopher?" that Waswo exaggerated the importance of a few isolated passages, and that Valla assumed a philosophical position largely consistent with that of the Scholastics in spite of his combative rhetoric.

Lodi Nauta's recent study *In Defense of Common Sense: Lorenzo Valla's Humanist Critique of Scholastic Philosophy* is a careful and judicious sally into this contested ground. Contrary to Waswo's claims, Nauta argues that Valla maintained a referential understanding of language: "The underlying assumption of much of what Valla wrote is that language refers to the world" (276). But while he is generally sceptical toward comparisons between humanism and twentieth-century linguistic theory, Nauta concedes that "a categorical prohibition against making such comparisons, within set limits, would greatly impoverish the study of the history of philosophy," and notes that, when compared with the work of Wittgenstein, Valla's "program of replacing philosophical speculation and theorizing with an approach based on linguistic practice and common sense" has "fundamental differences but also, at the level of basic convictions about philosophical theories and speculation, interesting affinities" (7, 276). It is these "affinities" between humanism and ordinary language philosophy that I wish to highlight here, without making the claim that they are absolutely definitive of Valla's philosophy or the humanist program more generally. Valla often operates under the assumption that language is an instrument for signifying the things of the world: "a speech," he writes, "consists of what is signified and what signifies – things and words" (*Dialectical Disputations* 27). But he makes the key distinction that common language – which for Valla implied both the *sermo eruditorum* of Latin authorities and the *sermo quotidiano* of the people – provided the best and most comprehensive image of the world, especially when compared with the arcane and overly schematic language of the philosophers.

While Valla attempted to refute the Scholastics on their own terms, later figures like Erasmus, though offering at times perfunctory affirmations of the theological and metaphysical assumptions of medieval philosophy, had little interest in such matters. Their aim was to fashion a pedagogical and rhetorical culture suited to the demands of civil society and the revival of classical literature. While it did not rise to the level of an explicit philosophical program or a thorough rejection of Scholastic philosophy, the humanist emphasis on the clarity of common language and the eloquence of the classics led them to focus on everyday linguistic practice in a manner that opposed the abstract theorization of the medieval grammarians. I contend that the focus on common language and everyday practice that we find in educational reformers like Erasmus led to the tendency of Renaissance writers to integrate grammatical and pedagogical language into their representations of worldly and affective experience. This characteristic of Renaissance literature may not represent a clear philosophical position, but it nevertheless has implications for the philosophy of language that I hope to describe in this study.

The Medieval Background

The rediscovery of Aristotelian philosophy in eleventh-century Europe provoked, among many other intellectual upheavals, a re-examination of the theoretical underpinnings of grammatical study. A number of major texts on grammar, the discipline that John of Salisbury called the "foundation and root" of the Scholastic curriculum, appeared in the high medieval period, typically taking the form of commentaries or glosses on the ancient grammarians Donatus and Priscian.[5] This tradition culminated in Peter Helias's *Summa super Priscianum*, an exhaustive commentary on Priscian and the first in the line of encyclopedic *summae* that would include Thomas Aquinas's *Summa theologica*.

Among the most important innovations of medieval grammar was the concept of the *modi significandi*, or "modes of signification." The *modi significandi*, basically identifiable with the formal properties of grammar, are the qualities that make individual words into parts of speech able to be integrated into syntactical statements. In medieval theory, a vocal expression or graphic mark becomes a meaningful word when it is joined to an object in the world and has the faculty of signifying "superimposed" upon it. A word then becomes a part of speech by a second act of superimposition through which it comes to bear the *modi significandi*. The word upon which the *modi significandi* has been superimposed carries with it its entire syntactical potential and is able to be joined with other words to form meaningful sentences. *Lapis*, for instance, is a word meaning "stone," but it also bears certain *modi significandi* making it a singular masculine noun in the nominative case, and thus able to form a proposition such as *lapis durus est*, "the stone is hard." Thomas of Erfurt explains the process: "a *word* is specified formally by means of the faculty of designating superimposed upon the expression, since a word is a significative expression. A part of speech exists formally by means of the active mode of signifying superimposed upon the word, because a part of speech is a word inasmuch as it possesses an active mode of signifying" (*Grammatica speculativa* 149). Jan Pinborg has called the theory of the *modi significandi* "the first systematic syntax in the history of Western linguistics" ("Speculative Grammar" 260).

In the late thirteenth and fourteenth centuries, a group known as the speculative grammarians or the *Modistae* developed the theory of the *modi significandi* into an ambitious theoretical framework based on perceived continuities between grammar, psychology, and ontology. The *Modistae* posited, alongside the *modi significandi*, another pair of modes known as the *modi intellegendi* ("modes of understanding") and *modi essendi* ("modes of being"). This tripartite structure traced what the *Modistae* saw as the direct correspondence between the worlds of being, intellect, and language. The summary statement of the movement is Thomas of Erfurt's *Grammatica speculativa*, which will be my primary focus here. The *Grammatica speculativa* was widely read in its own time and enjoyed influence into the twentieth century, in part because it was misidentified as a work of Duns Scotus until 1922. It was admired by Charles Peirce and was the subject of Heidegger's habilation thesis, "Duns Scotus' Theory of the Categories and of Meaning." Along with the work of earlier medieval grammarians, it is often credited with advancing a nascent form of the universal grammar popularized in the twentieth century by Noam Chomsky.[6]

In the *Grammatica speculativa*, Thomas writes that the *modi significandi* are immediately derived from the *modi intellegendi*, or the properties of things as understood in the intellect, and ultimately derived from the *modi essendi*, or the properties of the things themselves. Language is the result of a process in which the properties of things impress themselves upon the mind, and the mind in turn expresses these properties in grammatically complex words. According to this model, the *modi significandi* were not simply grammatical forms inherent in language: they were reflections of the world as mediated by the intellect. Such a claim extends linguistic naturalism beyond the usual correspondence of word and thing: even the most formal properties of grammar – person, number, gender, mood, and so on – originate from and correspond to the properties of the world. We may get a sense of Thomas's methods from his account of the noun and the verb, which he defines by reference to the Platonic division between being and becoming, "the condition and permanence inherent in the thing from which it has essence" and the "change and succession inherent in the thing, from which it has becoming."[7] The noun is derived from the former of these, the "mode of being of an entity which is the mode of condition and permanence" (153). A noun such as *murus*, "wall," would correspond to the wall's being, the enduring "wall-ness" that defines its nature. By contrast, the verb is derived from the latter part of the dyad: from becoming, or "the property of flux and succession which is opposed to ... the property of state and permanence" (211). In a Modistic analysis of the phrase *muri corruerunt* – "the walls collapsed" – the verb *corruo* would be derived from the walls' property of becoming, their mutability and potential for destruction and decay.

Thomas explains all the basic parts of speech and grammatical forms through this method of analysis, deriving each of them from some property of worldly existence. Most significant for our purposes is his analysis of mood (*modus*) and voice (*genus*). In regard to the former, Thomas maintains the classic position descending from Priscian through Peter Helias that mood is an expression of the affections of the mind. Closely echoing a formulation of Priscian's, Thomas writes that "mood is the changing inclination of the mind, demonstrating its various affections" (*modus est varia animi inclination, varios eius affectus demonstrans*).[8] Thus the imperative reflects an inclination to command, the optative to hope or desire, and so on. The voice of the verb is defined in similarly psychologizing terms. The passive verb, as I have noted in my Introduction, is "that which signifies passion" (*quod significat passionem*), reflecting a passive orientation toward the verb's object.[9] Like mood, voice is an "expression of a state of mind," as it derives from the state the subject assumes in relation to its object.[10] The claim that grammatical forms like mood and voice derive from the subject's state of mind privileges psychology over grammar, but it also establishes an important connection between linguistic structures and the psychic states from which they are thought to derive.

The *Grammatica speculativa* represents an exhaustive and largely successful attempt to unite the precepts of Scholastic philosophy to the forms of Latin grammar. In arguing that grammatical forms reflect the properties of the mind and the world, Thomas implies that the world is, in a sense, grammatical: that it has a formal structure analogous to the structure of language, even if this structure is thought to be somehow prior to the use of language. I offer this brief survey of Modistic theory, then, in order to illustrate the grammatical naturalism against which humanism reacted, but also for its own virtues in demonstrating the arresting similarities between grammar and traditional metaphysics. While we may not accept the Modists' belief in the ontological and psychological origins of grammatical forms, when viewed with the critical distance opened up by the intervention of humanism, the parallels it establishes between grammar and metaphysics become immensely suggestive of the interdependence of language and the world.

Lorenzo Valla and the Critique of Modism

Beginning in the fifteenth century, humanist grammarians and pedagogues began to reject the theory of the *Modistae*. The new humanist appreciation of Greek and of the varieties of Latin that appeared over the centuries cast doubt on the naturalist and universalist assumptions of the Modists, for had the rules of grammar truly emanated from the ideal structures of the mind and world, linguistic usage would not be so changeable and diverse. Where the Modist grammarians saw a system of grammatical forms corresponding directly to the properties of the world, humanist reformers began to see a contingent framework of rules and conventions established in order to represent and regulate the varieties of language as it is actually practised. The rules of grammar were not the ultimate principles of language, originating from the properties of the world: language itself assumed priority, and the rules came to be understood as abstractions created institutionally in order to better understand and organize the use of language. Emerging from this critique was a view of language as an ongoing activity, a practice guided by convention rather than derived from an immutable edifice of rules and principles. The humanist perspective on language was pragmatic, attentive to historical usage, and accommodated to the demands of civil society.

Among the earliest and most strident critiques of Modist grammar was that of the fifteenth-century Italian humanist Lorenzo Valla. Valla spoke derisively of "the petty reasonings of dialecticians, and metaphysical obscurities, and the nonsense about *modi significandi*," arguing that such absolute principles are untenable when one considers "how different is the situation of the Greek language from that of the Latin"

("In Praise of Saint Thomas Aquinas" 23). Against the notion that language is grounded upon the properties and things of the world, Valla wrote that "Human practice ... is the progenitor of words" (*hominum usum ... verborum est auctor*, 31–3). This claim, it must be said, is not so radical a rethinking of the nature of language as is may appear. It may simply echo Aristotelian conventionalism, which holds that words are related to things by convention rather than by some natural, inherent relationship between them.[11] It does not necessarily preclude the notion that language is a representation of the world, which Valla tends to accept. But there are nevertheless moments in Valla's writing, as I hope to show, in which the emphasis on convention and use shades into a more thorough critique of the referential understanding of language.

The text that I will focus on here is Valla's *Disputationes dialecticae* (*Dialectical Disputations*), an ambitious treatise that likely represents his most significant and sustained contribution to the philosophy of language. The *Disputationes* is directed toward distinct and sometimes contradictory aims. Foremost is the goal – suggested by the text's alternate title, *Repastinatio dialectice et philosophie* or "The Reploughing of Dialectic and Philosophy" – of reforming medieval dialectic by replacing the ungainly vocabulary of Scholastic logic and metaphysics with a more parsimonious system supported by a careful and knowledgeable account of Latin and Greek grammar. So, for instance, Valla reduces the ten categories of Aristotelian logic to a mere three: substance, quality, and action. This project, while it attempts to reform the errors and "barbarisms" of the Scholastics, is roughly in accord with their philosophical aims and principles. But the *Disputationes* also advances the thesis that linguistic use rather than philosophical or technical definition is the ultimate determinant of meaning. This argument is often in conflict with the text's philosophical goals, for while the philosophical work is dedicated to paring away extraneous concepts, Valla's philological efforts multiply words and meanings, discovering a variety of senses for terms he would otherwise like to fix in an orderly system.

We can see this tension between brevity and copiousness in Valla's analysis of the concept of *res*. The text begins with a discussion of the "six transcendentals," terms held by Scholastic philosophy to transcend categories as they apply universally to all things: *ens* ("being"), *unum* ("one"), *bonum* ("good"), *verum* ("truth"), *res* ("thing"), and *aliquid* ("something"). Valla argues that this scheme is redundant and clumsy, and that a single term can serve in the place of six recognized by the Scholastics. Playing on the similarity of *res* and *rex*, Valla writes that *res* is "emperor and king" of all terms and should be taken as the sole transcendental (*Dialectical Disputations* 19). Most of the other five Valla finds obviously redundant and easily done away with: "Does not 'something' signify 'some thing'? Does 'one' not mean 'one thing'; 'true' a 'true thing' or a 'truth,' which is also a thing; good a 'good thing' or 'goodness' or 'righteousness,' which itself is also a thing?" (19). But he concedes that "being" has a more convincing claim to primacy and demands greater consideration. Valla begins his argument against the priority of "being" with the observation that the Greeks commonly use the term as a participle, as in the phrase "the man being tired went to sleep." And participles demand antecedents: just as "a husband's loving" must have as its subject an antecedent – "a husband who loves" – so must "being" be rooted in a "thing which is." So even if we speak of "being" without explicitly observing an antecedent, we are still assuming the priority of a "thing" which has "being": thus "the whole meaning of 'being' is not innate but, I would say, begged and borrowed" (23). Why say "a stone is a being," meaning "a stone is a thing which is," when "'the stone is a thing' would be more explicit, less clumsy and better usage?" (23–5). This analysis is representative of Valla's practice throughout the *Disputationes*: it shows his reliance on rigorous grammatical analysis to interrogate the terminology of the Scholastics, and, in keeping with Valla's general desire to accommodate the language of philosophy to the practical demands of worldly life, it justifies metaphysical parsimony through an appeal to clearer and more elegant usage.

Valla's argument, as I have suggested, does not question the metaphysical foundations of Scholastic philosophy. The claim that the "thingness" of things encapsulates all their transcendental properties (being, unity, goodness, etc.) still assumes that the term *res* expresses a prior reality. Yet following the argument on the priority of *res* there is a turn in the course of the text: Valla the parsimonious philosopher gives way to Valla the philologist and humanist, who is less interested in rigour and economy than in variety of usage, in what Erasmus will later call *copia*. Valla goes on to list the many colloquial uses of *res* that differ widely from the metaphysical sense he explores elsewhere in the text. In this historical and philological account, a "thing" is not simply the basic element of reality: it may also be a cause ("because of that thing"), a deed ("the things of Augustus"), a conflict ("a thing between me and an angry man"), a sexual encounter ("a soldier with whom I was having a thing"), a possession or a piece of property ("greedy for things"), a suitable situation ("just the thing"), and so forth (29). This accounting of the varieties of linguistic use shows that, in spite of Valla's desire for surety and simplicity, the meaning of a word cannot be fixed by philosophical fiat. And it indicates a concern with the practical use of language that is everywhere apparent in Valla's writing.

We can see further evidence of this pragmatic concern in a remarkable passage that I will quote at some length. Here is Valla on the use of the word "empty" (*vacuum*):

> But let us see who speaks better, the ordinary person or the philosopher. The ordinary person says that he calls the barrel "empty" when it lacks liquid, the pool "empty" when it has no water or fish, the storehouse "empty" when it lacks grain or seed, the forum "empty" when people have left it, and also the kiln "empty" or the oven "empty" when the fire has gone out or has been extinguished or when the bricks and loaves are gone. The philosopher supposes that these things cannot be empty because they are full of air, so that if the air goes out, another body comes in, and when that leaves, air comes back in again: and so these things are never empty.
>
> Let the ordinary person respond that his is "the right to decide standards in language," and that he does not call such things "full" when there is nothing but air in them, except when the air itself is of some importance, as when the sails of ships or a ball or balloon for playing games are full, and when a wine-sack is said to be "full of wind" as the harvest approaches. For if you call a bowl without liquid "full" because there is still air in it, what need was there to boast about an astonishing fact unknown to ordinary people, declaring that "nothing empty is allowed in nature"? Don't children know that, especially those used to blowing into that balloon or bladder to inflate it?
>
> And yet if nothing is empty in nature, then surely there will not be anything full, just as there will be nothing hard unless something could have been soft, not light unless heavy, not bitter unless sweet, and so on. For the very thing that they say, "empty is not allowed in nature," is exactly the same as saying "air is not allowed in nature" on the grounds that it is nothing. The ordinary person speaks better than the philosopher, then, and all the best writers agree. (267–9)

In this passage, Valla grants priority to the use of language in the world, refusing to subordinate words to their objects of reference. His astute attention to the subtle differences in the uses of the word "empty" shows that its meaning cannot be reduced to an extralinguistic object or state of affairs such as the absence of matter. Valla observes that we call a bucket "empty" when it has in it only air, yet a sail similarly filled with air is called "full." This is because in the practice of sailing the air "is of some importance": it is not merely a material object, but a thing that has entered into our conscious awareness because of the value and interest it holds for us. Similarly, the bucket is not empty because it has absolutely nothing within it, but rather because it lacks that which it is intended to hold. The word "empty," then, does not simply designate some object or concept outside of itself: instead it functions in the world in a pragmatic way, allowing us to discriminate among objects of concern and use. Language acts in conjunction with our practical engagement with things, guiding us as we make our way through the world.

Valla's discussion of the term "empty" elegantly illustrates the function of language as a conventionally structured practice that unfolds within a form of life. It suggests, in Wittgensteinian terms, that linguistic meaning is established through use and contingent upon the ways of life with which it is enmeshed. This understanding of language is implied rather than explicit, and it never attains the level of a sustained philosophical argument. But it nevertheless has a considerable influence on later humanists like Erasmus who, as we will see, consistently emphasize the role of language as an activity in our lives rather than an abstract system of signification.

Erasmus and Renaissance Pedagogy

Valla's anti-Scholastic program would win an important advocate in Desiderius Erasmus, a figure of unparalleled influence in sixteenth-century letters. Erasmus praised Valla as one "unrivalled both in the sharpness of his intelligence and the tenacity of his memory" who had "refuted the stupidities of the Barbarians, saved half-buried letters from extinction, restored Italy to her ancient splendour of eloquence, and forced even the learned to express themselves henceforth with more circumspection" (*Epistles* 64, 71). He produced two abbreviations of Valla's *Elegentiae linguae latinae*, and in 1505 published an edition of Valla's controversial annotations to the New Testament, the *Adnotationes*, with a prefatory letter defending Valla against his theological enemies. In his own pedagogical writings, Erasmus took up Valla's campaign against medieval grammatical theory.[12] While he did not question the principles of logic or the metaphysical foundations of the world, he argued that such schema are irrelevant to the concerns of civil society and the liberal arts, and often serve only to confuse and entangle the distinctly human pursuits of everyday life. Here, in the pedagogical text *De pueris instituendis* ("On the Education of Children"), Erasmus laments the errors of the medieval educational program, which rushes from rudimentary instruction in the parts of speech to the obscure and difficult subjects of dialectic:

as soon as they have learned the declensions and the agreement between nouns and adjectives their study of grammar is finished, and they are introduced to the confusions of logic, where, in effect, they are forced to unlearn whatever skills of correct speech they may previously have acquired. An even more wretched state of affairs prevailed when I was a boy: students were cruelly tormented with modes of meaning and petty enquiries into the "virtue" of a word, and in the mean time acquired nothing but poor speaking habits. Indeed, the teachers of that time, afraid to teach anything that might seem fit only for boys, would obscure grammar with the complexities of logic and metaphysics. (345)

As an alternative to this stultifying pedagogical practice, Erasmus sets out a plan for liberal education which would minimize instruction in logic and expand training in grammar, which he understands to include not only knowledge of the Latin language but also the study of classical literary genres and extensive training in eloquent speech and writing. Under Erasmus, grammar becomes the foremost subject of liberal education and the gateway into the civic culture of the age.

In the reflections on nature and education that make up much of *De pueris instituendis*, Erasmus inveighs against the naturalism and foundationalism of the Modists. He acknowledges the predominant influence of nature in almost all things, but he makes a significant exception in the case of human acculturation. "Education," he writes, "is that special task which has been entrusted to us," the one domain in which nature abdicates her governing power. Erasmus goes so far as to privilege education over nature, writing that "while nature is strong, education is more powerful still" (301). He concludes with an arresting pronouncement: "Man certainly is not born, but made man," fashioned into human form through the methods of liberal education in which grammar held the primary place (304). For Erasmus, grammar is no less than the means by which we become human.

In *De ratione studii* ("On the Method of Study"), Erasmus provides a more detailed account the of his favoured method of instruction.[13] As in *De pueris*, he begins with a nod toward orthodoxy by asserting that the knowledge of "things" (*res*) is ultimately greater in importance than that of "words" (*verba*). But he inverts their standard order by insisting that one may only gain knowledge of things through the study of words.[14] The program of grammatical study set out by Erasmus in order to facilitate the acquisition of such knowledge assumes a significantly different understanding of grammar from that which prevailed in Thomas and the other medieval grammarians. Erasmus writes that "it is not by learning rules that we acquire the power of speaking a language, but by daily intercourse with those accustomed to express themselves with exactness and refinement, and by the copious reading of the best authors."[15] In forswearing the memorization of rules detached from the practice of language, Erasmus refutes the Modist view of grammar as a system of immutable principles rooted in the properties of the world. One learns to speak not by a set of rules, but by conversation and reading, by participation in a language as it is practised in the world. It is through such participation that one comes to understand the norms and standards of language, which are no longer conceived as *a priori* laws, but as conventions that emerge from linguistic use.

It is tempting to describe the difference between the medieval and the humanist perspectives on grammar as prescriptive and descriptive, respectively. But it would be wrong to think of the accounts of Erasmus and others as purely descriptive or empirical, for they are not merely detached reports of how language has functioned historically. Instead they are explanations of the way that linguistic usage provides the standards and conventions for future use. The model of learning through experience and example advocated by Erasmus and his followers assumes that the rules for proper linguistic use are inherent in established and accepted forms of language. As Cummings writes in his discussions of Erasmus, "grammar works by examples, and thereby sets an example. The true aim of instruction is not a theory of signification, but precepts for elegant composition and *flores poetarum*" (*The Literary Culture of the Reformation* 129). The humanist account of language remains prescriptive and normative, but it derives its rules from the shifting patterns of historical linguistic practice rather than from the fixed and rigid standards of ontology and psychology. Language, for the humanists, is normative, but its rules are native to itself.

A fascinating discussion of obscenity in *De copia* demonstrates how Erasmus derives the rules of language from historical practice rather than founding them upon an extralinguistic ground. Erasmus rejects the argument of the Cynics that obscene words are those that describe obscene acts, astutely observing that the worst vices – parricide, incest, and so on – are named without offence and thus demonstrating the absence of any clear correspondence between obscene words and that which they represent. Instead, Erasmus contends that the definition of obscene words must be gathered from qualified usage: "Whence then is derived a rule of obscenity? From nowhere else but from the usage, not of anyone whatsoever, but of those whose speech is chaste" (23). At first glance, the formulation appears to be circular: if obscene words are simply those avoided by the chaste, how do we define chaste speech but by the absence of obscenity? Erasmus's point, however, is simply that obscenity is defined by context, convention, and tradition. There are certain words we expect to hear as part of a vulgar proposal, a crude insult, or an oath: they are traditionally put to such purposes, and their use over the ages reinforces the association with such indecorous speech acts. Chaste speech is native to the church; obscene speech to the tavern or the brothel: they are defined by the ways in which they are used and the practices and forms of life to which they adhere. Obscene words strike us as offensive not because of what they signify, but because of the ways and contexts in which they are traditionally employed. Historical practice provides the standards for our interpretation and judgment of language.

Erasmus's pedagogical thought was particularly influential in England: writings like *De ratione studii* and his work with John Colet in establishing St Paul's Grammar School set the template for sixteenth-century English education.[16] Among his contributions was an influential grammar manual produced in collaboration with Colet and the scholar William Lily. Published under the titles *Brevissima institutio*, *Rudimenta grammatices*, and *The Short Introduction of Grammar*, it was known familiarly as "Lily's Grammar." In 1542, Henry VIII decreed that the text was to be used exclusively in English grammar schools, establishing it as the standard for Latin education and one of the most widely read books of its time (Shakespeare, as we will see, quotes from it habitually). Colet's arresting statement on the nature of the Latin language, included in some editions of the manual, gives a sense of the linguistic understanding that the Erasmian program helped to propagate in England. Colet writes:

> But howe and in what maner, and with what constructyon of wordes, and all the varietees, and dyuersitees, and chaunges in latyn speche, whiche be innumerable, if any man wyll knowe, and by that knowledge attayne to vnderstande latyn bokes, and to speke & to wryte the clene latyn. Let hym aboue all besyly lerne and rede good latyn auctors of chosen poetes and oratours, and note wysely howe they wrote, and spake, and study alway to folowe them, desiryng none other rules but their example. For in the beginning men spake not latyn bycause suche rules were made but contrary wyse, bycause men spake suche latyn, vpon that folowed the rules were made. That is to saye latyn speche was before the rules, not the rules before the latyn speche. (*Aeditio* D6)

Colet describes language as a historical practice, an infinitely varied tapestry of uses and meanings that confounds any attempt to reduce it to a set of abstract principles. While the idealized rules of grammar may at times adequately approximate this discourse, its constant flux and change and its limitless individual variation make it impossible to capture within a comprehensive system. As Cummings writes, "Humanist attention to usage raised the spectre of a grammar without limits. Every usage seemed to require a new grammar to explain it. At times – as in Erasmus's great work *De copia verborum ac rerum* (1512) – it seemed as if the only true grammar would consist in a list of all the possible ways of saying things within the language" (*The Literary Culture of the Reformation* 126–7). Such an image is appropriate in Colet's England, where English was undergoing changes of unprecedented rapidity, adapting words, structures, and idioms from classical languages, European vernaculars, and even the languages of the Americas. Though they may not be perfectly representative of a humanist enterprise that often sought to control such change through adherence to classical style, Colet's comments present us with a striking picture of an ever-shifting, protean field of language whose only law is accepted use.

Pedagogy and Poetry

Jeff Dolven's *Scenes of Instruction in Renaissance Romance* has demonstrated the profound influence of humanist pedagogy on early modern literature, tracing a relationship of both inspiration and rivalry between the period's poets and educators. Though writers like Sidney and Spenser recommended their own works as superior methods of teaching to those employed in the schools, Dolven's sensitive readings suggest that their writings often emphasize their own failures as pedagogical devices and reveal profound doubts about the possibilities of the humanist enterprise. I am not primarily concerned in this book with the successes and failures of literature as instrument of teaching, but I follow Dolven in the view that early modern writers are "haunted by the scene of their own instruction" (59) and find in early modern literature marks of the powerful impact that humanist pedagogy had on the thinking and writing of its students.

Humanism's conception of language as a conventional practice and the efforts of humanist schoolmasters to join grammatical instruction to broader practices of writing, speaking, and acting may help to explain the pervasiveness and persistence of its influence. In order to learn a language of the variety and versatility described by Colet, one could not study rules in isolation. Instead, one would have to learn through experience in speaking and writing, as Erasmus advised. Through such practices as imitation, translation, commentary, and discussion, one gains experience in a language and comes to understand its use: one is acculturated in the language, inducted into a community of speakers. By this method one comes to master and internalize a set of rules, but these rules are often implicit and manifest in practice rather than memorized in the abstract. They are fluid and context-dependent, and they may change over time as different situations and goals arise, unlike the unyielding laws of logic and mathematics.

This method did not eschew instruction in the traditional apparatus of grammar, but it sought to join this instruction to experience in conversation and reading so that the rules of the grammar book were understood in practice. In this way, the humanists argued, students came to learn the rules more comprehensively and to apply them more easily. In *The Scholemaster*, one of the most influential texts in the English pedagogical tradition, Roger Ascham explains the practice of "double translation" and how it inculcates a more thorough and deeply internalized knowledge of grammatical principles than one would gain through memorization and study of "the naked rewles" (Nii). Here Ascham provides an overview of the practice:

> First, let him [the schoolmaster] teach the childe, cherefullie and playnlie, the cause, and matter of the letter: then, let him construe it into English, so oft, as the childe may easilie carry away the vnderstanding of it: Lastly, parse it ouer perfectly. This done thus, let the childe, by and by, both construe and parse it ouer agayne: so, that it may appeare, that the childe doubteth in nothing, that his maister taught him before. After this, the childe must take a paper booke, and sitting in some place, where no man shall prompe him, by him selfe, let him translate into Englishe hys former lesson. Then shewing it to his master, let the master take from him his latin booke and pausing an houre, at the least, then let the childe translate his owne Englishe into latin agayne, in an other paper booke. When the childe bringeth it, turned into latin, the Maister must compare it with Tullies booke, and laie them both together: and where the childe doth well, either in chosing, or true placing of Tullies words, let the master praise him, and say, here you do well. For I assure you, there is no such whetstone, to sharpen a good witte and encourage a will to learning, as is prayse. (Cii)

The passage shows that Ascham conceives of grammar school instruction as an irreducibly social interaction between student and master. The master does not simply communicate to the child the definitions of Latin words and the rules of Latin syntax; he guides him through exercises that provide direct experience in the language, gently correcting his mistakes and praising his performance when it adheres to expectations. This practice relies as much on cheer and praise, which cultivate in the child "a will to learning," as it does on the knowledge of correct terms and principles.[17] Through this practice of experiential training and affective engagement, the child does not merely learn what he is told by the master; he also gains the desire and discipline necessary to extend his learning independently. He is thus inducted into the humanist community, acculturated in such a way that he conforms to its ethics and internalizes its aims and desires.[18]

As Ascham continues, he shows how this method of instruction will instil in the student a knowledge of grammatical rules more effectively than the traditional practices of memorization and parsing:

> In these few lines, I have wrapped vp, the most tedious part of Grammer: and also the ground of almost al the Rewles, that are so busilye taught by the Maister, and so hardlie learned by the Scholler, in all common Scholes, which after this sort, the maister shall teach without all error, and the scholer shall learne without great payne: the master being ledde by so sure a guide, and the scholer being brought into so plaine, and easie a way. And therefore, we do not contemne Rewles, but we gladly teach Rewles: and teach them more plainly, sensiblie, and orderlie, then they be commonly taught in common Scholes. For, when the Master shall compare Tullies booke with the Scholers translation, let the maister at the first, lead and teach his scholer, be able to fetch out of his Grammer, euery Rewle, for euery example: So as the Grammer booke be ever in the Scholers hande, and also vsed of him, as a Dictionarie, for euery present vse. Thys is the liuelie, and perfect way of teaching of Rewles: where the common way, vsed in common Scholes, to read the Grammer alone by itselfe, is tedious for the Maister, harde for the Scholer, colde and vncomfortable for them both. (Cii)

As the master compares the schoolboy's re-Latinized Cicero to the original, he teaches his student to name the rules that he has intuitively followed or unwittingly violated. The rules are thus learned in practice, joined to the student's experience in the language. In this way, Ascham argues, the student comes to internalize the rules, having them always at the ready for whatever situation arises. Ascham's claim extends the application of the rules beyond the matter of the grammar school curriculum. The grammar book, internalized in such a way that it is employed "for euery present vse," becomes part of the student's reflexive apparatus, instinctively recalled in a variety of situations. We can get a sense of the outcome of this training from Shakespeare's *Much Ado about Nothing*: when Benedick responds to the interruption of Hero and Claudio's wedding by quoting from Lily's lesson on the interjection – "How

now? Interjections? Why then, some be of laughing, as ha, ha, he"
(4.1.19–20) – he dramatizes the tendency described in Ascham to recur
habitually to the grammar book in the course of everyday life.[19]

Richard Mulcaster's *Elementarie* provides further evidence of the capacious application of grammatical instruction. Mulcaster describes the
importance of the exercises and the practices of learning outlined in the
book:

> Take exercise awaie, what then is the bodie, but an vnweildie lump? what
> vse of it hath either cuntrie in defence, or it self in delite? Remove precept
> and practis, and where then is vertew, which neither knoweth, what to
> do, if it be not directed, neither doth when it knoweth, if it faill of practis?
> Set these fiue principles [reading, writing, drawing, music, and playing]
> apart, what can the vnlearned eie judge of? the vntrained hand deall with?
> the vnframed voice please with? (26)

In Mulcaster's account, the precepts and practices of the grammar
school govern both knowledge and embodied practice. The judgment
of the eye, the assured gestures of the hand, the pleasing eloquence
of the well-trained voice: all fall under the schoolmaster's guidance.
Even the body itself is merely an "unweildie lvmp" without the "exercise" of the schoolyard, which here seems barely distinguished from
the verbal exercises through which one learns Latin grammar. Not only
linguistic statements, then, but also embodied actions and feelings such
as "delite" are understood to exist within a framework of rules and
conventions. They are conditioned and corrected by the master's precepts and patterned after his practices. While the Modists conceived of
linguistic rules as reflections of psychological structures, for teachers
like Ascham and Mulcaster the situation was reversed: linguistic training was a means of cultivating and refining the virtues and passions
of the schoolboys in their charge. For early modern schoolmasters, as
Enterline writes, "language precedes and shapes character rather than
the other way around" ("Rhetoric, Discipline" 175).

The efforts of Ascham and Mulcaster to integrate grammatical instruction with broader practices of composition and conversation provide context for the literary appropriations of grammatical terms that
we will encounter in the following chapters. They suggest how those
writers trained in the humanist educational program came to adopt
the language arts as a frame through which to view the world, understanding and representing lived experience, and especially affective experience, in grammatical terms. From the schoolboy's rehearsal of the
rudimentary "amo, amas, amat" to his imitation and performance of

the *Amores* of Ovid or the laments of Dido and Hecuba, the grammar school equipped its students with a set of conventions, models, and practices that served as the foundations of the Renaissance discourse of passion. It is this set of rules and conventions, this "grammar," to which writers such as Sidney allude in speaking of "the grammar rules of affection" or the "grammar" of the heart, lines that recall the scene of the schoolroom and testify to the essential role played by language and pedagogy in shaping affective experience.

Chapter Two

"Heart-Ravishing Knowledge": Love and Learning in Sidney's *Astrophil and Stella*

Philip Sidney's *Astrophil and Stella* (1591), a sonnet cycle of unparalleled influence in Elizabethan England, unites the traditions of Petrarchan poetry with the idioms of Tudor pedagogy. The Renaissance school-room was the site of a powerful combination of disciplinary and ama-tory experience, making it an appropriate metaphorical setting for the Petrarchan love affair. Thus in Sidney's cycle the kiss is "schoolmaster of delight," Love a wanton boy "School'd onely by his mother's tender eye," and Stella a "schoole-mistresse" who punishes those who fail to learn her lessons.[1] The love affair is figured as a relation between an adoring but tormented pupil and a mistress who is both disciplining instructor and object of desire.

Andrew Strycharski has recently addressed the prevalence and sig-nificance of *Astrophil and Stella*'s allusions to pedagogy. By Strycharski's count, references to grammar, learning, and scholarly practices such as recitation and translation appear in no less than thirty-four of the poems – more than a quarter of the cycle – suggesting an obsessive recurrence to the scene of the schoolroom ("Literacy, Education, and Affect" 48). These references often take the form of an implied equivalence between love and learning. Strycharski's principal example of this equation is *Astrophil and Stella*'s second song: in that poem, Astrophil encounters a recumbent Stella "Teaching sleepe most faire to be" (2). Overcome with desire, he approaches her with the intent to "invade the fort" (15) but relents upon considering the anger such an act would provoke (rather than its inherent violence). But he allows himself to steal a kiss, which he compares to the first lesson of the schoolboy: "Who will read must first learn spelling" (24). For Strycharski, the scene is exemplary of the way that learning is "tangled with desire, sex, violence, and mascu-line anxiety" in *Astrophil and Stella* ("Literacy, Education, and Affect" 45). The vicious image of the rape fantasy "reflects a psychic violence accompanying literature," recalling the disciplinary cruelty of the schoolroom and the anxieties attendant upon literary ambition (56).

Working in a tradition that runs from the pioneering scholarship of Walter Ong to William Kerrigan to Lynn Enterline's important recent work, Strycharski sees the early modern schoolroom as the site of a formative psychic and libidinal experience, echoing and altering the Oedipal relations that initially developed in the childhood home. Early modern education staged what Ong called "a Renaissance puberty rite," a ritual by which boys would abandon the mother tongue and enter into the masculine order of Latinity.[2] Through this process, the student would come to abandon his former affection for his mother and come to desire and identify with the *magister*, a masculine figure Strycharski calls the *alma pater*.[3] Stella – who appears throughout the poems in the garb of a schoolmistress, threatening Astrophil with the correction of the rod – represents the return of a repressed femininity.

In relying heavily on psychoanalytic theory, Strycharski's reading prioritizes an affective interior over the expressive realm of language and engagement. I do not wish to deny the psychological effects of grammar school training: practices such as the repeated pronouncement of the schoolboy's *amo* did likely occasion powerful feelings of desire and allegiance toward the schoolmaster in students like Sidney. But they also emphasized, I would like to argue, that such feelings are cultivated and sustained through language, manifest in the avowals and rehearsals that made up the daily practice of the schoolroom. Early modern students would have come to understand the effects of language and grammar in enabling social and affective relations, effects already available to them as English speakers but now thrown into relief by formal and deliberate instruction in a second language. To equate love and learning, as Sidney so often does, not only reveals the psychological marks left by the schoolroom, but also demonstrates an understanding of love as a linguistic practice, a social interaction extended over time and guided by conventional standards like the exercises of the schoolroom.

Heart and Book

I will begin my discussion of *Astrophil and Stella* with the first and best-known of the sonnets:

Loving in truth, and faine in verse my love to show
That the deare She might take some pleasure of my paine:
Pleasure might cause her reade, reading might make her know,

Knowledge might pitie winne, and pitie grace obtain,
I sought fit words to paint the blackest face of woe,
Studying inventions fine, her wits to entertaine:
Oft turning others' leaves, to see if thence would flow
Some fresh and fruitfull showers upon my sunne-burn'd braine.
But words came halting forth, wanting Invention's stay,
Invention, Nature's child, fled step-dame Studie's blows,
And others' feete still seem'd but strangers in my way.
Thus, great with child to speake, and helpless in my throes,
Biting my trewand pen, beating my selfe for spite,
"Foole," said my Muse to me, "looke in thy heart and write."

The command of the Muse – "looke in thy heart and write" – is often taken as evidence for the notion that authentic love is to be found in the heart rather than in the traditions and conventions of love lyric. Astrophil, it seems, harbours within him a passion that is prior to its expression in language, a passion entirely distinct from that celebrated in earlier love poems, which serve merely as obstacles in his path. Jacqueline Miller's fine essay "The Passion Signified" has shown that passion in early modern literature is often understood to be inseparable from the words and signs in which it is expressed. But in *Astrophil and Stella* 1, she argues, "The passion precedes the representation of it; it is, syntactically and otherwise, posited as the origin of all that follows"; the poem "posits a passion 'within' that exists independent of its representation" (407). Daniel Juan Gil, in accord with Miller, contends that *Astrophil and Stella* advances the view that "public poetry is a trifling distraction that should ultimately be abandoned in favor of the noble love that it cannot quite represent" (*Before Intimacy* 40). In Gil's insightful reading, Sidney, motivated by the unsure foundations of his aristocratic position, attempts to distinguish himself from rival poets by reserving a private space for himself and his beloved Stella (a clear version of Lady Penelope Rich, sister to the Earl of Essex). The poems only gesture toward the love that Astrophil shares with Stella, denying their readers access to a privileged realm of aristocratic intimacy. "A mode of cultural production adequate to high love," writes Gil, "would thus have to be as unavailable, as silent, as the elite love that passes show is. It would have to be – in Wittgenstein's parlance – a private language. Astrophil's love for Stella and his friend is socially distinctive only as long as it is not represented in a public language; it must remain a 'joy, too high for my low stile to show'" (39). Along with such texts as Shakespeare's *Hamlet*, to which Gil's comments allude, *Astrophil and Stella* is considered by these critics and others to be among the classic articulations of psychological and sexual privacy, a repository of passions that exist prior to and apart from the public expressions of language.[4]

A subtle allusion to the idioms of humanist pedagogy in sonnet 1, however, suggests that the cycle maintains a different understanding of the relation between public language and private passion from the one described by Gil and Miller. The reference appears in the demand that Sidney look to his "heart" rather than his books ("others' leaves") in order to find the proper language in which to declare his love. In the pedagogical discourse to which Sidney so often alludes, to know "by heart" rather than "by book" was not to possess some altogether different kind of knowledge, but rather to manifest a more thorough comprehension of the subject at hand.[5] When paired with the book, the heart was not the repository of an essential and objectified passion; instead, it was the seat of an internalized skill that contrasted with the rote learning of the initiate, either in love or in letters. We may see one example of the conventional pairing of heart and book in the *Colloquies* of the Swiss humanist Corderius, a popular collection of dialogues intended to train students in Latin. Here a student describes the morning ritual of the schoolroom:

> I sit in my Place: The Master enters, he enquires about the Absenters, then he sits in his Chair, and orders the Writing of an Authour to be pronounced. We pronounce Three with a clear Voice, as we use every Day, then he bids us render the Interpretation, some of the more ignorant read, others render the Interpretation, and that by heart.

While he uses the image of the head rather than the heart, John Brinsley makes even more explicit the dependence of poetic eloquence on a thorough practice of learning and inculcated understanding:

> To attaine to this facultie, to bee able to write or speake of anie matter, and so to come to all excellent learning, the verie first and chiefe fountaine, and that which is all in all is to vnderstand the matter wel in the first place. As for store of matter, the writings of learned men (such as Socrates was) will furnish you aboundantly therewith.
>
> And when you haue the matter throughly in your head, words will follow, as waters out of a fountaine, euen almost naturally, to expresse your mind in any tongue, which yon [sic] studie in any right order ... This was a principall cause that made Tully, Ouid, Virgil, and some others so to flowe in eloquence; and especially Virgil, whom men worthily account the chief of all Latine Poets, because they did vnderstand so fully whatsoeuer they writ of. (*Ludus Literarius* 43–4)

Brinsley makes it clear that the poetic eloquence to which Astrophil aspires is understood to be the result of a transformative practice of scholarship. To write articulately and naturally, "to flowe in eloquence" like the great poets of the past, one must have the matter of one's writing "throughly" within, internalized in such a way that it becomes second nature.

The difference observed in *Astrophil and Stella* 1 between the heart and the book, then, is not one of true interiority versus false outward show; rather, it is between the mastery of a discourse and the rote recitation of it. The poem is concerned with what Ian Green has shown to be a central preoccupation of early modern education: the distinction "between, on the one hand, the mechanical parroting of words and, on the other, a real understanding of their meaning and commitment to their implementation."[6] To know "by heart" was to have internalized erotic rhetoric, to have mastered the language of love in such a way as to make consultation with books entirely superfluous. To write from the heart was not simply to write in correspondence with some internal feeling, but to use a language and a style subtly distilled and synthesized from the totality of one's study, to show that one had achieved facility in a language that existed in relation to earlier traditions but was not mechanically copied from "others' leaves." Turning back to Corderius's *Colloquies*, we can see that while the heart was opposed to the book, to have knowledge in the heart was nevertheless the outcome of study: "I will write [my lessons] out as diligently as I can. / And what then? / I will get by Heart the very Text of the Authour" (98). The poem is not a rejection of the Petrarchan mode as artificial – it is hardly ashamed of its artful composition – but rather a claim that the writer is a proper student of the Muse, one who has gained such expertise through study and experience that he has no need to consult his library.[7] It announces that Astrophil has completed his initiation in love and writes as an acknowledged master. In Shakespeare's *Romeo and Juliet*, Friar Laurence makes a play on this opposition similar to that of sonnet 1 in describing the ignorant, unfelt love of the young Romeo for Rosaline: "Thy love did read by rote," he says, "that could not spell" (2.3.84).[8] Just as a child may recite passages of Latin without knowing what they mean, so has Romeo courted Rosaline mechanically and without understanding. But his love for Juliet, like Astrophil's for Stella, is that of an expert.

One might object that the figure of "step-dame Studie," whose punitive beatings leave Astrophil tongue-tied and demoralized, contradicts this reading. This appears to be an image of the tyranny of the schoolhouse, suggesting that in order for Astrophil to express his true feelings he must free himself of the constraints of learning and tradition. But the allegory is more complex than a simple opposition between Study and

Nature, for that to which Sidney aspires is "Invention," a figure that is no less native to the schoolroom than is Study. Invention, or *inventio*, is the first of the five canons of rhetoric, the practice of creative discovery by which the speaker finds out and selects an appropriate subject among the many that exist in the world.[9] As a learned method by which one navigates the world's storehouse of themes and things, Invention unites learning and nature. It represents the true kind of learning, one which is artful and creative but nevertheless conforms to the shape of the world. Distinguished from Invention, Studie appears as the kind of artificial and mechanical training that Sidney often condemns, the narrow pedantry axiomatically opposed to the true practice of learning.

Astrophil and Stella 15 continues the discourse on mechanical recitation and internalized mastery. The sonnet is addressed to those poets who rummage through old books for the language they use in their verse:

> You that do search for everie purling spring
> Which from the ribs of old *Parnassus* flowes ...
> You that do Dictionarie's method bring
> Into your rimes, running in ratling rowes:
> You that poore *Petrarch's* long deceased woes,
> With new-borne sighes and denisend wit do sing.   (1–8)

Such rhymers, according to the poem, betray "a want of inward tuch" (10) in their laboured and affected borrowings. The phrase indicates a different understanding of inwardness from the one to which we are accustomed. "Inward tuch" suggests a skill acquired through engagement with the world, internalized through experience and education: the truly skilled poet has ability "inside," while the pedant is always groping for external devices – like dictionaries, commonplace books, and other writers' poems – to aid in composition. Sidney makes the same point in *The Defence of Poesy*'s complaint against derivative writers: "truly I could wish ... the diligent imitators of Tully and Demosthenes, most worthy to be imitated, did not so much keep Nizolian paper-books of their figures and phrases, as by attentive translation (as it were) devour them whole, and make them wholly theirs" (246). The comparison of *imitatio* to digestion, implying that one should distil what is best from many writers just as the stomach derives nutrients from food, is itself a commonplace borrowed from Seneca's *Epistles*.[10] Its deft and instinctive deployment here performs the principle under discussion. The point is not to advocate that one eschew study in favour of an unmediated expression of inward passion. It is instead to encourage a more thorough and transformative practice of study, one that makes external aid unnecessary and allows one's learning to be worn lightly and without ostentation. This metaphor of digestion suggests that love and passion are formed through acculturation, through reading and social engagement, shifting our focus from inward objects to inculcated habits of thought and practice.

The light touch that Sidney opposes to labour and affectation is comparable to what Baldessare Castiglione calls *sprezzatura* in *The Book of the Courtier*. Most often translated as "nonchalance," *sprezzatura* is the paradoxical virtue by which the courtier, through studious practice, conveys an impression of effortlessness and ease, for "true art is what does not seem to be art, and the most important thing is to conceal it" (*The Book of the Courtier* 67). Sidney's verse has a similar quality: its efforts are concealed by the appearance of spontaneity and ease. The connection is unsurprising, as Castiglione's book had a pervasive influence in Renaissance Europe, and Sidney is frequently described as an exemplar of its courtly ideals. It is worth noting that Castiglione's vision of courtliness is explicitly influenced by the practices and values of humanist pedagogy. In explaining his choice to write the text as a dialogue, Castiglione writes that "we shall not follow any strict order or list a series of precepts, as is the normal practice in teaching. Instead, following many writers of the ancient world, and reviving a pleasant memory, we shall recount some discussions that once took place among men who were singularly qualified in these matters" (40). As opposed to "the normal practice in teaching," Castiglione adopts the novel methods of the humanists, instructing by example rather than precept and privileging participation in conversation over the memorization of rules and principles. His eloquent speakers model the courtly sensibilities he seeks to impart to his readers. The effortless grace of the Lombard courtier and the Elizabethan poet's eloquent expressions of love, then, are both products of a humanist pedagogy that emphasizes imitation and practice.

At the conclusion of sonnet 15, Astrophil advises those seeking inspiration to turn away from poems and reference manuals and toward the image of his beloved:

> But if (both for your love and skill) your name
> You seeke to nurse at fullest breasts of Fame,
> *Stella* behold, and then begin to endite.   (12–14)

To gaze upon Stella's face is simultaneously to inspire one's love and to refine one's skill as a poet. Like eloquence and poetic skill, love is cultivated through learning and experience: it is not a thing to be found ready made in the heart, but a skill to be mastered like a language. Love is something one learns and something one does, inherent in the practices of wooing and courtship. The cycle shows that what appears to be an appeal to an inward passion distinct from the traditions of erotic lyric is in fact evidence that love is enabled by and manifest in a set of linguistic and pedagogical practices. No space or difference is acknowledged between the internal state and its expression: "My words I know do well set forth my mind," as Astrophil has it in sonnet 44 (1). Far from the private language with which Gil associates the cycle, then, Sidney's use of pedagogical terms shows that the language and the practice of love are essentially public, acquired through instruction and social intercourse and made meaningful by their relation to existing rules and conventions.[11]

Sonnet 16 is particularly suggestive of the way that pedagogical language emphasizes the public and linguistic nature of the love affair. The poem recounts how Astrophil, finding himself charmed but hardly captivated by various women, decides that tales of the pangs of love were exaggerated and those who told them "babes" who "of some pinne's hurt did whine" (7). But upon beholding Stella, and feeling for himself the pain of unfulfilled desire, he comes to recognize immediately the truth of their complaints. Unable to grasp what love was when it is simply described to him, he achieves a perfect understanding of it through experience (I will discuss the importance of learning by experience in Sidney later in the chapter). The poem concludes by framing this lesson in the language of the grammar school:

> In her sight I a lesson new have speld,
> I now have learn'd Love right, and learn'd even so
> As who by being poisond doth poison know. (12–14)

In pronouncing his lesson in Stella's presence, Astrophil plays the schoolboy demonstrating that he has properly learned his mistress's teachings, showing that he, unlike the young Romeo who "could not spell," has properly internalized her instruction in love.

As Jeff Dolven has shown, it was of great importance in humanist pedagogy that the schoolboy should perform his understanding of a subject in this way. Dolven describes the centrality of what he calls "telling learning" to early modern pedagogy, drawing upon Wittgenstein's concept of the language-game:

> The scene of instruction that is the classroom is set up to specify more narrowly what counts as knowledge and what learning looks like: it is the

school-master's job to prove that the students learn ... The daily routines that provide the proof, the classroom's exercises, must be constructed in such a way that both the matter to be learned and the condition of knowing it take specific, agreed upon forms. (*Scenes of Instruction* 15–16)

Reviewing a basic example of an exercise in the repetition of *sententia*, Dolven continues:

The rules of this little game are simple and familiar: the students commit to memory maxims ("petty sentences") from texts read to them by the schoolmaster and his assistant, the usher, and at the appointed time (typically first thing in the morning) they render or recite those maxims back ... The point of playing this game is to produce a representation of the schoolboy's knowledge, in the form of the sentence he repeats. How do I know the student knows that love conquers all? That he can conjugate *vinco*? That he respects my authority? Because he says, "*amor vincit omnia.*" Saying these words, at least within the parameters of the game, is what it means to know, to have learned, to understand. (16)

To learn and to demonstrate one's learning are activities that take place in the world and rely upon certain rules and conventions. Knowledge, which we are tempted to imagine as an internal mental state, is thus embodied in performance, and the rules and rituals of classroom instruction provide the standards by which we may say that a child knows or does not know: "Out of a daily obligation, then, an exercise performed in the chill earliest hours of the school day in a long, drafty hall, it is possible to read an account both of knowledge and of knowing" (Dolven, *Scenes of Instruction* 17). As Dolven suggests, the scene of instruction, with its explicit rules and conditions for correct performance, is clearly comparable to the kind of primitive language-game described by Wittgenstein in the *Philosophical Investigations*. That sonnet 16 reproduces the scene of instruction in order to characterize Astrophil's experience suggests that Dolven's claim that knowledge is constituted by ritualized and rule-guided performance may be extended to an account of love. In representing the performance of love as the rehearsal of a schoolboy's learning, the pronunciation of a lesson under the disciplinary gaze of the schoolmistress, the poem shows that Sidney conceives of love as a practice, a rule-guided activity, analogous to that which goes on in the schoolroom. Love too is a language-game, bound inextricably to our language and action in the world.

"O Grammer rules"

The most explicit and sustained reference to the language of the grammar school appears in *Astrophil and Stella* 63. The sonnet begins with an apostrophe to the rules of grammar:

> O Grammer rules, o now your vertues show;
> So children still read you with awfull eyes,
> As my young Dove may in your precepts wise
> Her graunt to me, by her own virtue know.
> For late with heart most high, with eyes most low,
> I crav'd the thing which ever she denies:
> She lightning *Love*, displaying *Venus'* skies,
> Least once should not be heard, twise said, No, No.
> Sing then my Muse, now *Io Pean* sing,
> Heav'ns envy not at my high triumphing:
> But Grammer's force with sweet successe confirme,
> For Grammer sayes (o this dear *Stella* weighe,)
> For Grammer sayes (to Grammer who says nay)
> That in one speech two Negatives affirme.

In the sonnet, Astrophil mischievously claims that in answering "No, No," Stella has in fact granted his entreaty by virtue of a double negative. The poem is ironic, though it carries some of the sexually aggressive and coercive qualities apparent in the second song. While *Astrophil and Stella* has been lauded for occasionally granting Stella a voice, differentiating her from the typically silent mistress of Petarchan poetry, that voice is often manipulated: on multiple occasions, Astrophil attempts to alter the meaning of Stella's denials by shifting the context in which they appear or wilfully misinterpreting her intent.[12] In this case, however, the attempt is patently disingenuous: Astrophil knows full well that Stella's repetition was for clarity and emphasis, as he himself reports that she spoke twice "Least once should not be heard." In this way, the poem satirizes the strict prescriptivism of the grammarians by appealing to the rules of grammar as though they were the divinely ordained law: "to Grammer who says nay"?

By awkwardly attempting to force the patterns of everyday speech into the strict confines of grammatical rules, the poem may be read as a dismissal of grammar as mere pedantry. Indeed, Sidney often mocks strict adherence to the Byzantine rules and strictures delineated in the grammar book. He advocates English in the *Defence* as a proper language for poetry precisely because it lacks the complex inflections of Latin. Responding to the objection that English "wanteth grammar," Sidney writes: "Nay truly, it hath that praise, that it wants not grammar: for grammar it might have, but it needs it not, being so easy in itself, and so void of those cumbersome differences of cases, genders, moods, and tenses, which I think was a piece of the Tower of Babylon's curse, that a man should be put to school to learn his mother-tongue" (248). The schoolmaster Rombus in Sidney's courtly entertainment "The Lady of May," a prototype of Shakespeare's Holofernes, speaks in an absurdly affected and often incoherent style of Latinate English, as we may see in the way he introduces himself to the queen: "I am, *Potentissima Domina*, a schoolmaster, that is to say, a pedagogue; one not a little versed in the disciplinating of the juvental fry, wherein (to my laud I say it) I use such geometrical proportion, as neither wanteth mansuetude nor correction" (6). Both passages seem to privilege a "natural" English language over the affected and overwrought Latinism of the schools. The situation becomes more complicated, however, when we consider that such sentiments are common in humanist pedagogical discourse and that satire on pedantry was native to the educational culture of the Renaissance. At roughly the same time as *The Lady of May*, for instance, Latin dramas such as *Paedantius* and *Bellum grammaticale* that similarly parodied pedantic excesses proved popular with university audiences. The satire on pedantry was not a rejection of the ideals of Renaissance humanism, but an internal critique that enabled sophisticated humanists to guard against affectation and sophistry and to distinguish themselves from naïve, provincial schoolmasters. To mock the fustian style of the country pedant was to proclaim the refinement of one's own learning.

As we have seen, humanist grammarians rejected the naturalism that obtained in medieval grammatical theory. For the humanists, the rules of grammar were not the natural principles of language, laws that emanated from psychological and ontological structures, as they were for the medieval grammarians. They were instead conventions inherent in linguistic use. Early modern writers understood the rules of grammar as a means to attain fluency and eloquence: they were at best expedients, and at worst impediments, in reaching this end. So long as the rules remained an efficient and useful way of mastering eloquent speech, they were beneficial; when they became ends in themselves, they led to mere pedantry. As Ben Jonson writes, "It is not the passing through these learnings that hurt us, but the dwelling and sticking about them. To descend into those extreme anxieties and foolish cavils of grammarians, is able to break a wit in pieces" (*Discoveries* 561).

This understanding of the rules as derived conventions assumes a broader conception of grammar itself. As I have discussed in the Introduction, the term "grammar" typically referred to a wide-ranging set of scholarly, pedagogical, and literary institutions in the early modern period, including classical scholarship, education in languages, translation and interpretation, literary composition, and so on. In some cases, it could serve as a synonym for language itself. Grammar held a fundamental place within the liberal arts and served as the basis for all the disciplines that followed, from rhetoric, to logic, to theology. More than a set of strictly defined linguistic principles, grammar was an art and a practice that informed the whole of early modern linguistic and literary culture. Thus while *Astrophil and Stella* 63 satirizes the prescriptive power of grammatical "rules" to govern the use of language in a programmatic way, it nevertheless participates in the wider practice of grammar by analysing and interpreting Stella's language. Astrophil may be subject to Jonson's charge of "dwelling and sticking about" the rules of grammar, playfully exaggerating the deterministic power of codified linguistic standards. But despite the disingenuous nature of his appeals to the rules, he shows that the love affair is an event that takes place in the field of language, dependent upon expression and interpretation and involved in careful negotiations over the meaning of words. By asserting a legalistic interpretation of Stella's language, Astrophil is actively intervening in their relationship. He is making a move in the language-game of courtship: an attempt to win Stella's favour by his wit, to elicit a smile by the absurdity of his appeal, or, more darkly, to pressure her into acceding to his entreaties. This game has rules, but they are more subtle, variable, and contingent than those outlined in the grammar book.

Grammatical Mood

The linguistic form with which Sidney is perhaps most concerned is grammatical mood. Margreta de Grazia's insightful and important essay "Lost Potential in Grammar and Nature" argues that the distinction between history and poetry that underlies Sidney's poetic theory is aligned with a difference in grammar.[13] In *The Defence of Poesy*, Sidney writes in a well-known phrase that the historian is bound to the "bare 'was'" (224), compelled to recount the facts of history as they happened, without amendment or idealization. History is "captive to the truth of a foolish world" (225), restricted to representing the injustice of a world ruled by the whims of fortune, from which it is impossible to derive wisdom or instruction. The poet, on the other hand, is able to express "what may be and should be" (218), providing, through carefully crafted fictions, patterns for judicious readers to emulate. The distinction that Sidney draws between history and poetry, as de Grazia explains, is deliberately represented as a difference in grammatical mood. Sidney's emphasis on the "bare 'was'" shows that the writing of history depends on the indicative mood to express the facts of historical existence. Poetry, by contrast, employs the modal auxiliary verbs "may" and "should" in order to express the possibilities and ideals that poetry may realize and the obligations it may place upon its readers.[14]

Sidney's self-conscious reflections on grammatical mood and modal auxiliaries appear at a significant period in the history of English grammar. As Lynne Magnusson explains in "A Play of Modals" – a recent essay that expands upon the theoretical and historical dimensions of de Grazia's analysis – the early modern period saw the culmination of a long process of development and change in the use of modal auxiliaries. By the sixteenth century, words such as "may," "might," "can," "would," and "should" had transitioned from full to auxiliary verbs. Verbs such as the Old English *magan* and the Middle English *mowe* or *maye* – meaning, like the Latin *posse*, "to be able" or "to have power" – had become the modal auxiliary "may," losing the ability to take non-finite forms and non-verbal objects. For this reason, we may no longer use the term in the infinitive as it appears in the Middle English phrase quoted in the *Oxford English Dictionary*: "I haue denyed hym to may be knawen" (*OED* "may" v.1). But while the forms of these verbs narrowed, their use in conjunction with other verbs allowed a complex and novel range of meanings, producing new ways of speaking of possibility and necessity, permission and obligation, desire and duty. In order to account for this verbal shift, the humanist scholar Thomas Linacre introduced what he called the "potential mood" to the five moods traditionally observed in Latin grammar: the indicative, the imperative, the optative, the subjunctive, and the infinitive.[15] John Brinsley defined the potential mood as that which "sheweth an abilitie, will, or duetie to doe any thing," and is known by the "signes" "May, can, might, would, should, ought or could" (*The Posing of the Parts*). By the mid-sixteenth century, the potential mood entered into Lily's *Grammar* and became part of the official curriculum of the schools.

Magnusson's essay focuses on Shakespeare's early plays, but its implications are wider, as it illuminates the significant contributions of modal auxiliary verbs to the early modern literary enterprise. As Magnusson shows, the ambiguous and flexible senses of these new terms – suggesting both sanction and compulsion, possibility and necessity – facilitated the complex wordplay in which early modern writers so often delighted. The ability of modal auxiliaries to express possibility, probability, and necessity also aided in the crafting of possible worlds and dramatic cruxes. And finally, modal auxiliaries contributed to the techniques of dramatic characterization by manifesting a character's intentions, beliefs, and desires in speech.[16]

Sidney is keenly attuned to the effects enabled by grammatical modality, often drawing attention to and commenting on the use of modal verbs in his writing. Sonnet 33, for instance, begins with the exclamation "I might, unhappie word, o me, I might" (1). This obscure poem appears to lament Astrophil's failure to court and win Stella before her marriage; Katharine Duncan-Jones theorizes that it may have been inspired by an encounter between Sidney and an adolescent Penelope Devereux in 1576, before her marriage to Lord Rich.[17] "Might" is an unhappy word because it acknowledges the absence of that which Astrophil desires. What *is* – Stella's marriage to another – precludes what *might* have been. The line emphasizes the role of the modal verb in navigating between actuality and potentiality, exhibiting a keen awareness of the formal properties and functions of language.[18]

Sidney explicitly refers to another grammatical mood, the conditional, in sonnet 69. In that poem, another that engages in ironic hyperbole, Astrophil announces triumphantly to a friend that Stella has finally granted his entreaties: "*Stella* hath with words where faith doth shine, / Of her high heart giv'n me the monarchie: / I, I, O I may say, that she is mine" (9–11). Yet the poem's concluding lines reveal that his victory is a qualified one. Astrophil concedes that "she give but thus conditionly / This realme of blisse, while vertuous course I take" (12–13). Stella grants Astrophil the "monarchie" of her heart upon the condition that he takes a "vertuous course." Given the clearly erotic nature of his appeals, Stella's apparent assent is actually a denial: she responds to Astrophil's request for sex with an offer of chaste friendship. Astrophil finally admits this, coyly adding that even kings have certain checks on their authority in an effort to minimize her rebuke: "No kings be crown'd but they some covenants make" (14). In sonnet 33, the employment of the modal auxiliary "might" divided the existing state of things from an unrealized potential world. Here "while" provides the necessary conditions for the persistence of amicable relations between Astrophil and Stella. This accentuated use of grammatical modality shows once again that the pair's relationship is an artifact of social and verbal negotiation.

For de Grazia, the distinction between the indicative and the potential mood is highly moralized: "The indicative mood, the paltry 'bare *Was*,'" she writes, "marks for Sidney an almost fatalistic resignation to the givens of a fallen world – sense's bestial appetite and history's brute fact" (25). Poetry is superior to history for its ability to envisage the possibility of a better world, to privilege the ideal over the degraded and corrupt circumstances of the real, and to provide through its fictions models of virtuous action. Contrary to the values set out in *The Defence*, however, *Astrophil and Stella* is characterized by the prominent use of the indicative mood and the frequent invocation of the unadorned and unmoralized fact of sensual love. Poetry's role in imagining ideal worlds, according to de Grazia, is curtailed in the cycle: Astrophil is associated with the materialism of sense and appetite and resists the normative "oughts" and "shoulds" of Virtue. In many sonnets, as de Grazia shows, "Sense abruptly breaks off Wit's potential mood and always with the mood of affirmation or fact – the indicative ... The possibility held out by the potential is conclusively dashed. The switch to the indicative reflects a reversion to sense" (23). Following Alan Sinfield's argument that Sidney intended the cycle to provide a cautionary tale, "a warning against the dire effects of love," de Grazia concludes that the poems offer a subtle rebuke to Astrophil's adulterous and sensual desire.[19] The affair depicted in *Astrophil and Stella*, she claims, ultimately falls short of the poetic ideals delineated in *The Defence*: it is able only to provide "a negative example of the poetics of the *Defence*, an oblique line ... by which the straight is to be better known ... By formulating possibility grounded in sense rather than conceived in mind, [Astrophil] misuses language's power to project 'what may and should be.' In the process, he destroys his potential, extinguishes his 'inward light,' and falls sadly short of the promise he once showed" (35).

I wonder, however, if this reading does not exaggerate the rigour of Sidney's Platonism. Though it has its moments of suffering and anguish, *Astrophil and Stella* is not so tormented by desire as is the poetry of Petrarch: its tone suggests contentment with the exquisite pleasures and pains of the love affair. If we consider that Astrophil's indicative refers not to the conditions of the Fallen World but rather to the Golden World of poetry, we might detect a dialectical rather than an oppositional relationship between *Astrophil and Stella* and *The Defence*. Within the Golden World of poetry, the indicative points toward an already ideal state of being in such simple assertions as "I do Stella love" (a line modified in the subsequent poem as "I must Stella love," suggesting that the indicative has taken on the normative force of the potential:

his love for Stella is that which is and must be). The "mays," "musts," and "oughts" of Virtue, on the other hand, demand accordance with an often petty, scolding, and all too worldly moralism, paradoxically pointing back toward the Fallen World from which poetry departs. We may get a sense of this from sonnet 47:

> Vertue, awake: Beautie but beautie is,
> I may, I must, I can, I will, I do
> Leave following that, which it is gaine to misse.
> Let her go. Soft, but here she comes. Go to,
> Unkind, I love you not: O me, that eye
> Doth make my heart give to my tongue the lie.   (9–14)

In Melissa Sanchez's words, this is one of "the many sonnets in which Astrophil recites academic platitudes only to dismiss them as insufficient to erotic experience" ("'In my Selfe the Smart I Try'" 9). The sequence of modal verbs that expresses Astrophil's resolution to end his erotic reverie and return to the world of virtuous behaviour – "I may, I must, I can" – is immediately revealed as false pretence by the sensual encounter with Stella. De Grazia understands this as a descent back into the Fallen World. But by so concluding, the poem leaves us with the impression of Love triumphant: the simple couplet that undoes twelve lines of laboured moralizing leaves us with little doubt of the victor in the contest of Virtue and Love. Compared with the unresolved debates we find in Petrarch, Sidney tends to grant Love the last word.

Though poetry for Sidney is sensuous and material, it does not share in the corrupt matter of the postlapsarian world. Sonnet 25 suggests that poetry manifests Platonic and Christian ideals in material form:

> The wisest scholler of the wight most wise
> By *Phoebus'* doome, with sugred sentence says,
> That Vertue, if it once met with our eyes,
> Strange flames of *Loue* it in our souls would raise …
> Vertue of late, with vertuous care to ster
> Loue of her selfe, takes *Stella's* shape, that she
> To mortall eyes might sweetly shine in her.
> It is most true, for since I her did see,
> Vertue's great beauty in that face I proue,
> And find th'effect, for I do burne in loue.   (1–4, 9–14)

Here Stella's body and the Platonic ideal are one, and Astrophil's burning desire identified with the refining fire of enlightenment. Just as poetry, as Sidney explains *The Defence*, unites the philosopher's universal precept with the historian's particular example, so in Stella "Nature doth with infinite agree" (35.4). Poetry repairs the rift between the ideal world of the mind and the sensuous world of the body; it manifests the ideals of philosophy in its sensuous fictions. The philosopher's "would," which imagines the possibility of sensuous contact with the ideal, is realized by the poet's indicative "I do burn," which describes just such an encounter in the experience of the love affair.

Regardless of how one understands Sidney's moral position in regard to virtue, love, and sensual pleasure, what is most important for our purposes is to recognize is the implicit suggestion that the difference between the sensual world of the indicative and the transcendent world of the potential is not ontological but grammatical. These are worlds established by different ways of writing: the indicative mood enables historical description, while the modal verb provides access to the idealized worlds of poetry. By insisting that history is a mode that operates by means of the "bare 'was,'" Sidney shows that the historical, sensual world is not simply a given fact of existence, but something understood as such by the means of certain linguistic practices. We distinguish everyday existence from possible and ideal states of being by means of certain linguistic forms: what *is* differs from that which *may be*. Grammar provides the conditions under which we may speak of the actual and the potential, the present and the wished for, the real and the ideal. Sidney's frequent recourse to the terms of the grammar school makes such linguistic effects particularly visible.

Understanding and Experience

Like the comparison between poetry and history, the discussion of poetry and philosophy in *The Defence* considers the distinctive grammatical forms that the two disciplines employ. Here Sidney describes the practice of moral philosophers:

> These men casting largesse as they go, of definitions, divisions, and distinctions, with a scornful interrogative do soberly ask whether it is possible to find any path so ready to lead a man to virtue as that which teacheth what virtue is; and teach it not only by delivering forth his very being, his causes and effects, but also by making known his enemy, vice, which must be destroyed, and his cumbersome servant, passion, which must be mastered; by showing the generalities that containeth it, and the specialities that are derived from it; lastly, by plain setting down how it extendeth

itself out of the limits of a man's own little world to the government of families and maintaining of societies. (220)

Bringing to mind Maynard Mack's well-known description of *Hamlet* as a play "in the interrogative mood" ("The World of *Hamlet*" 504), Sidney characterizes the philosopher as one who wields "a scornful interrogative." In early modern grammar, the term typically refers to punctuation – the *punctus interrogativus* or "interrogative point" – or to pronouns such as *quis*. While it is not a form of inflection, the semantic function of interrogative markers like *quis* is similar to that of grammatical mood.[20] Sidney's use of the term suggests that the moral philosopher's language has a particular form that enables his questioning and analysis, his division into *genus* and *species*, and his identification of causes and effects. If the mode of the historian depends upon the "bare 'was,'" that of the philosopher relies upon the bare "what" and the bare "why."

Like historical description, this mode is found wanting when compared to that of poetry. While the philosopher provides definitions and taxonomies, the poet brings us into the presence of passion by illustrating its manifestations and contexts, revealing its place in our lives through a kind of thick description. As the discussion in *The Defence* continues, Sidney compares the poet's representations of passion to the philosopher's definitions:

> Tully taketh much pains, and many times not without poetical helps, to make us know the force love of our country hath in us. Let us but hear old Anchises speaking in the midst of Troy's flames, or see Ulysses in the fullness of all Calypso's delight bewail his absence from barren and beggarly Ithaca. Anger, the Stoics say, was a short madness: let but Sophocles bring you Ajax on a stage, killing and whipping sheep and oxen, thinking them an army of Greeks, with their chieftain Agamemnon and Menelaus, and tell me if you have not a more familiar insight into anger than finding in the schoolmen his *genus* and difference ... passions [are] so in their own natural seats laid to the view. (222)

As I have discussed in my Introduction, in poetry we find the passions in their own "natural seats," represented in the forms they take in everyday life. As passion is inherent in linguistic expression, to exhibit Ulysses grieving over his exile from Ithaca is not merely to describe or define his passion but to perform it, to realize his sorrow in the form of the lament. The poetic representation of passion is not mimetic or secondary, for we might look to Homer or Virgil, as Renaissance moralists often urged, for models to guide our own actions in the face of adverse circumstances, and we may learn from them idioms and cadences in which to express our own private sorrows. Poetry is among the practices by which passion is shaped and cultivated: it is fictive, but not therefore false. In *Shakespeare's Festive Comedy*, C.L. Barber observes that "the general Renaissance tendency frankly to accept and relish the artificiality of art, and the vogue for formal and 'conceited' love poetry ... made for sophistication about the artistic process. The sonneteers mock their mythological machinery, only to insist the more on the reality of what it represents" (141). Barber quotes from sonnet 5, which acknowledges that "It is most true, what we call *Cupid's* dart, / An image is, which for our selves we carve" (5–6). But the poem concludes by insisting that it is "True, and yet true that I must *Stella* love" (14). Here and elsewhere, Sidney is intent to dispel the distinction between artifice and authenticity. Love that is fashioned through linguistic practices – the poet's fictions or the suitor's entreaties – is no less real as a result.

Poetic representation, according to Sidney, provides an image of passion more conducive to true understanding than the "wordish description" of the philosophers:

> For as in outward things, to a man that had never seen an elephant or a rhinoceros, who should tell him most exquisitely all their shapes, colour, bigness, and particular marks ... might well make the hearer able to repeat, as it were by rote, all he had heard, yet should never satisfy his inward conceit with being witness to itself of a true lively knowledge; but the same man, as soon as he should see those beasts well painted ... should straightways grow, without any need of any description, to a judicial comprehending of them: so no doubt the philosopher with his learned definitions – be it of virtues, vices, matters of public policy or private government – replenish the memory with many infallible grounds of wisdom, which, notwithstanding, lie dark before the imaginative and judging power, if they be not illuminated or figured forth by the speaking picture of poesy. (*Defence* 222)

Here Sidney compares an account of atomistic facts and features with the totalizing representation one finds in poetry. One may enumerate in detail all the particular parts of a thing without ever producing a complete image of it. Poetry, by contrast, imparts "a true lively knowledge" and "a judicial comprehending" of its subject by portraying not only its particular parts but its entire appearance (222). Moreover, poetry is able to move its hearers as well as to educate them. Even if the philosopher were able to impart greater knowledge than the poet, it would be a fruitless and unproductive knowledge because it would not motivate action. "Moving is of a higher degree than teaching," Sidney argues, "For who will be taught, if he be not moved with desire to be taught? And what so much good doth that teaching bring forth ... as that it moveth one to do that which it doth teach? For, as Aristotle saith, it is not *gnosis* but *praxis* must be the fruit. And how can *praxis* be, without being moved to practise?" (226). Poetry is superior to history and philosophy in that it represents the full scope of lived experience and actively participates in it by exhorting its readers to virtuous behaviour.[21]

Sidney claims that while philosophical instruction may enable one "to repeat, as it were by rote, all he had heard," it will not facilitate true understanding. The comparison of understanding with rote repetition restores us once again to the space of the schoolroom. The notion that poetry furnishes its readers with an experiential understanding different in kind from both the descriptions of history and the definitions of philosophy has an important precedent in Renaissance pedagogical theory. As we have seen in chapter 1, humanist writers from Erasmus to Ascham stressed the importance of learning through reading and conversing rather than by memorizing the rules of grammar in isolation. In *The Scholemaster*, Ascham advocates his favoured method of "double translation" – by which a student would translate a text into English and then, after an hour's pause, back into Latin – as "the liuely and perfite way" to achieve knowledge of Latin, compared to which "the common waie, vsed in common Scholes, to read the Grammer alone by it selfe, is tedious for the Master, hard for the Scholer, colde and vncumfortable for them bothe" (Cii). In privileging poetry's "lively knowledge" – which strongly recalls Ascham's "liuely and perfite way" – over the "bare rule" (*Defence* 221) of philosophy, Sidney unites his poetic theory with humanist pedagogy's elevation of experience over rule-based learning.

Sonnet 45 further explores the ability of poetry to convey a more comprehensive understanding of its subject and to move its audience to action:

Stella oft sees the verie face of wo
Painted in my beclowded stormie face:
But cannot skill to pitie my disgrace,
Not though thereof the cause her selfe she know:
Yet hearing late a fable, which did show
Of Lovers never knowne, a grievous case,
Pitie thereof gate in her breast such place
That, from that sea deriv'd, teares' spring did flow.
Alas, if Fancy drawne by imag'd things,

> Though false, yet with free scope more grace doth breed
> Then servant's wracke, where new doubts honor brings;
> Then thinke my deare, that you in me do reed
> Of Lover's ruine some sad Tragedie:
> I am not I, pitie the tale of me.

Stella, by this account, is more inclined to pity the fictive misfortunes of a romance or tragedy than Astrophil's "genuine" sorrow, which she has herself occasioned. The feigning of poetry is somehow able to elicit tears from Stella, while her lover's pleas are met with indifference.[22] Once again we find the love affair represented as an event of linguistic engagement: the sonnet emphasizes that the ability to understand or pity Astrophil's woe is a matter of comprehension, a "skill" by which the beloved may properly "reed" the lover's distress.[23] And like *The Defence*, the poem advocates a kind of experiential understanding – a "true lively knowledge" and "familiar insight" – over the knowledge of definitions and essences conveyed by the philosopher. An acknowledgment of the bare fact of Astrophil's grievance is insufficient to provoke Stella's pity, for pity requires a familiarity with the entire story of his plight. The depth of his admiration for Stella's beauty, the sting of disappointment at her refusals, the agony of unsatisfied desire: all this is the poet's role to impart. Without such poetic elaboration and ornamentation, the true nature of Astrophil's distress "lies dark to the understanding," unable to inspire pity or sympathy in its audience.

The poem concludes with a remarkable formulation: "I am not I, pitie the tale of me." The phrase "I am not I" rejects an essentialized selfhood, refusing to identify the poet with the "pure subjectivity and individuality" often thought to be the innovation of Renaissance literature.[24] Astrophil replaces pure subjectivity with an understanding of the self as temporally extended and intimately engaged with the surrounding world. He is not merely a thing, but a "tale," a narrative: he can only be properly understood and pitied within the context of a lived experience. Sonnet 61 emphasizes the loving subject's necessary involvement with the world. Stella explains to Astrophil that his love should paradoxically lead him to cease courting her: the true lover should abandon his own desires for those of the beloved, denying his own longing and accepting her refusals:

> That who indeed infelt affection beares,
> So captives to his Saint both soule and sence,
> That wholly hers, all selfnesse he forbeares,
> Then his desires he learnes, his live's course thence.   (5–8)

Echoing the self-denial of sonnet 45, the poem suggest that the love affair empties out the lover's subjectivity: "wholly hers, all selfnesse he forbeares." Astrophil cannot be isolated from the actions he takes, the events he undergoes, and the objects with which he is involved: there is no subject apart from its experience in the world.

In this chapter, I have attempted to show that the use of pedagogical language in *Astrophil and Stella* implies a conception of love as a normative practice, an understanding similar to Wittgenstein's thinking on affect. I will conclude with a brief comment on a figure that both Sidney and Wittgenstein employ: the tapestry. As I have discussed in my Introduction, *The Defence* advances the well-known claim that "Nature never set forth the earth in so rich a tapestry as divers poets have done," while Wittgenstein writes that "'Grief' describes a pattern which recurs, with different variations, in the tapestry of life" (*Philosophical Investigations* 175). Though purely coincidental, the joint use of the image of the tapestry in Sidney and Wittgenstein suggests a similar conception of human life and culture. The "tapestry" furnished by Sidney's poet and Wittgenstein's "tapestry of life" (*lebensteppech*) both imply a conception of human experience as a unified and artfully ordered whole. Composed of individual threads yet presenting a fully coherent image, the tapestry is a holistic picture that cannot be reduced to its constituent parts: we must appreciate it in its totality in order for it to make sense. According to Wittgenstein, we do not speak of one suffering "a second ... of deep grief" because what we call grief occurs for certain reasons and entails certain enduring practices and behaviours. Similarly, Sidney's isolated "face of wo," divorced from a narrative context, fails to provoke its intended response of pity in its audience. Just as for Wittgenstein expressions of grief can only be understood as patterns within the larger tapestry of lived experience, so in Sidney can Stella only pity Astrophil's grief when she appreciates the entirety of his "tale," a narrative of the kind traced in tragedy. The figure of the tapestry shows the importance of context to the meaning of an affective image or expression, emphasizing the necessarily situated and social nature of affect.

Chapter Three

The Ablative Heart: Love as Rule-Guided Action in Shakespeare's *Love's Labour's Lost*

For much of its history, *Love's Labour's Lost* was among the most poorly regarded of Shakespeare's plays.[1] It was considered at best a kind of preparatory sketch for the later comedies, a work of juvenilia in which Shakespeare experimented with characters and motifs that would find full expression in mature plays like *Much Ado about Nothing*.[2] Critics chiefly complained of the play's extravagant language, which they considered baroque and overly self-conscious. But in the latter half of the twentieth century, it was precisely this linguistic self-awareness that attracted critical attention.

William C. Carroll's *The Great Feast of Language* was the first full-length study to address the play's concern with language. For Carroll, *Love's Labour's Lost* is not simply a play characterized by a profusion of voices, styles, and devices, a vehicle for self-indulgent rhetorical pageantry, as it had been understood by its detractors. "It is, rather, a play radically concerned with the very nature of language – with its history, its potential, its proper use by the imagination" (11). Its structure is that of a debate, a form exemplified by the dispute among the courtiers that opens its action and the counterposed poems on spring and winter with which it concludes. The play "offers in its characters a wide range of attitudes toward the power of language, from a skeptical positivism to an almost primitive belief in the inner life of words" (11). And by experimenting with these various perspectives, it engages with early modern theories of language, considering abiding questions about the relation between name and thing that descend from Plato and the text of Genesis. Keir Elam's *Shakespeare's Universe of Discourse* follows Carroll in focusing on the play's linguistic self-consciousness and situating it amidst the debates on the nature of language that took place in the early modern period. Elam also brings a Wittgensteinian framework to his analysis, considering comedy itself as a type of language-game, a "distinct form of language-use subject to its own rules and defined within a given behavioural context."[3] His reading emphasizes the way in which Shakespeare's language performs various acts, from the provision of the material for theatrical performance, to the deployment of rhetorical and poetic figures, to the fashioning of imaginative worlds.

More recently, the work of Katharine Eisaman Maus has offered a valuable synthesis of the approach of Carroll and Elam – sensitive to the linguistic complexities of the play but relatively indifferent to its sexual and class politics – and the traditions of feminist critique. Maus argues that "apparently abstract intuitions about linguistic meaning acquire psychological and political urgency in the court of Navarre ... some of the important linguistic issues in *Love's Labour's Lost* are inseparable from its generic, comic concern with sexual politics and with the construction of a gendered identity in a social context" ("Transfer of Title" 207). In this chapter, I hope to follow Maus in joining an analysis of the concern with language in *Love's Labour's Lost* with attention to its social and psychological aspects. Following several critics who have noted the prominence of performative speech acts in the play, I will argue that the play's exploration of the relation between word and thing results in a sophisticated sense of the agency of language, of the capacity of words not only to name but to effect worldly action and create social relations. Moreover, I argue that not only language but also love is conceived as a form of social action: this is a play, as its title informs us, concerned with love's labour. Drawing on the language of grammar and pedagogy to characterize the practice of courtship, the play suggests that love is a pattern of practices and behaviours rendered coherent by social convention, a weave of worldly activities that involves both verbal and physical expressions. This is most clear in the play's concluding scene, in which the lovers pledge to prove their devotion through a series of carefully stipulated actions, showing that love is defined by convention and consensus.

The Debate on Language

In the play's much-discussed opening scene, the King of Navarre announces his intent to establish within his court a "little academe," to dedicate himself and his courtiers to a program of scholarship and intellectual inquiry that will win them eternal fame. In order to secure this pursuit against worldly temptations, he demands that the members of his court sign an oath committing them to three years of fasting and abstemious behaviour:

> Let fame, that all hunt after in their lives,
> Live registered upon our brazen tombs,
> And then grace us in the disgrace of death;
> When, spite of cormorant devouring time,
> Th'endeavour of this present breath may buy
> That honour which shall bate his scythe's keen edge,
> And make us heirs of all eternity.
> Therefore, brave conquerors – for so you are,
> That war against your own affections
> And the huge army of the world's desires –
> Our late edict shall strictly stand in force.
> Navarre shall be the wonder of the world,
> Our court shall be a little academe,
> Still and contemplative in living art.   (1.1.1–14)

Navarre envisions a scholarly community opposed to worldly things, both in its disavowal of physical comforts and in its focus on transcendent objects and ideas. The first seven lines of the speech concern the triumph of fame over death, a traditional poetic topos that may be traced at least as far back as Horace's *Odes* and serves as one of the major themes of Shakespeare's own sonnets.[4] There may also be a more specific reference to Petrarch's *Trionfi*, a cycle of six allegorical poems narrating the sequential victories of Love, Chastity, Death, Fame, Time, and Eternity which first appeared in English in Lord Morley's mid-sixteenth-century translation, *The Tryumphes of Fraunces Petrarcke*. The key terms of the speech's opening – "fame," "death," "time," and "eternity" – name precisely the final four of Petrarch's triumphs, suggesting a direct allusion to the cycle. Navarre departs from Petrarch's model, however, in making Fame victorious over both Death and Time and ultimately the equal of Eternity. Though Fame triumphs over Death in Petrarch, it succumbs to Time eventually, as the succeeding ages gradually erode even the greatest reputations. Time itself finally submits to Eternity, and the world is made new and changeless by God's final judgment. In this context, to claim the inheritance of Eternity shows remarkable pride on Navarre's part and foreshadows the failure of the academy and the violation of the oath intended to ensure its success. Indeed, the "still and contemplative" scene of "living art" that Navarre invokes could hardly be more remote from what follows: while Navarre proposes a life of quiet, ascetic contemplation, the greater part of the play

is characterized by feverish love affairs and a cacophony of often incoherent speech. And while he imagines that the fame his court will win
through its intellectual endeavours will allow it to triumph over death,
the play concludes with news of the King of France's untimely passing,
a melancholy reminder of human finitude that forestalls the expected
comic resolution.

As Maus has observed, Navarre's declaration that the academy will
allow the courtiers to become "brave conquerors" of "the huge army
of the world's desires" is consistent with the shift in aristocratic identity that took place in the Renaissance, when a peerage that had defined itself by martial prowess began instead to seek distinction in
learning and refinement. But even as Navarre's aspiration to scholarly
fame associates him with Renaissance humanism, the ascetic isolation
he avows and demands of his followers clearly recalls the *contemptus
mundi* of medieval monasticism. And as I will discuss further, the understanding of language assumed by the speech is consistent with the
medieval idealism that I have detailed in chapter 1.

Navarre's commitment to scholarly asceticism is challenged by the
courtier Berowne, who refuses to sign the oath and balks at its demands
of strict self-denial: "O, these are barren tasks, too hard to keep: / Not
to see ladies, study, fast, not sleep" (1.1.47–8). His opposition to the oath
provokes a debate with the other courtiers, who take up the cause of the
"academe" against Berowne's advocacy of love and pleasure. Navarre
insists upon the importance of study, which he defines as a practice that
transgresses the limits typically placed upon human comprehension
and ascends toward a god-like state of knowledge, in keeping with the
ambitions of his opening speech. To study is "to know that which else
we should not know"; to apprehend "Things hid and barr'd ... from
common sense" is "study's god-like recompense" (1.1.56–8). Against
this grandiose vision, Berowne characterizes study as a laborious and
ultimately vain pursuit of glory:

> Why, all delights are vain, but that most vain
> Which, with pain purchased, doth inherit pain:
> As painfully to pore upon a book
> To seek the light of truth, while truth the while
> Doth falsely blind the eyesight of his look.
> Light seeking light doth light of light beguile;
> So, ere you find where light in darkness lies,
> Your light grows dark by losing of your eyes ...
> Study is like the heaven's glorious sun,
>   That will not be deep-searched with saucy looks;

Small have continual plodders ever won,
    Save base authority from others' books.
These earthly godfathers of heaven's lights,
    That give a name to every star,
Have no more profit of their shining nights
    Than those that walk and wot not what they are.
Too much to know is to know naught but fame,
And every godfather can give a name.   (1.1.72–93)

The speech progresses through a sequence of images related to the light of the sun and stars: study is compared to the sun that rewards sustained scrutiny with blindness, and scholars become mere "earthly godfathers," arbitrarily assigning names to the stars but gaining no benefit by the practice. Berowne's second conceit makes it clear that the contention between the courtiers draws upon early modern debates on the nature of language, and on the nature of names in particular. Navarre's belief that the object of scholarship is the attainment of secret and transcendent knowledge recalls the widely held belief that words have a natural and essential relation to their objects of reference and that to know the true name of a thing is to gain a quasi-magical power over it. "The prevailing linguistic theory," writes Carroll, "held that there is an inherent rightness in names, that names are not arbitrary signs but are in some sense themselves the essence of what is named" (*The Great Feast of Language* 12). For Navarre, names provide access to the true nature of things and allow us to partake in "god-like" wisdom. Berowne rejects the naturalist perspective in favour of conventionalism that considers words and things to be united only by arbitrary human practice. Those astronomers who in naming the stars believe they have gained knowledge of the heavens have in fact simply affixed to them names of their own choosing: they are no different from the humble godfathers who engage in the everyday practice of naming children.

The principal source for these positions in the Renaissance was Plato's *Cratylus*, a dialogue in which Socrates attempts to adjudicate between the positions of two other interlocutors, the naturalist Cratylus and the conventionalist Hermogenes. According to the perspective of Cratylus,

everything has a right name of its own, which comes by nature, and ... a name is not whatever people call a thing by agreement, just a piece of their own voice applied to the thing, but ... there is a kind of inherent correctness in names, which is the same for all men ... the power which gave the first names to things is more than human. (383b, 438c)

Hermogenes counters this position by claiming that names are the result of groundless custom:

> There is [no] correctness of names other than convention and agreement. For it seems to me that whatever name you give to a thing is its right name ... no name belongs to any particular thing by nature, but only by the habit and custom of those who employ it and who established the usage. (384c–384d)

Socrates interrogates both of these positions, seemingly inclining toward naturalism for the majority of the dialogue, but ultimately abstaining from judgment on the matter, instead declaring that the question of names is a distraction from a more important concern with the nature of the things themselves (439b). The debate between naturalism and conventionalism persisted into the early modern period: the sixteenth-century French humanist Louis Leroy writes of the "controuersie" over "whether words were imposed at the will and pleasure of them that speake, or els by art, and natural reason." Proponents of the former position, arguing that the relation between words and things was "arbitrarie, founded on the consent and custom of men," pointed to the "varietie and continuall mutation which is seen in tongues"; advocates of the latter argued "that the true names did not change after our pleasure: but were agreeable to the things signified, whose essence, and similitude they did imitate." Leroy's description of those who pursued naturalism to its extreme ends, seeking to find divine wisdom in the nature of names, accords well with the scholarly ambitions of Navarre's academe: "Which opinion some haue so farre beleeued, that they haue gone about to inquire, and search out the proprietie of things, by the proprietie of words; and to insinuate so far, by the secret vertue which they deemed in them, as to do miracles in pronouncing them" (*Of the Interchangeable Course* 19). Leroy himself remains agnostic, declining to offer any definitive judgment on the matter.

Berowne's comments on the mundane quality of naming, which is the right of any godfather, make a point similar to one made by Maus: that naming is not simply the establishment of an abstract relation between a word and a thing, but an activity bound up with gender roles, familial structures, and property rights. The name "Navarre," as Maus points out, is not the exclusive property of the character that currently possesses it. It is shared among the king, his kingdom, and his ancestry, a title inherited from his predecessor and, presumably, to be passed on to his heir. The invocation of the custom of christening draws attention to the questions of power and property to which language is so firmly bound. Berowne's critique restores us to the space of practices and institutions, providing a reminder that names are dependent on social relations. But as the debate continues, Berowne fails to pursue the social implications of his claims, instead pursuing his conventionalism to radical ends that threaten to deprive speech of any meaning whatsoever. After Berowne delivers his speech, the academy's supporters unite in attacking him:

KING

How well he's read, to reason against reading.

DUMAINE

Proceeded well, to stop all good proceeding.

LONGAVILLE

He weeds the corn, and still lets grow the weeding. (1.1.94–6)

Berowne responds to these assaults with what appears to be a *non sequitur*: "The spring is near when green geese are a-breeding" (1.1.97). While the allusion to spring may obliquely endorse the pleasures of love and courtship against the cold studiousness of the other courtiers, the line nevertheless disrupts the logical course of the argument. Dumaine asks why he has offered such a capricious answer:

DUMAINE

How follows that?

BEROWNE

Fit in his place and time.

DUMAINE

In reason nothing.

BEROWNE

Something then in rhyme. (1.1.98–9)

Berowne concedes – and perhaps even flaunts – the nonsensical nature of his rejoinder, but he emphasizes its poetic qualities. His line is "rhyme" without "reason": it maintains the rhyme scheme and metrical pattern of the dialogue while abandoning its content. The outward and sensory elements of Berowne's words obscure the inward "light of truth" that Navarre seeks with his proposed academy. The form of language has eclipsed its content.

The utter arbitrariness of the line emphasizes Berowne's scepticism regarding the relation between word and thing: he seems to imply that the meaning of language is ultimately up to each speaker to determine. In this, he follows Plato's Hermogenes in understanding naming not only as a conventional but also as a private and individual practice: "Whatever name we decide to give each particular thing is its name ... Whether the giver be a private person or a state" (*Cratylus* 385a). And just as Berowne's scepticism glosses over the gender dynamics of his own example, missing the fact that it is specifically a god*father* that is authorized to name a child, so too does Hermogenes, in advancing a private understanding of language, unwittingly employ an illustration closely tied to the social and economic structures of slave-holding Athens: "whatever name you give to a thing is its right name; and if you give up that name and change it for another, the later name is no less correct than the earlier, just as we change the names of our servants" (384d). Both perspectives overlook the essential role of consent and authority in determining linguistic usage and the way that language is bound up with other social institutions. Naming is an act intimately related to the dynamics of power, accomplished only by one invested with the appropriate authority. In a patriarchal society like early modern England, the godfather grants a name to the child; in a slave-holding society like ancient Athens, the master determines what the slave is to be called.

In spite of these oversights, Berowne's deliberate division of "rhyme" and "reason" inaugurates a persistent motif in the play: the separation of form and content, word and thing, signifier and signified. The spectre of meaninglessness that Berowne conjures leaves us with radically polarized views on the nature of language. Language is either entirely subordinated to an essential meaning that somehow subsists outside of it, as in Navarre's view, or it is reduced to meaningless vocalization and opaque hieroglyph, as in Berowne's: it is either pure reason or mere rhyme.

Rhyme and Reason

The distinction between the formal properties of words and that which they are intended to signify – variously referred to as "rhyme" and "reason" (1.1.99), "word" and "matter" (1.1.190), "form" and "content" (5.2.515–17), and other similar formulations – recurs throughout the text of *Love's Labour's Lost*.[5] In the early scenes, the distinction is generally associated with the dialogue of the minor characters, who are defined either by a tendency toward vacuous rhetorical inflation or by crude literalism. When the courtiers agree to hear a suit brought by Armado, a Spanish knight enamoured with "the music of his own vain tongue" (1.1.164), Berowne expresses his hope of finding amusement in the discrepancy between Armado's bombastic language and the petty case he brings to the court: "How low soever the matter, I hope in God for high words" (1.1.190). Armado satisfies his expectation, presenting his case in a letter filled with archaism, ostentation, and clumsy rhetorical devices. Armado's bombast associates him with characters similarly prone to empty verbiage, such as the parson Nathaniel and the schoolmaster Holofernes. As Carroll observes, the characteristic feature of these characters' dialogue is synonymy: in an exaggerated version of Erasmian *copia*, they typically employ a long sequence of unnecessary and often inappropriate terms to describe something. Armado, for instance, refers to Jaquenetta as "a child of our grandmother Eve, a female, or, for thy more sweet understanding, a woman" (1.1.252–3). This expansion and variation of terms has an aesthetic rather than a communicative purpose, calling attention to the sound rather than the sense of words and emphasizing the distance between them.

Opposed to the play's verbally ostentatious dandies and pedants are figures like the peasant Costard and the constable Dull, characterized by their blunt speech and propensity for malapropism. An exchange between Armado (whose words are relayed in a letter read aloud by Navarre) and Costard demonstrates the deliberate juxtaposition of rhetorical inflation and reductive literalism represented by these two camps:

KING
> *There did I see that low-spirited swain, that base minnow of thy mirth –*

COSTARD
> Me?

KING
> *That shallow vassal –*

COSTARD
> Still me?

KING
> *Which, as I remember, hight Costard –*

COSTARD
> O, me! (1.1.239–47)

Armado describes Costard with a catalogue of flamboyant phrases, each of which the peasant answers with the deflationary reply "me." In a later scene, when Costard is presented with "remuneration" for the delivery of a latter, he again demonstrates a tendency toward reductive literalism, assuming that the word describes the precise quantity of money he has received: "Now will I look into his remuneration. 'Remuneration'! O, that's the Latin word for three farthings. Three farthings – remuneration" (3.1.133–5). And the malapropism for which

later Shakespearean characters like Dogberry and Mistress Quickly are
well known is equally on display in the garbled dialogue of *Love's Labour's Lost*:

DULL
>   I myself reprehended his own person, for I am his grace's
>   farborough ... There's villainy abroad. This letter will tell you more.

COSTARD
>   Sir, the contempts thereof are as touching me. (1.1.181–7)

Synonymy and malapropism are strangely similar in the way they manipulate the relation between word and meaning: both multiply sig-
nifiers while maintaining a consistent signified, providing a profusion
of terms that often depart from what the speakers are attempting to
convey. But if synonymy suggests concern only with the formal properties of words, then the malapropism and misunderstanding associated
with Costard and Dull imply the opposite: an indifference to the form
of words and an exclusive focus on the things they signify. Armado and
Holofernes care too much for words; Costard and Dull too little.[6] The
division of the minor characters into those bewitched by the sound of
words and those solely concerned with their sense mimics the polarized views on language rehearsed in the debate among the courtiers,
reiterating the contention between reason and rhyme.

   As the main plot advances, the divorce of sound and sense that characterizes the language of the comic figures begins to corrupt that of
the major characters as well. When Navarre and the members of his
court find themselves enamoured with the Princess of France and her
followers, they engage in a practice of courtship that echoes the affectation and inflation of Armado and Holofernes. The women of the French
court meet their flattery with withering scorn, as we may see in Rosaline's reaction to the sonnet sent to her by Berowne:

ROSALINE
>   Nay, I have verses too, I thank Berowne;
>   The numbers true, and, were the numbering too,
>   I were the fairest goddess on the ground.
>   I am compared to twenty thousand fairs.
>   O, he hath drawn my picture in his letter!

PRINCESS
>   Anything like?

ROSALINE
>   Much in the letters, nothing in the praise.

PRINCESS
   Beauteous as ink. A good conclusion. (5.2.34–41)

The "numbers" – that is, the metrical qualities of the verse – are "true," consistent and well crafted. But the "numbering" – that which the verse portrays – is false, misrepresenting Rosaline, who has a dark complexion, as the stereotypical "fair maiden" of Petrarchan lyric. Like the derivative poets scorned by Sidney, Berowne has failed to write poetry appropriate to its object and occasion, instead allowing established tradition to determine its form mechanically. In fact, as Rosaline observes, the only properly representative aspect of the poem is the black ink in which it is written, which resembles her features far more than the image that the poem describes.[7] Here once again the outward and formal qualities of language – the rhythm of the verse and the physical substance of writing – are emphasized at the expense of its content: the matter of the verse eclipses its meaning. While Berowne mocked Armado for the distance between his "high words" and the "low ... matter" they conveyed, he has himself opened up a similar divide by succumbing to the seductive power of Petrarchan rhetoric.

   Later in the same scene, the gap between word and thing is again exploited for humorous effect at the expense of Navarre and his followers. The suitors plan to approach and court their mistresses in the guise of Russian travellers, but their designs are overheard and betrayed to the French court by Boyet. The women play along, but they disguise their own identities by donning masks and exchanging the love-tokens they have received from their lovers, leading each to pledge his devotion to the wrong woman in something like a chaste version of the conventional bed-trick. When the deception is uncovered, Berowne ruefully observes: "The ladies did change favours: and then we, / Following the signs, wooed but the sign of she" (5.2.468–9). The episode acts as an allegory for the bedazzlement of signs. Labouring under the same illusion that inspired Berowne's clumsy Petrarchism, the courtiers allow themselves to be misled by the emblems and rituals of courtship, pursuing an abstraction of femininity – the "sign of she" – rather than a person.

   Following this episode, the persistent motif of word and thing is given perhaps its most complex expression in a speech delivered by the Princess. When a group led by Holofernes offers to enact a pageant for the assembled courtiers, Navarre initially refuses, expecting that the incompetence of the local performers will embarrass the Navarrese in front of the French. But the Princess intervenes, suggesting that the players' very ineptitude will provide entertainment:

Nay, my good lord, let me o'errule you now.
That sport best pleases that doth least know how –
Where zeal strives to content and the contents
Dies in the zeal of that which it presents;
Their form confounded makes most form in mirth,
When great things labouring perish in their birth.   (5.2.513–18)

Here the Princess addresses the question of form and content in a speech that demonstrates her own mastery of language. The players, she expects, will be so eager to "content" or please their audience that the "contents" of the play will fail; the ruin of the pageant's "form" will make "form in mirth," or pattern for laughter. By punning on both "form" and "content," she demonstrates precisely the control over the relationship between word and thing that the comic characters and courtiers lack.[8] Excessive synonymy and malapropism both suggest that language has slipped the reins, that the speaker has lost control over words or their meanings. The pun, on the other hand, shows the speaker's capacity to direct language to her own ends, to make a word mean whatever she intends.

The distinction between form and content so often invoked in *Love's Labour's Lost* was a frequent point of discussion in humanist pedagogy and the debates surrounding it. As Richard Halpern has observed, humanists faced with ancient literature that early modern sensibilities considered obscene invoked the distinction, emphasizing the writing's formal and stylistic qualities at the expense of its content. Halpern quotes the scholar and schoolmaster Robert Cawdrey, who defends the "forme" of classical poetry in spite of its "ill matter" through an analogy with painting: "As in slaughter, massacres or murther, painted in a Table, the cunning of the Painter is praysed, but the fact it selfe, is utterly deplored: So in Poetrie wee follow elocution, and the proper forme of wordes and sentences, but the ill matter wee do worthily despise."[9] To the critics of humanism, however, the tendency to emphasize linguistic form was a sign of the superficial nature of the program. In *The Right Teaching of Useful Knowledge*, a reform-minded pedagogical text that sought to provide a more pragmatic course of study for the children of the merchant class, George Snell accused his humanist predecessors of being "empty Nominalist and verbalists only" who knew not "the verie things and matters themselves."[10] And as I will discuss further in the following chapter, Francis Bacon famously derided the humanists for their elevation of form over content, writing in the *Advancement of Learning* that their rhetorical excesses caused them

> to hunt more after words than matter; and more after the choiceness of
> the phrase, and the round and clean composition of the sentence, and the
> sweet falling of the clauses, and the varying and illustration of their works
> with tropes and figures, than after the weight of matter, worth of subject,
> soundness of argument, life of invention, or depth of judgment. (139)

It should be noted, however, that Bacon employs the tools of rhetoric
even as he condemns it: his rebuke is a masterful example of the figure
of antithesis.

Love's Labour's Lost participates in the critique of rhetorical inflation
in its mockery of the courtiers' affected language and in its satirical
representation of characters like the schoolmaster Holofernes. But it is
no less disparaging of the position represented by Snell and Bacon: that
"matter" alone is important and that words have only an instrumental
value in directing us to things. Snell's emphasis on mathematical training for the merchant class resonates with the crass acquisitiveness of
Costard, whose interest in Latin words only extends to what he believes
they may say about his finances. And the play delights in mocking the
hypocrisy of those like Bacon who praise plain speaking in elevated
language, as we can see in Berowne's declaration of his intent to woo
in the plain style:

BEROWNE
    Henceforth my wooing mind shall be expressed
    In russet yeas and honest kersey noes.
    And, to begin: wench, so God help me, law!
    My love to thee is sound, *sans* crack or flaw.
ROSALINE
    Sans "*sans*," I pray you.   (5.2.412–16)[11]

The play's engagement in the debate on language and humanism is
ambivalent, condemning both the intoxication with the "Sweet smoke
of rhetoric" that we find in characters like Armado and the incompetence in the verbal arts on display in Dull and Costard (3.1.60). By
simultaneously rejecting a verbalism that is solely concerned with
words and an empiricism interested only in things, the play implicitly
advocates an understanding of language in which word and thing exist in harmony.[12] I would like to suggest that it is a humanist-inspired
understanding of language as rule-guided action that serves to reconcile form and content in the play. This perspective reveals the inade-
quacy of both the naturalist and conventionalist positions rehearsed in
the play's opening scene, which in spite of their opposition similarly

conceive of language as a system of naming, neglecting its role as action and practice.

The most important and extensive account of the active role of language is the speech-act theory of J.L. Austin, a follower of Wittgenstein whose work has been more influential in literary criticism than that of his predecessor.[13] Austin's theory contends that utterances he called "performatives" – which include promises, christenings, marriage vows, and other ritualistic expressions – do not simply refer to objects or events in the world, but are themselves events, actions that create new social relations and identities. Such statements can be neither true nor false; instead, they are "felicitous" or "infelicitous," in Austin's words, depending on whether they fulfil the expectations that surround them. Several critics have noted the prevalence of performative speech acts in the play, best exemplified by the oaths which bookend its action.[14] Maus writes that "*Love's Labor's Lost* begins with edicts proclaimed, contracts endorsed, and promises extracted – a flurry of what J.L. Austin calls 'performative utterances.' This kind of language is not referential; it performs actions rather than describe or point to an extralinguistic reality. As such, performative utterances seem to close the gap between signifier and signified, *verba* and *res*, word and world" ("Transfer of Title" 209).

As Maus suggests, performative speech acts unite word and thing because they are verbal actions that have tangible effects in the world. Though the courtiers eventually betray the oath to which they swear, it nevertheless serves to regulate their behaviour for a time, compelling them, for instance, to refuse to host the French embassy on the grounds of the court. And their failure to keep the oath carries real-world consequences, leading them to feel shame for their actions and exposing them to the ridicule of the women of the French court. In this way, the oath is distinct from the feckless speechifying of Armado or Berowne's futile attempt to woo Rosaline with formulaic verse, examples of language divorced from the world. The oath that opens the play and the one that concludes it – of which I will have more to say later in the chapter – provide a model of linguistic action that exorcises the spectre of meaninglessness haunting the play.

The invocation of Austin may seem anachronistic, but there were at least general anticipations of his thought in the early modern period. The intellectual historian Ian Maclean has argued that something very much like Austin's understanding of performative speech was at work in Renaissance theories of legal discourse, a type of language that was understood not simply to describe the world but to act upon it.[15] The term employed by Renaissance legal theorists to indicate the effect of legal language was *vis* or "force," suggesting the way that law compels and constrains action in the world.[16] Remarkably, Navarre uses precisely this term in demanding that members of his court sign a binding document, claiming that the oath "shall strongly stand in *force*" against worldly temptation (1.1.11, my emphasis). While it seems unlikely that Shakespeare would have been directly acquainted with the legal theory that Maclean cites, the use of the term "force" suggests that he shared with the jurists of his day a clear sense of the agency of language, the way that language can regulate behaviour and effect social relations.[17] This awareness is especially prominent in the play's depiction of courtship.

Passion, Performance, and Pedagogy

In his later lectures on speech act theory, Austin divides the performative utterance into three distinct acts: the locutionary act, or the pronouncement of the statement itself; the illocutionary act, the social action accomplished by the pronouncement of the statement; and the perlocutionary act, the indirect effects the statement may have beyond its immediate purpose, especially the way it may influence the feelings and attitudes of the speaker and her audience. To say the words "I promise" is a locutionary act; to commit oneself to an action with these words is an illocutionary act; and to acquire a feeling of resolve and determination in making this commitment, or to inspire confidence in the person to whom the promise is made, is a perlocutionary act. Austin considers the illocutionary act to be the heart of the performative utterance. The perlocutionary act, by contrast, is incidental and unnecessary, and other types of statements may have the same effects on thoughts and feelings.

Stanley Cavell has critiqued this dismissal of the perlocutionary force of the performative and Austin's neglect of the affective aspect of language in general. To address this oversight, Cavell proposes the concept of the "passionate utterance," a type of statement that is not a description but lacks the strictly delineated illocutionary effect of the performative.[18] Considering examples such as "I'm bored" and "I love you," Cavell defines passionate utterances as statements that single out another person and propose an exchange of feelings; it is "a mode of speech in or through which, by acknowledging my desire in confronting you, I declare my standing with you and single you out, demanding a response in kind from you, and ... so making myself vulnerable to your rebuke" ("Passionate and Performative Utterances" 195). Unlike performative utterances, such statements do not immediately enact social actions: while saying "I promise" has the concomitant and necessary effect of committing the speaker to a course of action, there are no such guarantees involved with a statement like "I love you." Passionate utterances seek to persuade or evoke feeling, inviting the interlocutor to share in an experience with the speaker. Though they lack illocutionary effects, they are fundamentally perlocutionary: the feelings they may evoke or the changes in attitude they may produce are not merely incidental but serve as their central purpose. Cavell argues that passionate utterances have conditions of felicity just like those of more traditional performance speech acts, though they are less clearly defined than those of the performative. Among these conditions are the presence of a specific person to whom the passionate speaker appeals and the existence of passionate experience within the speaker: the passionate utterance "is grounded in my being *moved* to speak, hence to speak in, or out of, passion" (193).

In his recent book *Shakespeare, Love and Language*, David Schalkwyk draws upon Cavell's concept of the passionate utterance in his sophisticated analysis of love in Shakespeare, emphasizing the verbal and performative nature of love in the plays. Rejecting what he calls the "essentializing of love as desire" in the long philosophical tradition, the reduction of love's complexity to simple lack and longing, Schalkwyk argues that love in Shakespeare "is a complex attitude or disposition established and developed over time through forms of behavior in relation to another person who is regarded as unique and incapable of substitution." This amatory attitude necessarily involves passionate utterances, expressions that call upon another to reciprocate the lover's attention. "Love is therefore primarily a performative concept: love *acts* rather than simply is or feels. The theatrical medium of Shakespeare's plays shows repeatedly that it is an embodied, performative concept" (6–7). In the remainder of the chapter, I will follow Cavell and Schalkwyk in thinking about the relation between performativity and love, considering the ways that *Love's Labour's Lost* represents the passion of love as a meaningful, rule-guided action, as a practice that forges affective bonds and social obligations. Love in this sense necessarily involves language – promises and praise are among its foremost features – but it is not exclusively a matter of words.

The relation between the performativity of speech and the labour of love emerges most clearly at those moments at which the play engages with the tradition of the grammar school, drawing on its language of rules and instruction to depict the relations of courtship. Of all the plays of Shakespeare, *Love's Labour's Lost* is perhaps most closely connected to the discourse of early modern pedagogy. Its ornate speeches, formal dialogues and debates, and theatrical set-pieces – only loosely united by any narrative logic – resemble nothing so much as a collection of schoolroom exercises. Moreover, as Kathryn Moncrief has shown, many of the play's exchanges and relationships have a pedagogical character, often inverting the standard gender hierarchy in such a way that women become teachers of men ("'Teach us, sweet madam'"). As I have suggested, part of this engagement with the culture of pedagogy is satirical, like the mockery of the pedant Holofernes, a character descended from Sidney's Rombus and the pompous and ridiculous *dottore* of the *Commedia dell'arte*. But the play also makes productive use of the pedagogical tradition, deriving from it a sophisticated sense of the interrelations of love and language, bodies and words.

An exchange between Armado and his young page Moth offers an arresting example of the play's appropriation of grammatical and pedagogical terms and helps to demonstrate that *Love's Labour's Lost* conceives of love as a rule-guided activity rather than a psychological or physiological state. When Armado admits to momentarily forgetting his beloved Jaquenetta, Moth adopts the role of schoolmaster, chastising Armado for failing to properly learn his lessons:

MOTH

Negligent student! Learn her by heart.

ARMADO

By heart and in heart, boy.

MOTH

And out of heart, master. All those three I will prove.

ARMADO

What wilt thou prove?

MOTH

A man, if I live; and this "by," "in" and "without" upon the instant. "By" heart you love her, because your heart cannot come by her; "in" heart you love her, because your heart is in love with her; and "out" of heart you love her, being out of heart that you cannot enjoy her. (3.1.33–42)

Moth catalogues the various affective relations that exist between Armado and Jaquenetta, describing the lover's longing, ardour, and disappointment in the pursuit of his beloved. In doing so, he speaks of Armado's heart as if it were a noun in the ablative case, adapting a lesson from Shakespeare's grammar book, Lily's *Short Introduction of Grammar*. Here is the relevant passage in Lily:

The Ablatiue case is commonly joyned with Prepositions seruing to the Ablatiue case: as De magistro, *Of the Maister*. Coram magistro, *Before the Maister*.

Also In, with, through, for, from, by and then, after the comparatiue
degree, be signes of the ablatiue case. (A6v)

Lily's curiously tautological definition (the "Ablatiue case" is defined by
the association with "Prepositions seruing to the Ablatiue case") stands
in contrast to the more substantive accounts of the other five cases: he
describes the nominative, for instance, as the case which "aunswereth
to this question, Who or What" (A6v). This is likely the result of the
fact that the ablative case is unique in lacking a single distinct function.
In Latin, the ablative case – from *ablatus*, "carried away" – combines
the functions of three earlier cases: the true ablative, indicating separation and used with the preposition "from"; the comitative, indicating
association or instrumentality and used with "with" or "by"; and the
locative, indicating position or placement and used with "in" (Ruck,
Latin 71–5). Moth's complex joke plays on each of these three senses,
suggesting the instrumental role of the heart ("'By' heart"), its position
as the site of love ("'in' heart"), and the way the heart is removed from
the object of its desire ("'out' of heart," a phrase that also suggests the
disappointment this distance occasions).

Moth's description of the loving heart has several significant implications. First, it suggests that love, like language, is an action made meaningful by conventional rules and standards. By representing the heart
as a noun in the ablative case, Moth implies that the love relationship
has an established structure, and those who participate in it have conventional roles, just as the parts of speech have established functions
within a sentence. Armado, the nominative lover, courts Jaquenetta, the
accusative beloved. The ablative heart is the instrument and site of his
love, the means by which he loves and the state in which he loves. By so
"grammaticalizing" their relationship, Moth shows that love is an action
in which the lover, beloved, and heart jointly participate. It might also
be said that by drawing attention to the role of the heart in the practice
of love, Moth underlines what Cavell calls the conditions of felicity of
the passionate utterance. Among the conditions that must be in place for
expression of passion to be effective, Cavell lists sincerity of feeling: "In
speaking from my passion I must actually be suffering from the passion"
("Passionate and Performative Utterance" 193). For the declaration of
love to have its intended effect, the speaker must convey the truth of her
experience, demonstrating that her "heart is in it," as the phrase goes. The
ablative role of the heart, the fact that one must speak "by heart" and "in
heart," is thus a necessary condition of the passionate expression of love.

The application of the rules of noun declension to the loving heart
also makes an important point about the relation between language

and the body. It is worth recalling at this point that Austin advanced the performative theory of language against what he saw as a persistent and pernicious fallacy: the belief that statements such as promises named some object or event, some resolution that takes place in the secret recesses of the speaker. He exemplified this belief with a line of from Euripides' *Hippolytus* that he translated as follows: "my tongue swore to, but my heart ... did not" (*How to Do Things with Words* 9–10). Euripides' formulation is premised on the idea that language is essentially descriptive, that vows are representations of beliefs or resolutions held within heart. Moth's account of the heart offers a different perspective: language does not *describe* the heart; language *involves* the heart and acts in conjunction with it. The lover's heart works alongside his vows and expressions to give shape to the practice of love.

Words and Bodies, Assemblages and Patterns

Moth's adaptation of the lesson in the ablative case advances the play's effort to bridge the divide between word and thing by applying the rules of grammar to the body. Other invocations of learning and pedagogy in the play have a similar effect. When the courtiers realize that they have all fallen in love in spite of their vows to commit themselves exclusively to scholarship, Berowne delivers a speech claiming that the true objects of their study should be women's eyes:

> O, we have made a vow to study, lords,
> And in that vow forsworn our books;
> For when would you, my liege, or you, or you,
> In leaden contemplation have found out
> Such fiery numbers as the prompting eyes
> Of beauty's tutors have enriched you with?
> ...
> From women's eyes this doctrine I derive:
> They sparkle still the right Promethean fire;
> They are the books, the arts, the academes,
> That show, contain and nourish all the world;
> Else none at all in aught proves excellent.   (4.3.292–328)

In lines that recalls *Astrophil and Stella*, Berowne calls the courtiers to attend to the teachings of the body, the instruction and inspiration found in their lovers' eyes.[19] We can see another example of the pedagogy of the body in the courtiers' instructions to Moth, which are described to the Princess and her followers by Boyet:

Their herald is a pretty knavish page
That well by heart has conned his embassage.
Action and accent did they teach him there:
"Thus must thou speak and thus thy body bear."   (5.2.97–100)

Here Moth has taken on the position of the schoolboy, a role appropriate to his stature if not his intellect, ceding the place of the schoolmaster
to Navarre and his court. They have led him to learn the speech he is
to deliver "by heart," just as a schoolboy might memorize a passage
out of Cicero or Terence, and instructed him in the accents and gestures
with which he is to present it. Just as Moth's play on the ablative case
applied grammatical rules to the heart, so does the courtiers' instruction apply equally to words and bodies, ranging across the text of the
message Moth is to convey to the Princess, the heart that serves as its
repository, the tone of voice in which he is to pronounce it, and the way
he will comport his body in delivering it. These scenes of instruction
knit together language and the body, showing that social and affective
practice depends equally upon them both.

In his recent book *The Melancholy Assemblage*, Drew Daniel observes an
intersection of words and bodies similar to what I have described here
(67). Daniel analyses the Renaissance tradition on melancholy, which
is derived from a set of diverse and at times contradictory discourses,
including the pseudo-Aristotelian tradition that associates melancholy
with inspired genius and the Galenic understanding of melancholy
as morbid illness. In order to characterize the complexity and fluid-
ity of early modern melancholy, Daniel draws upon Gilles Deleuze's
theory of the assemblage, a dynamic concretion of objects drawn from
different ontological categories, with particular emphasis on the inter-
mingling of words and bodies. The assemblage's ontological plurality,
the fact that it is composed of fundamentally different kinds of things,
differentiates it from more conventional theories of complex systems,
making it a useful means of approaching the diversity of the discourse
on melancholy. Daniel cites Jaques's diagnosis of his own particular
strain of melancholy in *As You Like It* as a paradigmatic example of the
humour's heterogeneity: "it is a melancholy of mine own, compounded
of many simples, extracted from many objects, and indeed the sundry
computation of my travels, in which my often rumination wraps me
in a most humorous sadness" (4.1.15–18).[20] Like the Deleuzian assemblage, Jaques's melancholy is a composite form made up of a diverse
range of objects, from the material to the social to the discursive.

In his reading of *Love's Labour's Lost*, Daniel notes a similar moment
of ontological crossing in Berowne's reflection on the effects of love,

which has overtaken him in spite of himself: "By heaven, I do love, and it hath taught me to rhyme, and to be melancholy. And here [indicating his sonnet] is part of my rhyme, and here [indicating his breast] my melancholy" (4.3.11–13). The sonnet and the heart are equally expressive of Berowne's passion: "Eliding the discursive and the somatic," writes Daniel, "[Berowne's] survey of evidence alleges a similarity between the paper and the breast as equally demonstrable, and therefore equally persuasive, proofs of love" (*The Melancholy Assemblage* 83). The love poem and the melancholic breast exist alongside one another: the former is not the sign of the latter, but each acts in its own way to demonstrate Berowne's love. We know that Berowne is in love because he writes sonnets and because his body is afflicted with melancholy: like the poem, the melancholic breast is "a means of representation" (Wittgenstein, *Philosophical Investigations* §50).

Though their philosophies are very different, Deleuze's concept of the assemblage is analogous to what Wittgenstein has called a "pattern." Both terms suggest loosely connected constellations of practices, signs, and physiological events, and both cut across the boundaries that divide language from the body. In the *Philosophical Investigations*, Wittgenstein writes that practices traditionally assigned to the realm of language and culture are essentially equivalent to those actions that seem to belong to the body: "Giving orders, asking questions, telling stories, having a chat, are as much a part of our natural history as walking, eating, drinking, playing" (§25). Consistent with assemblage theory, the comment demonstrates a refusal to subordinate the discursive to the biological or vice versa: language and the body are conceived as essentially parallel to one another, jointly contributing to what Wittgenstein calls our "natural history."[21] In a speech conceding that he has fallen in love in spite of his intentions, Berowne characterizes the practice of courtship with a list of actions similar to that of Wittgenstein: "Well, I will love, write, sigh, pray, sue and groan. / Some men must love my lady, and some Joan" (3.1.199–200). Like Wittgenstein, Berowne observes no distinction between the linguistic practices of writing and praying and such physical expressions as sighing and groaning, non-verbal actions that are often involuntary and lack determinate meaning: these actions are all equally significant elements of his courtship.

Love Put to the Test

Berowne's love is not an object or feeling within him. The sensation in his breast bears witness to it, but the testimony of the poetry he has composed for Rosaline is no less significant. His love, according to his own report, is a pattern of actions, experiences, and expressions: "I will love, write, sigh, pray, sue and groan." This weave of practices is given coherence and shape by a set of practical conventions that allow it to be recognized as love, as Moth suggests with his play on the rules of the loving heart.

The idea of love as rule-guided action is explicitly dramatized in the grim episode that concludes the otherwise light comedy of *Love's Labour's Lost*. After Holofernes' pageant descends into farce, a messenger arrives to inform the Princess of her father's sudden death. As the mourning Princess prepares to return to France, Navarre pleads with her to pledge her love to him before she departs: "Now, at the last minute of the hour, / Grant us your loves" (5.2.781–2). But the Princess refuses, fearing that the king's words of love, like his devotion to scholarship, will prove false in time:

> Your oath I will not trust, but go with speed
> To some forlorn and naked hermitage,
> Remote from all the pleasures of the world,
> There stay until the twelve celestial signs
> Have brought about the annual reckoning.
> If this austere insociable life
> Change not your offer made in heat of blood;
> If frosts and fasts, hard lodging and thin weeds,
> Nip not the gaudy blossoms of your love,
> But that it bear this trial and last love;
> Then, at the expiration of the year,
> Come challenge me, challenge me by these deserts,
> And, by this virgin palm now kissing thine,
> I will be yours.   (5.2.788–801)

Echoing the opening scene, but shifting from a comic to a tragic vein, the Princess demands that Navarre swear an oath to withdraw from the world, spending a year in a state of anchoritic solitude. Katherine and Maria require similar commitments from their lovers, and Rosaline, to put his wit to good purpose and dull its cynical edge, assigns to Berowne the charge of comforting the sick on their deathbeds: "your task shall be / With all the fierce endeavour of your wit / To force the pained impotent to smile" (5.2.840–2). In this melancholy scene, the women stipulate the standards by which their suitors' love is to be judged, carefully detailing the criteria by which love will be distinguished from idle desire. The truth of the suitors' declarations of love, then, is established not by conformity with some inward object, but by faithful practice, by behaviour that conforms to a set of social standards.

At this point, I would like to recall Wittgenstein's comments on love discussed in the Introduction: "Love is put to the test, pain not. One does not say: 'That was not true pain, or it would not have gone off so quickly'" (*Zettel* 504). Among other characteristics, love is typically defined by an enduring and exclusive dedication to its object. Should a state that appears to be love prove to be easily deterred, or should it be directed toward a variety of objects in rapid succession, we would tend to identify it as some other phenomenon: as lust, as caprice, as a passing fancy. Those involved in romantic relationships routinely interrogate and appraise their own experiences to determine if what they feel is worthy of the name. How long has it lasted, and might it soon fade away? How does it compare to other such feelings? What is truly motivating it? It is only when such questions are satisfied that we call a particular feeling or experience "love." Such standards are what Wittgenstein would call the grammar of love, the rules that define what love is and establish its place in our language and our lives.

At the conclusion of *Love's Labour's Lost*, the suitors' love is "put to the test" in an unusually overt and formalized way. The scene illustrates the idea of love as a normative, situated practice with remarkable clarity and detail. The practical nature of love is clear from its temporal extension: that the suitors' affection must "bear this trial and last love" shows that it is not an object or state of being, but an action that takes place over time. Love is also defined by its situation within a specific form of life, the way it is related to other cultural practices and institutions. In this case, love is defined in contrast to the closely adjacent yet illegitimate form of physical desire that the Princess associates with "the heat of the blood," a desire that will exhaust itself in sexual satisfaction. It is this physical lust against which the women's demands are intended to guard, ensuring that the suitors follow a proper course of love culminating in marriage. Throughout the play we see the ways that love is bound up with such institutions as courtliness and lyric poetry, and here we even see an oblique relation to asceticism, penance, and modes of self-interrogation, as the Navarrese courtiers are expected to repent for their errors and reflect upon their motivations.[22] Finally, and perhaps most importantly, the scene demonstrates the normative dimension of love, which is judged according to explicit standards of devotion and fidelity. The scene thus shows that love is not only a practice, but a practice subject to rules and conventions that define its nature.

As Maus observes, the turn to practice and performance has the potential to buttress the existing state of gender relations:

the Princess and her ladies are not revolutionaries. They do not want to undermine or escape from patriarchy, but to find themselves a secure and relatively advantageous position within it. Thus Berowne's skepticism, with its refusal to acknowledge a connection between words and practice, is despite its apparent tolerance at least as threatening to their interests as Navarre's rigid misogynist exclusivism. For the happiness of their lives will depend upon their husbands' scrupulous fulfillment of their contractual obligations in marriage. ("Transfer of Title" 218)

But the turn to performance can have a radical side as well. A focus on performativity tends to undermine universal truth-claims and reveal the conventional nature of social roles and structures. Judith Butler has famously adapted Austin's speech act theory to argue that gender itself is a performance, an identity created through the routine iteration of normative gestures and behaviours.[23] While *Love's Labour's Lost* falls well short of such a claim, it nevertheless makes the heroic love associated in the period with aristocratic masculinity into a very ordinary thing, a matter of custom and contractual arrangement. Unmoored from any particular property held within the heart or quality possessed by the mind, love ceases to have a role in class and gender distinction: just as "every godfather can give a name," so may anyone love, so long as they adhere to the standards imposed upon them by culture and society. In this way, the women's pragmatism may ultimately be more radical than Berowne's scepticism, which neglects social and historical institutions in favour of an embrace of abstractions and absolutes. In the following chapter, I will consider Shakespeare's most famous sceptic, Hamlet. Like Berowne, Hamlet rejects social convention, seeking instead to distinguish himself by recourse to an ineffable inwardness. Yet even as he attempts to transcend the social and the linguistic realm, gesturing toward an interior state that seems to exist entirely apart from it, he borrows from the discourse of the grammar school, betraying the debt to humanist pedagogy that he is often at pains to deny.

Chapter Four

"Shapes of Grief": The Ineffable and the Grammatical in Shakespeare's *Hamlet*

Ye know not, what hurt ye do to learning, that care not for wordes, but for matter, and so make a deuorse betwixt the tong and the hart.
— Roger Ascham, *The Scholemaster*

Readers of *Hamlet* have for some time observed "the intensely critical, almost disillusionist, attitude of the play towards language itself."[1] This is especially true of the play's protagonist, who in his professed clumsiness with poetic "numbers" and his impatience with the tedium of "words, words, words" adopts a traditional anti-rhetorical position, a dismissal of the outward qualities of language in favour of the things they strive to represent but often only obscure (*Hamlet* 2.2.119, 192). The position draws on the long-standing opposition between words and things, a dichotomy frequently raised in early modern discourse on grammar and pedagogy. As we have seen, Erasmus addresses the distinction between *verba* and *res* in *De ratione studii*, associating the former with the basic pedagogy of the grammar schools and the latter with university-level study (162). Early comedies like *Love's Labour's Lost* – in their adolescent eroticism, delight in wordplay, and frequent allusions to Latin pedagogy – may be said to belong to the world of *verba* and the grammar schools. In Hamlet, however, there appears a Shakespearean hero who is at home not in the grammar school like the lovers of the comedies but in the rarefied realm of university discourse, here denoted by the image of Wittenberg. Hamlet is an intellectual who has ascended beyond the matter of the *trivium*: already a master of *verba*, he desires to grapple with *res*.

The play itself, however, draws attention to its own artifice, its own verbal constitution, through its insistent metatheatricality, undermining its protagonist's campaign against the limits of language. Thus while

Hamlet the character is intent on transcending linguistic representation, *Hamlet* the play revels in it, ostentatiously parading its status as an edifice of "mere words."[2] The tension between Hamlet's desire for unmediated access to things and the play's linguistic self-consciousness has been insightfully explored by such critics as Richard Waswo, Robert Weimann, and Bruce Danner.[3] But a crucial area of this conflict has so far escaped notice. Hamlet's desire to transcend language is most clearly represented by his attempts to adumbrate an interiority that lies beyond the power of verbal signification. It is in his inward passions, those privately held feelings and impressions that he struggles to translate into outward action, that Hamlet locates a realm beyond language, as we see in his insistence that "I have not art to reckon my groans" (2.2.120). But the very opposition of passion and action that defines this ineffable inwardness is derived from the structure of language, and the terms used to explore it are borrowed from the discourse of grammar. The clearest evidence of this debt to grammar appears in Hamlet's "To be or not to be" speech: in this famous meditation on being, this deliberation on whether it is better "to suffer" or "to stand against a sea of troubles" (3.1.57–9), the text employs a set of terms and verbal configurations that Shakespeare would have learned not from reading Montaigne or some other philosopher, but from the lessons of the grammar school: "The Infinitive signifieth to do, to suffer, or to be" (Lily, *A Short Introduction* B3). Thus we find in *Hamlet* an important connection between the culture of the grammar school represented in the early comedies and the drive toward the ineffable that has, since its own time, established the play as a work "to please the wiser sort."[4] And it is precisely at those moments when the text strives to indicate a realm beyond language that the debt to grammar becomes most apparent.

Sarah Beckwith's recent study *Shakespeare and the Grammar of Forgiveness* offers an artful and perceptive reading of Shakespeare's late drama, arguing that while tragedies such as *Hamlet* bear witness to the destructive consequences of "a split between a self that 'passeth show' and a face and body that can only betray a mind too lonely and inaccessible to be expressed," the later plays heal this rift by cultivating a language of forgiveness, pioneering what Beckwith calls a "theater of embodiment" in the union between inward being and outward expression (1). Beckwith's "grammatical investigation," which draws upon the philosophy of Wittgenstein and Cavell, entails an understanding of "language as act, as event in the world, and so asks us to extend our conception of the work of language beyond the work of representation" (7). With this principle in mind, Hamlet's claim that he has "that within which passes show" becomes something more than a mere gesture toward an interior space: it is a demand for acknowledgment, an appeal to sympathy, a subtle chastisement of the heartless world around him. As such, his words are not inadequate, as they paradoxically claim, for they exert a profound influence upon the world of the play and manifest Hamlet's own being in that world.

Beckwith's reading of Shakespeare unfolds within the context of the Reformation, in the wake of the traumatic interruption of the rituals and practices that for centuries gave form and meaning to the lives of the medieval English. Of particular significance is the loss of the sacrament of penance, which according to Beckwith served a central role in establishing and maintaining communal relationships. Shakespeare's late drama works to remedy this loss by developing a new language of acknowledgment and reconciliation, a "grammar of forgiveness," within the secular arena of the theatre.

This chapter provides a different historical and institutional context for a Wittgensteinian reading of *Hamlet* by demonstrating the play's engagement with the pedagogical and rhetorical culture of its age. *Hamlet* emerges from a humanist culture steeped in grammar and rhetoric, a culture that understands human action and experience through the framework of the language arts. It reaches the stage at a time when this rhetorical culture is being challenged by empirically minded critics such as Francis Bacon, for whom the autonomy of language that prevailed under humanism was a "distemper of learning, when men study words and not matter" (*The Advancement of Learning* 139). Although the play is marked by this new distrust of the primacy of language, it is nonetheless a product of a humanist education and habitually recurs to the discourse of the language arts, even in its attempts to evoke an extralinguistic interiority.[5] I am convinced by Beckwith's argument that we are still too quick to take Hamlet at his word when he claims a self beyond the scope of words (*Shakespeare and the Grammar of Forgiveness* 16). In celebrating an inner being that purports to lie outside the text, we neglect the play itself, privileging a self-abnegating metaphysics over the forms of life so vividly realized in its language. We also fail to see that Hamlet's claims of a private and ineffable interiority are themselves verbal acts, rhetorical gestures that operate within a particular tradition and abide by the rules of a particular grammar.

The Declension of Melancholy

Outside the character of Hamlet himself, the world of *Hamlet* is one in which, to quote Anne Ferry's characterization of the Renaissance, "man's inward and outward experiences [are] viewed as closely parallel ... no great separation [is] consistently conceived to exist between them."[6] We do not get the sense from most of the characters in the play that there is an unbridgeable gulf between outward expression and inward states, between words and behaviours and that which they may signify. When Hamlet's inscrutable conduct confounds the court, Claudius does not attribute their confusion to a discrepancy between Hamlet's outward behaviour and his inward thoughts; instead, he assumes the two to be transformed in concert: "nor th'exterior nor the inward man / Resembles what it was" (2.2.6–7). Even Claudius's private confession that "Words without thoughts never to heaven go" (3.3.98) suggests not an absolute distinction between words and their meanings, but rather the insufficiency of his own performance of repentance, as he has not renounced the prizes won by his treachery:

> That cannot be, since I am still possess'd
> Of those effects for which I did the murder –
> My crown, mine own ambition, and my queen
> May one be pardoned and retain the offence? (3.3.53–6)

What Claudius's words lack, then, are practical actions: the abdication and confession that would constitute genuine repentance. His words fail not because they lack some inward or outward object of reference, but because they are pronounced apart from the context and circumstances necessary for the practice of repentance.

We can see the harmony of inward and outward states with particular clarity in Polonius's account of what he takes to be Hamlet's pining for Ophelia. This is of course a misdiagnosis: what he believes to be love melancholy is in fact the half-feigned madness brought on by Hamlet's encounter with the ghost. Nevertheless, the lines demonstrate the way that affective states such as melancholy are understood to be manifest in their expression. Polonius explains that upon being rebuffed in his advances toward Ophelia, Hamlet

> Fell into a sadness, then into a fast,
> Thence to a watch, thence into a weakness,
> Thence to a lightness, and, by this declension,
> Into the madness wherein now he raves
> And all we mourn for. (2.2.147–51)

Hamlet's melancholy advances through a series of stages in a familiar and recognizable pattern: first sadness, then lack of appetite and sleeplessness, then fatigue and light-headedness, and finally madness. Its beginning is disappointment in love; its end, insanity. I want to place particular emphasis on the use of the term "declension" to describe this sequential pattern. "Declension" is a technical term in grammar, referring to the successive forms of an inflected noun, pronoun, or adjective. In addition to this specialized definition, the *Oxford English Dictionary* lists the more general senses of a "deviation or declining from a standard, falling away," and "sinking into a lower or inferior condition" ("declension, *n.*") citing the speech of Polonius and lines from *Richard III* (we might add a similar usage in *Henry IV, Part Two*).[7] Certainly there is the suggestion of "decline" in the passage, for Hamlet's state progressively deteriorates in Polonius's account. But the only other contemporary uses of this wider sense come from Shakespeare himself: all other instances of the term cited by the *OED* prior to 1660 are confined to the technical discourse of grammar. It seems safe to assume, then, that the lines are intended to recall the grammatical sense of "declension," associating the progressive stages of Hamlet's melancholy with the forms of the Latin noun. There are, we should note, six stages demarcated in Polonius's speech, mirroring six cases of Latin nouns observed in the Tudor grammar school.[8] The analogy that Polonius establishes here between grammatical and affective positions is highly significant.

In one of the key aphorisms of the *Philosophical Investigations*, Wittgenstein writes that "Grammar tells us what kind of object anything is" (§373). For Wittgenstein, as I have discussed, "grammar" names the set of rules and conventions that guide the use of language. Since the meaning of a word in Wittgenstein is derived from its use rather than from its object of reference, the rules that guide the use of a word also establish its meaning. Grammar provides the necessary conditions under which an object may be publicly recognized and understood. Grammar is no less fundamental to the phenomena of inner life than to any other object, for "An 'inner process' stands in need of outward criteria" (§580). We are accustomed to thinking of the phenomena of inward life as existing prior to their expression in language: we imagine that we feel some pain or desire, and subsequently use a word to name that feeling. Wittgenstein inverts this process, arguing that we first learn how to speak of pain and desire from the world around us, and then accommodate this way of speaking to our own inward states. As David Schalkwyk writes, "the language of inwardness is constituted by public life. The meanings of the words used of inward states are not those states themselves, but rather publicly derived rules and uses" (*Speech and Performance* 109). In a well-known discussion that has come to be known as the private language argument, Wittgenstein contends that for a language to be meaningful, it must conform to standards of correct usage, a publicly sanctioned "grammar." A private language, in which words "refer to what only the speaker can know – to his immediate private sensations" (§243), lacks such a grammar and consequently cannot function:

> But what does it mean to say that he has "named his pain"? – How has he managed this naming of pain? And whatever he did, what was its purpose? – When one says "He gave a name to his sensation," one forgets that much must be prepared in the language for mere naming to make sense. And if we speak of someone's giving a name to a pain, the grammar of the word "pain" is what has been prepared here; it indicates the post where the new word is stationed. (§257)

To speak of pain we must first understand the grammar of pain: the words and constructions we use to speak of pain, the situations in which it makes sense to have pain, the proper responses to another's pain (such as sympathy and pity), and so on. Even what may appear to be a private, inward sensation such as pain requires a particular grammar by which it may be publicly known.

I would like to suggest that Polonius's "declension of melancholy" is analogous to Wittgenstein's grammar of pain. To describe the progress of Hamlet's melancholy as a "declension" is to imply that melancholy has a particular grammar in which it is expressed and by which it is understood. Like the forms of the inflected noun, melancholy progresses in a coherent pattern: it has a kind of verbal logic that makes it intelligible. In representing Hamlet's melancholy in grammatical terms, Polonius implicitly identifies melancholy with the form of its expression. For melancholy to have a grammar, a system of rules and conventions by which it abides, it can be neither simply a material object like black bile nor an abstract state of mind that subsists solely in the interior. It must be a public practice, extended over time and enacted in the world, like a spoken or written language. Melancholy is thus not simply indicated by melancholic behaviour, but inherent in it, manifest in the "forms, moods, shapes of grief" (1.2.82) by which it is publicly known. As Wittgenstein writes, "We do not see facial contortions and *make the inference* that he is feeling joy, grief, boredom. We describe a face immediately as sad, radiant, bored, even when we are unable to give any other description of the features. – Grief, one would like to say, is personified in the face."[9] Here we find no distance between one's inward state and the shows and signs that lend it material form.

I acknowledge the risk of perversity in attributing such insight to Polonius, a figure of fun throughout the play and the most frequent object of Hamlet's scorn. The use of the grammar school term is probably intended, in part at least, to suggest Polonius's pedantry. But I believe that Polonius represents an exaggerated form of an idea that we find latent throughout the play, and even in Hamlet himself, despite his protestations: that inward states, far from being inexpressible, are "grammatical," structured by conventional rules and manifest in characteristic patterns of language and behaviour.

This perspective is represented in many of the early plays of Shakespeare, which often use grammatical terms to trace affective states and relationships. We have already seen how Moth's appropriation of the grammar book in *Love's Labour's Lost* served to delineate the structure of the love affair. *Titus Andronicus* furnishes us with another significant example of the grammatical representation of passion. Like *Hamlet*, *Titus Andronicus* prominently features the problem of expression, but in *Titus* the failure of expression is attributable to the physical destruction of the organs of speech rather than to the divide between feeling and expression. Observing his brother Marcus with his arms crossed, Titus describes his own manner of mourning after the loss of his hand:

> Marcus, unknit that sorrow-wreathen knot.
> Thy niece and I, poor creatures, want our hands,
> And cannot passionate our tenfold grief
> With folded arms. This poor right hand of mine
> Is left to tyrannize upon my breast,
> Who, when my heart, all mad with misery,
> Beats in this hollow prison of my flesh,
> Then thus I thump it down.   (3.2.4–11)

To "passionate" one's grief is to give it material form in the gestures and motions of the body: lacking his left hand, Titus must beat his breast with his right in order to properly perform his sorrowful state.[10] Lavinia's dismembered body, deprived not only of its hands but of its tongue as well, is an even greater obstacle to articulacy, but she is nevertheless able to express herself in silent action. Mute and mutilated, her body has become a "map of woe" (3.2.12), manifesting its grief in the wounds it bears and the postures and positions it assumes. Titus pledges to train himself in her particular manner of expression, adopting the language of grammar school pedagogy in order to do so:

> Speechless complainer, I will learn thy thought.
> In thy dumb action will I be as perfect
> As begging hermits in their holy prayers.

Thou shalt not sigh, nor hold thy stumps to heaven,
Nor wink, nor nod, nor kneel, nor make a sign,
But I of these will wrest an alphabet,
And by still practice learn to know thy meaning.   (3.2.39–45)

In Titus's account, "thought" is parallel to "dumb action" and "meaning" to "alphabet": there is no distinction between the sorrow Lavinia feels and the gestures in which that sorrow is expressed. The difficulty of understanding does not result from a gulf between outward sign and inward feeling, but from the strange and novel grammar Lavinia is forced to adopt in her damaged condition. Titus has once again become a student in studying this new tongue: imagining himself in the grammar school, he vows to learn the "alphabet" of Lavinia's passion.[11] Like Hamlet's melancholy, Lavinia's sorrow is represented as possessing a particular grammar, a set of rules and structures by which it is rendered legible and coherent. I take the allusions to the discourse of the grammar school in the two plays as evidence of a worldview profoundly influenced by humanist pedagogy, a worldview that, to quote Bacon's censure, is more concerned with "words than matter" (*Advancement of Learning* 139). Within this worldview, the art of grammar provides a vocabulary with which to understand and express human existence.

In "Fiction as 'Grammatical' Investigation," Schalkwyk argues that "it may be fruitful to regard fiction, or at least certain kinds of fiction, as being already engaged in the kind of grammatical investigation with which Wittgenstein was concerned in his philosophical work. If Wittgenstein opens the doors of philosophy to fiction, it may be that his kind of philosophy has long been a guest in its house" (288). Literature, like the language jokes that held particular interest for Wittgenstein, provides us "with a glimpse of the way in which our sense of the world is embedded at the intersection of our language and our historical and practical being in the world" (292). It produces this insight in a variety of ways: "it may seriously question or disturb grammatical forms, it may simply expose them to view, or it may highlight them in order to explicitly endorse or confirm them" (292). Through its innovative and self-conscious uses of language, literature already engages in a method analogous to that of Wittgenstein, questioning, revealing, and emphasizing the forms and functions of language. I would like to suggest that, owing to the centrality of grammatical study in humanist pedagogy, early modern literature performs these tasks in a particularly insistent way. In using the terms of grammar to represent the passions of characters like Hamlet and Lavinia, the plays of Shakespeare emphasize the interdependence of inward states and the language in which they are expressed.

Hamlet's Inexpressible Passion

Throughout much of the Shakespearean canon, the inward life of passion is inseparable from the outward mode of its expression. In the character of Hamlet, however, we find articulated with arresting and seductive eloquence the idea that outward expression is merely the garb of passion, more apt to conceal passion's truth than to convey it. Passion, Hamlet claims, is precisely that which cannot be conveyed through language or performance: it is the definitive characteristic of an interiority that surpasses outward expression, that which, in Bruce Danner's words, "cannot be represented, cannot be named, and therefore cannot be translated into the world without the taint of mediation" ("Speaking Daggers" 31). The language and gesture previously understood as coextensive with passion become shallow ostentation to Hamlet, who insists again and again that mere words cannot fathom his feeling, that his inner life is ultimately inexpressible.

Hamlet thus moves from a rhetorical and grammatical understanding of the world, an understanding characteristic of sixteenth-century humanism, to a metaphysical one in which reified "things" assume priority over "words." As I have suggested, this need not be taken as an epochal shift toward modernity: Hamlet's perspective accords with the reaction against humanism taking place at the beginning of the seventeenth century and with such venerable discourses as the Pauline language of Word and Spirit.[12] It does, however, signal a shift within Shakespearean drama, a transition from a theatre often defined by self-conscious displays of polished rhetoric to one characterized by a complex and often baroque syntax that seems to reflect "the spontaneous rhythms of a mind in motion" (Greenblatt, Introduction to *Hamlet* 105). The pleasure that was once taken in lyricism and rhetorical flourish gives way to a pronounced discomfort with the conventions of language that we see exemplified in the character of Hamlet. But the anti-rhetorical position, as Russ McDonald observes, is paradoxically achieved not by the rejection of the language arts, but through a more accomplished and sophisticated use of rhetoric itself (*Shakespeare and the Arts of Language* 41).

The exemplary case of the tension between language and inwardness is, of course, Hamlet's speech in act 1, scene 2. His first extended piece of dialogue, the speech seems intended to define his character against the world of the court in which he moves. Claudius and Gertrude are dismayed by what they perceive as Hamlet's excessive mourning, which violates the traditionally moderated and circumscribed performance of grief for a lost parent. Gertrude asks why Hamlet's practice of mourning "seems ... so particular" (1.2.75) when it is part of the natural order of things for a son to lose his father. Hamlet responds:

> Seems madam? Nay, it is. I know not "seems."
> 'Tis not alone my inky cloak, good mother,
> Nor customary suits of solemn black,
> Nor windy suspiration of forced breath,
> No, nor the fruitful river in the eye,
> Nor the dejected haviour of the visage,
> Together with all forms, moods, shapes of grief,
> That can denote me truly. These indeed "seem,"
> For they are actions that a man might play,
> But I have that within which passes show,
> These but the trappings and the suits of woe.   (1.2.76–86)

Hamlet's speech surveys his appearance in the wake of his father's death, detailing the gestures and postures of his grief: black clothing, tears, laboured breath, a downcast demeanour. These are the conventional signs and practices that comprise what we might call "the grammar of mourning." But for Hamlet, these practices cannot entirely "denote" his particular experience of sorrow. As Katharine Eisaman Maus writes, the speech emphasizes the gulf "between signs ('trappings and suits') and what they signify ('that within')" (*Inwardness and Theater* 1). The outward shows of grief are merely signs of an inward phenomenon that ultimately surpasses signification.

Though it is often read solely as a contribution to philosophy or intellectual history, the speech serves a number of rhetorical purposes in the context of the scene. It displays Hamlet's loyalty to the memory of his father and offers a subtle but caustic rebuke to the hypocritical courtiers whose grief so quickly gave way to celebration of the new king's marriage. Beckwith's reading of the speech emphasizes the relationship with Gertrude, suggesting Hamlet is motivated by the sting of his mother's betrayal. Hamlet's speech is "a response to a felt abandonment by the mother who has theatricalized his deepest feeling [by implying that it is mere "seeming"]. He has lost his father, and now apparently his mother too is vanishing from him" (*Shakespeare and the Grammar of Forgiveness* 18). Schalkwyk notes that the speech establishes Hamlet's singularity and idiosyncrasy, casting him as a melancholic and moralistic figure at odds with the corruption of the court: "If losing fathers is common, then Hamlet asserts the uncommonness of his persistent grief in contrast to those around him that have been happy to turn from death to life" (*Speech and Performance* 116). One important point that is easy to overlook is the fact that Hamlet's performance of grief is not minimized but exaggerated. Though the speech dismisses the importance of his mournful behaviour, we learn from the reactions of Claudius and Gertrude that this behaviour has been especially pronounced. Hamlet has violated the conventions of mourning not by refusing to participate in what he derides as empty ritual and ceremony, but by performing his grief in an especially emphatic way. Calling this performance inadequate is in effect to emphasize it yet again: "if only you knew the full extent of my grief: these outward shows, extravagant as they are, are only the shadows of its substance." These readings focus on the function of the speech rather than its referential content.

It should be noted that Hamlet never explicitly names his inward state, referring to it only obliquely as "that within." Though this nebulous phrasing has provoked a variety of theories, both sound and extravagant, about what occulted thing Hamlet might harbour within himself, it should most likely be read as a strategy of occlusion intended to emphasize the inexpressibility of his sorrow.[13] I would like to propose that the missing term in Hamlet's language is "passion," conceived as an inward affection opposed but intimately related to outward action. This specific term is implied by Hamlet's use of the term "actions" to describe the outward gestures and expression opposed to "that within." "Action" is a richly significant word in the speech: adjacent to "play," it suggests play-acting and theatricality, the occupation of the stage actor. But in this context, the word also suggests a general metaphysical category, a mode of active being opposed to passion. This becomes clear when the speech is compared to contemporary discourse on passion and action. Robert Burton employs remarkably similar language in writing that "Weeping, Sighing, Laughing ... are motions of the Body, depending upon these precedent motions of the minde: Neither are tears, affections, but actions" (*The Anatomy of Melancholy* 422). Thomas Wright makes the same distinction in writing that "In many externall actions may be discouered internall passions" (*The Passions of the Minde* 197). If the outward gestures of mourning and other performances of feeling are "actions" in the language of Shakespeare, Burton, and Wright, than "that within" is perfectly aligned with Burton's "affections" and Wright's "internall passions."

The discussions of Burton and Wright rely on a binary opposition between passion, conceived as a passive experience or suffering, and action, understood an outward performance or gesture. Passion and action are organized along the same lines as "body" and "mind," and "external" and "internal." According to this model, the sorrow Hamlet passively experiences upon the death of his father is opposed to the action he takes to express or convey this sorrow, such as mourning or weeping (though it may motivate these actions).[14] Hamlet's speech on the inexpressibility of his sorrow thus relies upon the formal opposition of inward passion and outward action, of the passive affections and impressions of the mind or soul and the actions and gestures of the body.

Passion and action are common terms in Renaissance intellectual discourse, appearing as rhetorical topoi, logical oppositions, and metaphysical categories.[15] The frequency with which they appear in the text of *Hamlet* has led scholars to speak of the play's "preoccupation with passion and action."[16] Shakespeare would have almost certainly first encountered the technical sense of the terms in his grammar lessons: Lily defines the verb as a part of speech that "betokeneth doing: as Amo, I love. or sufferinge: as Amor, I am loved. or Being: as Sum, I am" (*A Short Introduction* Bii). Like Polonius's description of Hamlet's melancholy, then, the speech is marked by the influence of the grammar school, albeit in a more subtle way. Through its explanation of the voice of the verb, the grammar book provides a basic model for the opposition of "doing" and "suffering" that may be accommodated to broader discourse on human agency and experience. When Hamlet, to cite but one example of the terms in the play, reproaches himself for overindulgence in passion and a consequent lack of action, he alludes to this model:

> Do you not come your tardy son to chide,
> That, laps'd in time and passion, lets go by
> Th'important acting of your dread command? (3.4.107–9)

To suggest an essential distinction between what Wright calls "external actions" and "internal passions" is to allude to an oppositional structure derived from linguistic use and formalized in the traditions of grammar. The negative space of the interior, that which "passes show," can only be constructed in opposition to the actions of the exterior. The reason Hamlet can darkly, yet nevertheless meaningfully, gesture toward this inward space is that it is already understood as the opposite of outward action. The passion-action antinomy allows the elided passion to be recognized, its space already established by the schema of grammar. Though the speech insists upon the inexpressibility of inward passion, it communicates this passion by reference to the conventional oppositions of grammar: ineffability is paradoxically enabled by the structure of language. Hamlet's passion, in spite of his refusal even to pronounce its name, abides by a particular grammar.

That Hamlet's "that within" speech, "the *locus classicus* of early modern 'interiority'" (Schalkwyk, *Speech and Performance* 115), draws on the language of the grammar school is telling evidence of the harmony of language and inwardness in the play. It is also symptomatic of a wider relationship between language and metaphysics, for the metaphysical categories of passion and action themselves, I would argue, are abstracted from linguistic use. As I have discussed in the Introduction, Aristotle's *Categories*, perhaps the first systematic theorization of passion and action, derives the concepts from the use of passive and active verbs. Observing that we say a thing "cuts" or "is cut," "burns" or "is burnt," Aristotle derives the general categories of action and passion through what is essentially an exercise in descriptive grammar: "'Cuts' or 'burns,' again, indicates Action [*poieîn*], 'is cut' or 'is burnt' a Passion [*páschein*]."[17] The more familiar sense of passion as a psychological state is likewise abstracted from the everyday use of language: when a man is angry, writes Aristotle, "We say 'Such a man is affected.' Such states are passions [*páthe*]."[18] In drawing on the language of the grammar school to depict the inward passions of its characters, *Hamlet* highlights the relationship between grammar and metaphysics that has persisted throughout the long tradition of Western philosophy.[19]

Metatheatre and the Antic Disposition

Though we often find Hamlet adopting an anti-rhetorical and anti-grammatical pose, at times he too evokes the atmosphere of the grammar school, especially in the antic scenes. The first encounter with the ghost features both of these positions and demonstrates the tension between them. Upon meeting with this truly transcendent being, a thing undreamt of in the philosophy of the age, Hamlet swears to put behind him the learning of his youth:

>   Remember thee?
> Ay, thou poor ghost, whiles memory holds a seat
> In this distracted globe. Remember thee?
> Yea, from the table of my memory
> I'll wipe away all trivial fond records,
> All saws of books, all forms, all pressures past
> That youth and observation copied there,
> And thy commandment alone shall live
> Within the book and volume of my brain,
> Unmix'd with baser matter.   (1.5.95–104)

Here it seems the commonplaces and *sententiae* of humanist pedagogy have been rendered irrelevant by a being beyond human comprehension. The existence of the ghost demands a radical revaluation of all learning: it is a "thing" of which no "word" can give an adequate account. But immediately upon the pronouncement of this vow against learning, Hamlet turns to his tables to record a commonplace learned from the ghost's tale: "My tables. Meet it is I set it down / That one may smile, and smile, and be a villain" (1.5.107–8). In their article "Hamlet's Tables," Peter Stallybrass, Roger Chartier, J. Franklin Mowery, and Heather Wolfe note the irony that a play based upon an earlier version of the Hamlet story would evince such hostility toward the traditions of *imitatio* and commonplacing: "While Hamlet scorns the audience's table-books in Q1, the scripts through which he comes into existence are themselves the products of writing tables and commonplace books" (414). The irony is emphasized by Hamlet's reference to the "book and volume of my brain." Even the vow to forswear the practices of humanism, then, suggests how deeply the methods and materials of learning are embedded in early modern discourse, providing the vocabulary in which thought and memory are conceptualized.

When Horatio and the guards re-enter the scene, Hamlet begins to adopt that performance of madness he calls his "antic disposition," and the reverence and awe he had displayed toward the ghost suddenly give way to wry mockery. As Hamlet asks the assembled witnesses to swear to conceal what they have seen, the ghost echoes his request, repeatedly calling out "Swear" from below the stage. Each of these commands is met with an impertinent reply from Hamlet, beginning with "Ah ha, boy, say'st though so? Art thou there, truepenny? Come on, you hear this fellow in the cellarage. Consent to swear" (1.5.158–60). In addition to their surprisingly jocular quality, given Hamlet's usual veneration of his father, the lines are noteworthy for the way they draw attention to the theatrical situation. The reference to the ghost as a "fellow in the cellarage" reveals him to be an actor crouching beneath the floor of the stage rather than a spirit journeying back to Purgatory. (Coleridge, in a rare criticism of the play's artistry, found this scene "hardly defensible" [*Lectures and Notes* 358].) Hamlet's name for the ghost, "truepenny," is a reference to Tom Truepenny, the loyal servant figure from *Ralph Roister Doister*, a sixteenth-century comedy by the schoolmaster Nicholas Udall intended for performance in the grammar school. The reference recalls the pedagogical culture that featured prominently in Shakespeare's early comedy.

This dryly ironic and self-consciously theatrical performance is punctuated by a simple Latin tag: "*Hic et ubique?*" (1.5.164), Hamlet asks in regard to the ghost's seemingly ubiquitous presence. The phrase has no definite origin, but scholars have proposed a number of possible sources, typically invoking theological and devotional traditions.[20] Stephen Greenblatt – suggesting that the phrase recalls the discourse of Purgatory, clearly relevant to the scenes with the ghost – cites a prayer for the dead that was part of the ritual practice of Catholic England: "Avete, omnes animae fideles, quarum corpora hic et ubique requiescunt in pulvere" ("Hail all faithful souls, whose bodies here and everywhere do rest in the dust").[21] In addition to this echo of Catholic devotional practice, Greenblatt also notes that the phrase would have suggested "that Hamlet, like his friend Horatio, is something of a scholar" (234). But in an age of Latin learning, one would not need to be a scholar to articulate such a simple expression. I believe the phrase would have recalled the basic exercises of the grammar school rather than the kind of scholarship one would associate with Wittenberg. Between the reference to Udall's grammar school play, the echo of schoolboy Latin, and the generally irreverent tone of the scene, we might be led to consider Hamlet's "antic disposition" as a kind of schoolboy demeanour, an attitude prone to wordplay and self-consciousness of the kind prevalent in the early comedies. This attitude is in dramatic contrast with the seriousness of the vow to put away childish things that Hamlet pronounces upon the ghost's initial departure. By dryly describing the otherworldly presence of the ghost in the terms of the schoolroom, the text emphasizes the tension in the play between the ineffable and the ordinary.[22]

Being, Suffering, Acting

Hamlet's "To be or not to be" soliloquy – almost certainly the best-known passage in Shakespeare, and perhaps all of English literature – raises once again the question of passion and action, and again recalls the language of the schoolroom. The speech appears during the execution of Hamlet's plan to expose the king's guilt by means of the play, though it seems to have little dramatic bearing on the events that surround it. Performed between the resolution to stage the play and the instructions to the players, the speech is a moment of contemplation and reflection that interrupts the course of the Hamlet's most pragmatic activity:

> To be or not to be, that is the question:
> Whether 'tis nobler in the mind to suffer
> The slings and arrows of outrageous fortune,
> Or to take arms against a sea of troubles
> And by opposing end them.   (3.1.56–60)

Despite the reference to "the question," the speech actually raises two questions, two rhetorical topoi of the kind debated in the schools. The first of the two – "To be or not to be" – is descended from the question of whether an unhappy life is better than none at all. As Harold Jenkins observes, this was a traditional topic for dialectical argument, and Augustine's discussion of it in *De libero arbitrio* closely parallels the language of the speech: "It is not because I would rather be unhappy than not be at all, that I am unwilling to die, but for fear that after death I may be still more unhappy."[23] The second question – whether it is nobler "to suffer" or "to take arms" – concerns the opposition of passion and action, which as we have already seen is one of the play's preoccupations. Critics have associated this question with the long tradition of ethical debate on the opposed virtues of patient endurance and active valour.[24] Proposing such topics gives the speech "the structure of a formal academic debate," recalling the traditions of humanist pedagogy (Greenblatt, Introduction to *Hamlet* 105).

The precise relationship between these two questions is ambiguous and has provoked considerable critical argument. The second question is presented as a gloss or restatement of the first, but the opposed terms under consideration in the questions – "being" and "not being" in the first, "suffering" and "acting" in the second – are not easy to reconcile with one another. The order of the terms as they are presented would associate "being" with "suffering" and "not being" with "acting," contrary to our likely expectations. As "being" is typically taken for human life or existence, it should imply a kind of activity. Some have claimed that this must be the case, and that the order of the terms is simply inverted in the second statement.[25] But the simplest reading equates being with suffering: as Jenkins puts it, "the alternatives are to 'suffer' or to 'end', to endure or to die; and these are what the body of the speech discusses."[26] Being is thus represented as perpetual sufferance: to be is to endure the slights, oppressions, and disappointments of life in an ongoing exercise of "patient merit" (3.1.74).

In elaborating this view, the speech moves from the broad and abstract terms of the opening lines to an intimately detailed, if jaundiced, account of life's experiences, enumerating such hardships as the frailties of the body, the injustices inflicted by the great, the frustrations of legal process, and the disappointments of love. One's only available relief within this darkly inflected worldview, in which life is merely a succession of hardships and failures, is self-slaughter or a show of vain resistance that leads inevitably to death. Thus "end" bears a bitter double meaning: to end one's troubles is not to overcome them, but to confront them in an act of futile heroism that will end one's troubles and one's life by the same stroke. In its uncompromising refusal to accept the injustices and indignities of the world, the speech is poised between defiance and despair. Significant for our purposes is the way the speech represents a variety of forms of life and ways of engaging with the world, drawing evocative if economical portraits of the disappointed lover, the humiliated servant, the petitioner denied access to justice. These scenes of humble, ordinary existence stand in contrast with the exalted abstractions with which the speech begins.

In addition to the resemblance to Augustine, critics have noted echoes of Plato, Cicero, Plutarch, and Montaigne in the speech.[27] Aristotle's discussion of "being and not being" in the *Metaphysics* – perhaps filtered through Marlowe's *Doctor Faustus*, which quotes the Greek "*on cai me on*" – is often cited as an influence.[28] I would like to propose an additional source for the speech's terms, a humble one amidst this philosophical pantheon: Lily's lesson in the infinitive, "The infinitive signifieth to do, to suffer, or to be."[29] Lily's "to do," "to suffer," and "to be" closely parallel Hamlet's "To be," "to suffer," and "to take arms." It would be too much to say that Lily is a source for the speech, but, given the frequency with which Shakespeare cites Lily and the resemblance of the terms, it may be that the lesson was at least echoing in Shakespeare's memory when he composed the opening lines.

The nature of human being, agency, and passivity expressed and elaborated with such eloquence in the speech may thus be traced to a simple lesson in verbal voice. The echo of Lily shows that the abstract terms with which the soliloquy opens, which have led many critics to associate the speech with various metaphysical schemata, are not only "modes of being" but also ways of speaking.[30] The metaphysical categories of being, action, and passion are abstracted from grammatical positions: as we have seen, Aristotle derives the categories of *poiein* and *paschein* from the fact that we say a thing *does* or *suffers*, and the first category – *ousia*, "substance" or "essence" – is abstracted from the statement that a thing *is* (as Wittgenstein writes, "*Essence* is expressed in grammar").[31] That the background of what is often considered Shakespeare's most philosophical speech may be traced through Aristotle and Plato to his adolescent training in grammar seems an apt allegory for this process, vividly representing the way that the concepts of philosophy emerge from the everyday uses of language.

As P.M.S. Hacker writes, capacities such as reason, deliberation, and memory – though we may attribute them to animals in a rudimentary or attenuated form – "presuppose possession of a language. The limits of thought and knowledge … are the limits of the possible expression of thought and knowledge" (*Wittgenstein: Connections and Controversies*

61). To act and to understand ourselves as temporal beings, for instance, we must have a grammar of temporality, or tense: it is "the use of a tensed language and of devices for temporal reference, that constitutes the primary criteria for ascribing to a creature knowledge, memory, thought, and belief involving such reference to the past or future" (62). Our sense of temporality is predicated on the fact that our language is a tensed language, for only by the mechanism of tense may we speak of what is, and was, and is to come. Without a tensed language, we would exist in time, but we would not be able to plan for the future, to ruminate on some distant memory, or – by means of the future anterior tense that intrigued those in the Heideggerean tradition – to project ourselves into the future and consider what we will have been.

Just as temporality relies upon tense, the portrait of human agency and passion on display in Hamlet's speech is dependent upon the mechanism of verbal voice, the ability of active and passive grammars to express the position of the subject as one who acts or suffers in the world. Shakespeare's "dance of human passions"[32] relies upon passive grammar to express that one is stricken by "The pangs of dispriz'd love" (3.1.72), stymied by "the law's delay" (3.1.72), or compelled to endure "the proud man's contumely" (3.1.71). The suffering of the subject in these constructions is manifest in the structure of language. In prefacing its detailed narrative of lived experience with paradigmatic verbal forms ("to be," "to suffer," "to stand against") that echo the grammar book, the speech invites us to consider, citing Schalkwyk again, "the intersection of our language and our historical and practical being in the world." In this way, the speech constitutes something like a "grammatical investigation": its rumination on being, suffering, and acting is an exploration of the power of grammar to express these concepts and an arresting reminder of the interrelation of language and worldly existence.

Chapter Five

"Drunken Custom": Rules, Embodiment, and Exemplarity in Jonson's Humours Plays

For without doute, *Grammatica* it selfe, is sooner and surer learned by examples of good authors, than by the naked rewles of Grammarians.

— Roger Ascham, *The Scholemaster*

The 1604 edition of Thomas Wright's influential psychological treatise *The Passions of the Minde in General* includes a prefatory poem by Ben Jonson. The two men may have been close: there is evidence suggesting that it was Wright, a Jesuit priest, who converted Jonson to Catholicism when he was imprisoned in Newgate Gaol.[1] But whatever their personal relationship, Jonson likely had an intellectual interest in the book, as his writing for the public stage drew heavily upon Galenic medicine and the psychology of the passions. The poem, one of Jonson's few sonnets, praises Wright for his judicious account of the passions and their effects, comparing his facility in psychological diagnosis to the skill of a painter:

> In picture, they which truly understand
>   Require (besides the likeness of the thing)
>   Light, posture, heightening, shadow, colouring,
> All which are parts commend the cunning hand;
> And all your book (when it is throughly scanned)
>   Will well confess; presenting, limiting,
>   Each subtlest passion, with her source and spring,
> So bold, as shows your art you can command.
>   But now, your work is done, if they that view
>   The several figures languish in suspense
>   To judge which passion's false, and which is true,
>   Between the doubtful sway of reason and of sense;
>   'Tis not your fault, if they shall sense prefer,
>   Being told there, reason cannot, sense may, err. ("To the Author")

Like the artist who has mastered all the techniques of the craft, Wright is able not only to describe a particular passion but also to show its situation and environment, detailing its causes, tracing its effects, and describing the subtle shadings that distinguish it from adjacent affections. In the concluding sestet, Wright's readers are imagined lingering "Between the doubtful sway of reason and of sense," unsure if they should follow the rational guidance that the book provides or trust the uncertain evidence of their own impressions. Should they prove receptive to his teaching, Wright's careful account of the passions and affections will lead them away from the errors of sense and toward the better guidance of reason. As the passions themselves are more closely aligned with sense than reason, Wright's clinical analysis works to lessen passion's effects.[2] Wright's book, according to the poem, unites diagnosis with therapy: he represents the passions in order to chasten them.

Jonson situates Wright's book at the meeting point of art and medicine, the diagnostic and the therapeutic. I would like to suggest that Jonson's own writing stands at a similar crossroads. While Jonson praises Wright the physician for possessing the skill of an artist, in his own work he aspires to the clinical precision of a physician: he often frames his artistic aims in the language of medical diagnosis, promising that those who attend his plays "shall see the time's deformity / Anatomized in every nerve and sinew" (*Every Man Out* Induction 118–19). And as in Wright's work, diagnosis is not merely descriptive, but takes on a therapeutic function. The satirical representation of humour and affectation that we find in the plays seeks to correct these vices by exposing them to the mortifying effects of laughter and scorn, and Jonson's dramas conclude with ritualistic scenes in which the characters are disburdened of the humours that plagued them. Jonson thus fulfils the Horatian demand that poetry both delight and instruct, joining the mimetic function to the didactic.

Ben Jonson's *Every Man In His Humour* (1598) and *Every Man Out of His Humour* (1599) are the best-known examples of the "humours play" or "comedy of humours," a dramatic genre inaugurated by George Chapman in the mid-1590s.[3] The comedy of humours marked a turn away from the romantic comedies favoured by Shakespeare and others in the late Elizabethan period and catered to the tastes of an increasingly urbane London audience. It synthesized the humoral temperaments described in Galenic medicine – the sanguine, the phlegmatic, the choleric, and the melancholy – with the stock characters of classical and Italian comedy, exhibiting a panoply of ludicrous figures for satire and ridicule. But the comedy of humours also engaged with a new sense of the term emerging at the end of the sixteenth century: humour as folly, affectation, idiosyncrasy, or caprice. As the various humoral temperaments were associated with eccentric behaviour, personal whims began to be known as "humours."[4] Jonson's satire is particularly focused on this novel usage: while he treats those characters who truly suffer from the pathologies of humoral imbalance with a measure of sympathy, those who simply affect a fashionable melancholy or who flaunt their eccentricities to draw attention to themselves are subjected to unalloyed scorn.[5] Poised between the medical and the social, the term "humour" directs our attention to a complex of tensions that are crucial to a thorough understanding of Jonson's work. "Humour" in Jonson stands at the intersection of medicine and poetry, the material and the ideal, and the descriptive and the normative. Humours are simultaneously physical pathologies to be diagnosed and social vices to be amended; they demand the satirical tools of the poet no less than the care of the physician. And as they are represented in order to be corrected, Jonson's humours unite the descriptive and the normative, serving as examples intended to guide the behaviour of the spectators.

In the previous three chapters, I have argued that early modern writing represents the passions and affections as rule-guided practices, actions and experiences made meaningful by social standards and norms. In my analysis of Jonson's humour plays, I hope to clarify the nature of the rules themselves. Jonson's theatre, as the chorus in *Every Man Out* has it, is "allied to the time" and "accommodated to the correction of manners," employing realistic depictions of Renaissance city life in order to discipline the customs or behaviours of his audience (3.1.521, 528–9). Jonson makes it clear that he presents images of the humours as rules: his representations of affective habits and behaviours are intended to guide the actions of the spectators, leading them to renounce such vices and vanities in their own lives. By employing images of humorous behaviour as the instruments of correction, Jonson suggests that the rules that guide and give shape to the passions, affections, and humours are nothing other than the artifacts of past practices, actions that have acquired the force of example over time. This understanding is consistent with the exemplary pedagogy and poetics of the Renaissance and with the pragmatism of Wittgensteinian philosophy.

Classical Ideals, Grotesque Bodies

Even amidst the often frank and bawdy work of his contemporaries, Jonson's writing stands out for its Rabelaisian physicality. The characters of his plays, from the lecherous Volpone to the grotesque Pig Woman of *Bartholomew Fair*, are marked by their conspicuous fleshliness, and his poetry is no less saturated than his theatre with carnal imagery and scatological language.[6] As Julian Koslow has shown, critical approaches to Jonson's representations of the body have undergone a shift in recent years. Jonson scholars traditionally accepted his avowed commitment to Stoic ethics, considering him "a poet who valorizes the disincarnate ideality of language over merely material forms of social being."[7] According to this reading, the purpose of Jonson's grotesque imagery is to expose the body to the mortification of satire, elevating the ideal and the rational while debasing the material and sensory. More recent critics, however, have rejected this moralizing reading, taking an approach that "represents Jonson's linguistic practice as partaking in, rather than distancing itself from, the life of the flesh."[8] Gail Kern Paster, Patricia Fumerton, and Bruce Boerher have all argued that Jonson's depictions of the body are more than simply objects of censure: Jonson represents the body with a vitality and delight and often eclipses his Stoic moralizing. We can get a sense of this from the introduction to the folio version of Jonson's *Hymenaei*, a masque celebrating the marriage of Robert Devereaux, the third Earl of Essex, and Lady Frances Howard. The introduction begins with a characteristically Stoic declaration of the superiority of the ideal over the material: "It is a noble and just advantage that the things subjected to understanding have of those which are objected to sense, that the one sort are but momentary and merely taking, the other impressing and lasting" (667). Yet as Jonson continues, he defends his masque against those who would prefer lighter entertainment by comparing his intellectualism to a feast that is too rich for the stomachs of the unlearned:

> howsoever some may squeamishly cry out that all endeavour of learning and sharpness in these transitory devices ... is superfluous; I am contented these fastidious stomachs should leave my full tables, and enjoy at home their clean empty trenchers, fittest for such airy tastes; where perhaps a few Italian herbs picked up and made into a salad may find sweeter acceptance than all the most nourishing and sound meats of the world. (667)

That even this declaration of idealism depends upon the metaphor of digestion suggests the degree to which Jonson's writing is suffused with the imagery of the body.

Koslow's own reading offers a valuable synthesis of the neoclassicist and materialist perspectives on Jonson. While he agrees that the body is central to Jonson's poetics, he contends that recent criticism has been too quick to dismiss Jonson's idealism. Koslow focuses upon the relation between the material and the ideal, the way that "bodies and words react upon and inform each other" in Jonson's writing ("Humanist Schooling" 123). He further argues that it is humanist pedagogy that facilitates this contact by embodying ancient texts in present-day social practices. "Jonson's encounter with the classics as a boy centered on a set of intense, emulative, literary practices," he writes, "a way of treating texts as if they were living persons after whom one patterned one's own behavior, both literary and social" (128–9). The grammar school thus represents the point at which the linguistic and the physical intersect: it is the meeting place of a classical literature that has transcended the material circumstances of its production and the physical revivification of that literature in the practices and performances of the schoolroom. Jonson's theatre recalls and reproduces the fusion of classical values and embodied practices that took place in the Westminster School of his boyhood, bringing the language of the ancient poets, and in some cases even the figures of the poets themselves, onto the modern stage:

> By using these poets as dramatic characters and mediating his classicism through a vivid theatricality, Jonson profoundly complicates the relation between the realm of a putatively ideal textuality and that of a corruptible corporeal materiality. In essence, he finds a material means of accommodating his linguistic idealism by staging his schooling in this play as a theatrical performance, giving the texts from which he had once been taught body and life. In doing so he works to turn the theater itself into a schoolroom, one in which his vernacular poetry can claim the same authority over everyday, contemporary social life as the poetry of the ancients had within the walls of the school. (Koslow, "Humanist Schooling" 125–6)

Like the early modern schoolroom, in which students gave new life to the speeches of Cicero and the plays of Terence through performance, Jonson's theatre embodies the values of the ancient world, granting physical form to what might otherwise be understood as transcendent ideals.[9]

To illustrate the way that humanist pedagogy bridges the divide between language and the body, Koslow turns to a scene in Jonson's 1601 satire *Poetaster*. When the poetaster Crispinus, modelled on Jonson's rival John Marston, fails in his plot against Horace, a version of Jonson himself, he is punished by being forced to take an emetic of hellebore, causing him to vomit up his grandiose vocabulary. Horace attends him with a basin, catching the fustian words that had fattened his discourse:

CRISPINUS

 Oh, I am sick –

HORACE

 A basin, a basin, quickly! Our physic works. – Faint not, man.

[*A receptacle is brought and held up for Crispinus.*]

CRISPINUS

Oh – retrograde – reciprocal – incubus –

CAESAR

What's that Horace?

HORACE

"Retrograde" and "reciprocal incubus" are come up.   (5.3.411–15)

The remarkable scene imagines words as bodies that can be regurgitated, seeming to subordinate the verbal to the physical and provide strong evidence of Jonson's materialism. But Koslow notes that the play in fact downplays the therapeutic effects of purgation: "These pills can but restore him for a time" (5.3.468). For Crispinus to be truly cured of his poetic ills, he must submit to a program of Latin scholarship, beginning with Cato's aphorisms and the plays of Terence. The regimen of literary therapy that Horace prescribes is, as Koslow observes, identical to the typical grammar school curriculum, in which the writings of Cato and Terence were standard introductory texts. The scene demonstrates the thorough intertwining the physical and the discursive in Jonson. Crispinus's pompous poetic style is imagined as a physical malady, but that illness is in turn cured by exposure to classical literature.

The meeting of medical discourse and grammar school pedagogy that Koslow observes here recurs throughout Jonson's writings. Another example appears in the *Hymenaei*, which includes an allegory of the conflict between reason and the humours and passions. The latter are represented by eight male masquers "gloriously attired" and distinguished by "their several ensigns and colours," who dance to "a kind of contentious music" and threaten to interrupt the marriage ceremony with their swords (671). They are chastened by the figure of Reason, allegorized as "a venerable personage, her hair white and trailing to her waist," dressed in clothing decorated with mathematical figures and bearing a lamp and sword (672). In the folio version of the masque, Jonson includes a footnote addressing complaints that he received over the decision to represent the humours as men, presumably resulting from the traditional association of women with the passions and humours.[10] He writes:

That they were personated in men hath already come under some grammatical exception. But there is more than grammar to release it. For besides that *humores* and *affectus* are both *masculine in gender*, not one of the specials but in some language is known by a masculine word; again, when their influences are common to both sexes, and more generally impetuous in the male, I see not why they should not so be more properly presented. (671)

Jonson's principal defence is that the humours are to be found in both men and women, and that their effects are more prominent in men, a surprising claim, perhaps, from a frequently misogynistic writer. But it is the other justification, presented as an aside, that is more interesting for our purposes. Jonson dismisses the complaint about the allegory as a "grammatical exception," or pedantic criticism. But he counters that grammar itself excuses the conceit, and that the "grammatical" objection actually betrays an ignorance of grammar. This is because the words *humores* and *affectus* are both masculine, and thus anyone with even "small Latin" should expect them to be allegorized as male figures.[11] The rules of grammar dictate the organization of bodies in the masque.

Jonson's invocation of grammatical gender to defend his representation of the humours demonstrates once again the intertwining of linguistic and affective vocabularies that we have already seen in Sidney and Shakespeare. It provides further support for Koslow's argument, as it seeks to ground embodied performance in the knowledge of classical languages cultivated in the grammar school. But the passage may also help to clarify the manner in which linguistic ideals and material bodies relate to one another in Jonson by invoking the concept of rules. By dividing up male and female bodies in accordance with the gender of the words *humores* and *affectus*, Jonson imposes a rule upon the world, allowing a linguistic principle to govern the body's behaviour. Yet the humanist philosophy in which Jonson was educated held that concepts like grammatical gender were nothing other than abstractions derived from the historical practice of language. To allow the rules of grammar to govern embodied action is thus to engage in an ongoing dialectic between linguistic ideals and material practices: embodied action gives rise to rules, which in turn govern embodied action.

Exemplarity and Embodied Rule-Following

In order to explore this interaction between linguistic rules and material bodies, I will turn to an important concept in Renaissance pedagogy and poetics: the example. As Jeff Dolven puts it, the example is "a compromise between experience and maxim," "a sample cut from the world's cloth in such a way that it somehow bears a lesson" (*Scenes of Instruction* 136). Humanist pedagogy, as we have seen, emphasized exemplary rather than prescriptive instruction, maintaining that language learning should take place through the imitation and translation of model texts rather than the memorization of abstract grammatical rules. A similar principle held sway in Renaissance poetics, which pointed to the exemplary instruction that poetry provided in order to justify its moral value.

Sidney's *Defence of Poesy*, which I have discussed at length in chapter 2, provides one of the most sophisticated accounts of poetic exemplarity in the period. For Sidney, the instruction of the poets, like that of the humanists, is essentially exemplary: it is a way of providing images of "virtuous action" upon which readers will be inspired to model their own behaviour (220). These images, however, are not simply invented out of whole cloth, for Sidney agrees with Aristotle that the function of poetry is *mimesis* or the imitation of nature: "a representing, counterfeiting, or figuring forth" (217). Poetry, then, is simultaneously normative and descriptive, standing at the border between "ought" and "is." It represents embodied actions and events that take place in the world, but it presents them in such a way that they take on significance beyond themselves, offering them up as ideals to be imitated or cautionary examples to be shunned. If the schoolroom is the usual space in which an embodied action is imbued with normative significance, the institution of poetry takes on a similar role in Sidney's account, providing the setting in which an image of life may become a pattern for living, a body may become a rule.

We have seen how Sidney situates the practice of poetry between the prescriptivism of the philosopher and the descriptive accounts of the historian. While the philosopher may set out "the bare rule" by which one may achieve a virtuous life, the purely abstract and didactic language of philosophy is without the motivating and acculturative power of poetry. On the other hand, the detailed and compelling narratives of the historian have the capacity to capture the imagination but lack the moral structure and purpose of philosophy. Bound to describe events as they have actually happened, the historian is restricted to representing the injustice of a world ruled by the whims of fortune, a world from which it is impossible to derive wisdom or instruction. The poet alone is able to unite the captivating power of history with the precepts of philosophy; poetry presents images and narratives that enthral their readers but are judiciously arranged in such a way as to provide moral instruction.[12] As the space in which the ideal intersects with the empirical, it is in poetry, to quote *Astrophil and Stella* once more, that "Nature doth with infinite agree" (35.4). The example is the formal device by which this union of the ideal and the material is accomplished. We may get a clear sense of this from Sidney's description of Xenophon's life of Cyrus. Sidney emphasizes that while the account of Cyrus is founded upon the facts of his life, it is presented in such a way as to motivate its readers to action, to condition their behaviour through an inspiring and judiciously crafted example:

> Which delivering forth also is not wholly imaginative, as we are wont to
> say by them that build castles in the air; but so far substantially it worketh,

not only to make a Cyrus, which had been but a particular excellency as
nature might have done, but to bestow a Cyrus upon the world to make
many Cyruses, if they will learn aright why and how that maker made
him. (*Defence* 216–17)

Xenophon's account makes Cyrus into a heroic ideal, but at the same
time it embodies the ideal of heroism in the person of Cyrus. To represent Cyrus in such a fashion is not only to describe the life of a particular embodied individual but also to establish a pattern by which bodies
will be governed in the future, "to bestow a Cyrus upon the world to
make many Cyruses." The example of Cyrus joins the material to the
ideal, making the historical figure of Cyrus into a rule and embodying
that rule in the person of Cyrus.

The most common way of representing exemplarity in the Renaissance was through the figure of the mirror. As Debora Shuger has
shown, the mirror was understood in the Renaissance not only as a
reflection of life, but as a standard to be followed. Hamlet is the "glass
of fashion" because he embodies in his way of life a particular ideal
that serves as a pattern for others to imitate: the other courtiers look to
him, as one looks to a mirror, to regulate their own appearances and
manners of comportment.[13] Jonson himself employs the figure in this
manner in his "Epistle to Katherine, Lady Aubigny," a poem that presents to its subject her "truest glass: / Wherein your form you still the
same shall find; / Because nor it can change, nor such a mind" (243). As
Ian Donaldson writes, the poem provides Lady Aubigny with "a standard against which to measure her life. In a similar sense, well-known
contemporary handbooks furnished so-called 'mirrors' for princes and
magistrates: ideal exemplars or patterns for living" (*Ben Jonson* 11). The
mirror is simultaneously descriptive and normative: it reflects life as it
is, but it also conditions life by serving as a standard and guide to those
who view it. As I will discuss later in the chapter, Jonson understands
the function of satire in precisely this manner and employs the figure of
the mirror to characterize his own practice as a dramatist.

The concern with exemplarity in Renaissance pedagogy and poetics
resonates with Wittgenstein's interest in the nature of rules. The question of how ideal rules may apply to embodied practices was central
to Wittgenstein's late work, and his discussion of the issue has engendered extensive debate in analytic philosophy.[14] Wittgenstein ad-
hered to the well-established philosophical position that meaningful
action, as opposed to reflexive or machine-like behaviour, depends
upon a framework of rules or norms, for in order to ascribe intention
or purpose to an action we rely upon rules that establish how a person

should or should not act in pursuit of a particular goal. This normative understanding of human action dates back at least to Kant, who held that rules were essential to conceptual thought and moral agency. Yet for Kant, the rules were universal, *a priori* principles that determined whether or not a particular action was right or wrong, a particular judgment correct or incorrect. Wittgenstein rejects this idealized understanding of rules, arguing that the conception of rule-following as the application of an *a priori* principle to a particular action entangles us in an infinite regress. To determine whether an action conforms to an *a priori* rule – to interpret a rule – is itself an action, and thus subject to its own set of rules. "Can't we imagine a rule regulating the application of a rule; and a doubt which *it* removes – and so on? ... This was our paradox: no course of action could be determined by a rule, because every course of action can be brought into accord with the rule" (*Philosophical Investigations* §84, §201). Wittgenstein's solution to this paradox is to invoke the notion of practice: "[T]here is a way of grasping a rule which is *not* an interpretation, but which, from case to case of application, is exhibited in what we call 'following the rule' and 'going against it' ... 'following a rule' is a practice" (§§201–2). He also refers to rule-following as a "custom," a "usage," and an "institution" (§199). To follow a rule is not simply to act in accord with an *a priori* principle; instead, it is to engage in an activity consistent with the customs, institutions, and expectations of one's socio-cultural situation. Rules, then, are not principles that exist independently of the practices that they govern, but standards implicit in those practices and interwoven into the life of a community.

Maintaining Kant's normative understanding of human action but rejecting his rationalism and idealism, Wittgenstein holds that the horizons of experience are established not by what Kant called "the eternal and unalterable laws of reason" (*Critique of Pure Reason* Axii) but by the contingent and conventional standards that guide our everyday lives. "The application of the concept 'following a rule,'" he writes, "presupposes a custom" (*Remarks on the Foundation of Mathematics* 322). This immanent and historical perspective on human experience leads Wittgenstein to adopt the crucial formulation I have discussed in my Introduction: "form of life." For Wittgenstein, a form of life is the social, cultural, and material setting within which our languages and practices take place and upon which their meaning ultimately rests: "What has to be accepted, the given, is – one might say – *forms of life*" (*Philosophical Investigations* 238). While it is only within a form of life that our practices may have meaning, it is our practices that define the contours of our forms of life. A form of life, then, is neither simply a set of rules nor an index of practices, but a unified whole that cannot be reduced to the ideal or material elements of which it is composed. As Theodore Schatzki puts it, "In Wittgenstein, life is a 'weaving ... stream' ... of activity transpiring within particular forms of life. These forms of life, however, are the products of past activity, extended by the current activity, and only as such constitute the context for further action" ("Wittgenstein + Heidegger" 308). Wittgenstein presents us with an image of life as a cascading sequence of practices, each taking place within an existing framework of rules, yet also altering that framework by establishing new precedents and standards for action.

In his comments on language-learning, Wittgenstein offers a description of embodied rules and exemplary instruction strikingly similar to what we find in Renaissance pedagogy and poetics. According to Wittgenstein, we are inducted into a form of life by mastering its rules and conventions.[15] These rules, however, are not learned through explicit instruction: we learn by doing, by imitating the exemplary actions of our instructors. At one point in the *Philosophical Investigations*, Wittgenstein imagines a scene in which he instructs a student in the use of unfamiliar words, emphasizing that the student must be trained in their use in order to adequately grasp their meaning: "if a person has not yet got the *concepts*, I shall teach him to use the words by means of *examples* and by *exercises* ... I do it, he does it after me; and I influence him by expressions of agreement, rejection, expectation, encouragement. I let him go his way, or hold him back, and so on" (§208). By means of this process of acculturation, the student and teacher come to accord not only in language but in practice, behaviour, and culture: the student is initiated into a form of life. This manner of acculturation functions not by precept but by a process of guided participation in which exemplary actions are borrowed from everyday life in order to serve a didactic purpose. A phrase, gesture, or expression is removed from its ordinary context and performed in such a way as to teach someone how it is to be used: "I do it, he does it after me." Rule-following is situated and embodied. The rules do not have an existence apart from the actions and practices that abide by them: embodied actions are proffered *as* rules and establish the standards for subsequent action. Every practice is a potential rule, and every rule an ossified practice.

Rule and Convention in the Humour Plays

Jonson's humour plays function in a manner consistent with the accounts of Sidney and Wittgenstein, presenting images of actions and behaviours drawn from the world of late Elizabethan London and investing these images with normative value in order to discipline the conduct of his spectators. The highly self-conscious nature of Jonson's theatre makes it an ideal space for considering such themes: the metatheatrical moments in the plays directly engage with the questions of the nature of humour, the relation between representation and instruction, and the role of convention in theatre and language. *Every Man Out of His Humour* opens with such a scene, an Induction in which Asper, the supposed author of the play, rages against the vices he intends to satirize while his companions Mitis and Cordatus attempt to assuage his anger.[16] As Asper rants intemperately against the corruption of the court and the sins of the city, his interlocutors plead with him to calm himself: "this humour," explains Mitis, "will come ill to some. / You will be though to be too peremptory" (Induction 71–2). Asper seizes on this use of the term "humour," which seems to crystallize the vanities that have so enraged him. Vowing to "give these ignorant well-spoken days / Some taste of their abuse of this word *humour*" (Induction 77–8), Asper launches into a speech defining the original sense of the term and tracing the degenerative process that has made it into a watchword of fops and dandies:

ASPER

> Why, *humour* (as 'tis, *ens*) we thus define it
> To be a quality of air or water,
> And in itself holds these two properties:
> Moisture and fluxure …
> … and hence we do conclude
> That whatsoe'er hath fluxure and humidity,
> As wanting power to contain itself,
> Is *humour*. So, in every human body,
> The choler, melancholy, phlegm, and blood,
> By reason that they flow continually
> In some one part and are not continent,
> Receive the name of humours. Now thus far
> It may by metaphor apply itself
> Unto the general disposition;
> As when some one peculiar quality
> Doth so possess a man that it doth draw
> All his affects, his spirit, and his powers
> In their confluxions all to run one way:
> This may be truly said to be a *humour*.
> But that a rook, in wearing a pied feather,
> The cable hatband, or the three-piled ruff,
> A yard of shoe-tie, or the Switzer's knot

> On his French garters, should affect a humour,
> O, 'tis more than most ridiculous!
>
> CORDATUS
>
> He speaks pure truth. Now, if an idiot
> Have but an apish or fantastic strain,
> It is his humour.
>
> ASPER
>
> Well, I will scourge those apes,
> And to these courteous eyes [*Indicating audience*] oppose a mirror
> As large as is the stage whereon we act,
> Where they shall see the time's deformity
> Anatomized in every nerve and sinew,
> With constant courage and contempt of fear. (Induction 86–120)

Derived from the Latin word for fluid or moisture, the strictest sense of the term should apply to liquid bodies: "whatsoe'er hath fluxure and humidity … is *humour*."[17] The fluid components of the body – blood, phlegm, choler, and melancholy – are called humours in this precise sense, as "they flow continually" and "are not continent." While the psychological states that share their names with the body's humours are not fluids in the literal sense, Asper allows that they may be called humours "by metaphor" because of the way they imitate the humours' effects: just as black bile may flow throughout the body and affect all of its functions, so may a melancholy mood suffuse the mind and direct the spirits and affections. But now the term is promiscuously applied to personal idiosyncrasies, novel habits of dress, and other trivialities that have nothing to do with its original meaning.

Asper's name is borrowed from Aemilius Asper, a Latin grammarian who produced commentaries on Terence, Virgil, and Sallust. The association emphasizes Asper's concern with language, which we may see in his complaints about the abuse of the word "humour" itself. He laments that modern usage has ruined the venerable medical term: the "poor innocent word" has been "racked and tortured," stretched out of shape in order to accommodate the novel senses it has acquired in the modern age (Induction 82–3). Asper's strict policing of terms would seem to make him a linguistic prescriptivist. His survey of the uses of "humour" exhibits increasing frustration as the term moves farther away from its original sense, implying that linguistic change is a process of corruption by which words fall away from their true foundations and acquire merely conventional meanings. What Asper perceives as the degradation of the word exemplifies the debasement of manners and behaviours that his satire is intended to oppose. He conceives of his role as a satirist to free the world from the arbitrary rule of what he memorably derides as "drunken Custom," to reform a world governed by social convention and restore an order founded on reason and virtue (Induction 28).

Yet as the scene continues, it suggests that comedy itself, the weapon Asper wields against "drunken Custom," is purely customary in form. After Asper leaves the stage, Mitis asks Cordatus about his play, inquiring whether it adheres to the rules of classical drama:

MITIS

Does he observe all the laws of comedy in it?

CORDATUS

What laws mean you?

MITIS

Why, the equal division of it into acts and scenes, according to the Terentian manner; his true number of actors; the furnishing of the scene with *grex* or chorus; and that the whole argument fall with compass of a day's efficiency. (Induction 231–7)

Cordatus objects to this rigid understanding of the comic form:

CORDATUS

O no, these are too nice observations.

MITIS

They are such as must be received, by your favour, or it cannot be authentic.

CORDATUS

Troth, I can discern no such necessity.

MITIS

No?

CORDATUS

No, I assure you, signor. If those laws you speak of had been delivered us *ab initio* and in their present virtue and perfection, there had been some reason of obeying their powers. But 'tis extant that that which we call *comedia* was at first nothing but a simple and continued satire, sung by one only person, till Susario invented a second; after him Epicharmus a third; Phormus and Chiomides devised to have four actors, with a prologue and chorus, to which Cratinus long after added a fifth and sixth; Eupolis, more; Aristophanes, more than they: every man in the dignity of his spirit and judgment supplied something. And, though that in him this kind of poem appeared absolute and fully perfected, yet how is the face of it changed since Menander, Philemon, Caecilius, Plautus, and the rest, who have utterly excluded the chorus, altered the property

> of the persons, their names, and natures, and augmented it with all
> liberty, according to the elegancy and disposition of those times wherein
> they wrote! I see not then but we should enjoy the same *licentia* or free
> power to illustrate and heighten our invention as they did, and not be
> tied to those strict and regular forms which the niceness of a few (who
> are nothing but form) would thrust upon us. (Induction 238–65)

With this lengthy history of the gradual development of comedy in ancient
Greece and Rome, we find the opposite of Asper's strict prescriptivism.
The laws of comedy are not universal principles that determine the genre's
proper form, but instead a set of conventions derived from historical precedents. The comic poets of the past did not follow established precepts;
they wrote according to their own intuitive judgment and the materials
available to them, adapting the genre in reaction to what had come before
and in accordance with the tastes and expectations of their times. Precisely
the kind of fluid alteration and innovation that so infuriates Asper has, in
Cordatus's view, governed the history of his chosen form.

Given that Asper is the supposed author of the play, one would expect
his views to be representative of Jonson's.[18] The long-standing comparison between the "artful" Jonson and the "natural" Shakespeare,
a tradition inaugurated by Jonson himself and acquiring the force of
axiom over time, would also seem to associate Jonson with strict ne-
oclassicism.[19] Yet in his prose writings, Jonson clearly supports the
more liberal perspective of Cordatus, rejecting the idea that the rules
of classical drama should be unthinkingly obeyed. In the *Discoveries*, a
commonplace book interlaced with personal reflections, he maintains
a conventionalist perspective on language and literature, contending
that the principles of both derive from historical example and social
consensus. Adapting passages from the Dutch humanist Daniel Hein-
sius, Jonson writes:

> I am not of that opinion to conclude a poet's liberty within the narrow
> limit of laws, which either the grammarians or philosophers prescribe. For
> before they found out those laws there were many excellent poets that ful-
> filled them; amongst which none more perfect than Sophocles, who lived
> a little before Aristotle. Which of the Greeklings durst ever give precepts
> to Demosthenes? Or to Pericles, whom the age surnamed "heavenly," be-
> cause he seemed to thunder and lighten with his language? Or to Alcib-
> iades, who had rather nature for his guide, than art for his master? (586)

Echoing Cordatus's claim that the laws of comedy are not "delivered us *ab initio*," Jonson contends that the rules of grammarians and

philosophers are not *a priori* principles, but rather descriptive accounts of the works of exemplary poets and orators. Sophocles had already mastered the art of tragedy before Aristotle set down its characteristics in the *Poetics*, and Demosthenes never had to consult with the *Rhetoric* to perfect his skill as a speaker. These figures did not follow the rules of their crafts: they defined them. As Jonson continues, however, he defends the theory of Aristotle as a guide that facilitates the acquisition of poetic ability in those without the inspiration of a Sophocles or a Demosthenes:

> But whatsoever nature at any time dictated to the most happy, or long exercise to the most laborious, that the wisdom and learning of Aristotle hath brought into an art because he understood the causes of things, and what other men did by chance or custom, he doth by reason; and not only found out the way not to err, but the short way we should take, not to err. (586–7)

Aristotle's theory is a post-hoc systematization of the practice of exemplary artists, establishing as rules the techniques that successful writers have employed in the past. As such, it has great pragmatic value, providing an efficient way for writers to hone their ability, the "short way we should take" to excel as poets, dramatists, and rhetoricians. Yet Aristotle's is far from the final word on the subject: as Cordatus suggests, modern poets should follow the spirit of the ancients in adapting the rules as they see fit, enjoying the right "to illustrate and heighten [their] invention as [the ancients] did," rather than uncritically adhering to those "strict and regular forms" imposed by classical orthodoxy. As Wittgenstein argued, the rules do not precede practice, for to abide by a rule is to work within an established tradition, following, extending, and transforming it.

As Mitis and Cordatus continue their discussion of the laws of comedy, they begin to wonder why the play has yet to begin and express relief when the Prologue finally enters the scene. Cordatus scolds him for his lateness: "Now, sir, if you had stayed a little longer, I meant to have spoken your prologue for you" (Induction 285–6). The Prologue takes the offer seriously and begins to leave: "with all my heart, sir, you shall do it yet, and I thank you" (Induction 287–8). While Cordatus implores him to remain and perform what is presumably the only function for which he exists, the Prologue flatly refuses and abandons the stage, leaving the baffled Cordatus to face the audience: "'Sdeath, what a humorous fellow is this? Gentleman, good faith, I can speak no prologue" (Induction 309–10). Finally, the "incomprehensible epicure"

Carlo Buffone, one of the main characters in the drama itself, enters the scene and performs the role of the Prologue, introducing the play with a toast of Canary wine (Induction 351–2). In addition to its metatheatrical wit, the encounter with the "humorous" Prologue and a fugitive from the main action of the play emphasizes Cordatus's description of the conventional and contingent nature of "the laws of comedy." The Prologue, a figure who should have a purely instrumental function in the play, displays precisely the kind of eccentricity that Asper intends to satirize, suggesting that the formal machinery of comedy is no less distempered than the society it seeks to critique. Like Asper's "drunken Custom," the Prologue's susceptibility to humoral imbalance suggests that what appear to be ideal principles may in fact share in the embodiment of the material world. The appearance of Carlo Buffone similarly subverts the rules of theatre, transgressing the boundary between frame narrative and main action and blurring the line between the satirist and the object of the satire.

The Induction thus stages a progression from strict moralism and orthodox aesthetics to an almost anarchic state of confusion. It begins with Asper's expression of indignation at the humours and eccentricities of the age and his desire to enforce a rigorous moral order through the disciplinary power of comedy. We then learn that the form of comedy itself is a product of historical convention, undermining its power to impose any strictly defined law upon the world. Finally, we encounter a "humorous" Prologue and a debauched character from the main narrative who usurps his role, suggesting that even the most abstract of dramatic functions are embodied and contingent. Taken together, this sequence of events challenges an idealist view of the comic theatre. Comedy cannot be understood as a mechanism for enforcing *a priori* laws, for it is itself a conventional practice, operating by custom rather than precept, adapting its principles from historical precedent.

Another passage in the *Discoveries* suggests that Jonson's conventionalist perspective on comedy extends to language as a whole. Paraphrasing Quintilian's *Institutio Oratoria*, Jonson writes:

> Custom is the most certain mistress of language, as the public stamp makes the current money … Yet when I name custom, I understand not the vulgar custom, for that were a precept no less dangerous to language, than life, if we should speak or live after the manners of the vulgar; but that I call custom of speech, which is the consent of the learned, as custom of life, which is the consent of the good. (563)

Jonson affirms that linguistic meaning is determined by custom rather than some natural relation between words and things, adopting a perspective on language similar to that which we have seen in Erasmus and others. To explain the position, the passage proposes a comparison with coinage: just as public authority endows a piece of metal with the value that makes it a coin, so does the sanction of a community of speakers transform a sound or image into a meaningful word.[20] Yet the analogy suggests that it is not simply the popular will that determines the meaning of language, for in Jonson's time, as in Quintilian's, money was marked with the image of the sovereign and depended upon the power of the state to guarantee its value. Jonson equates the political authority that creates monetary value with the aesthetic and ethical authority that defines eloquence and good manners, the "consent of the learned" and the "consent of good."[21] The passage reconciles the rule of custom with the authority of learning, suggesting that the judgment that distinguishes between eloquence and vulgarity is provisional and contingent. Just as playwrights compose within an ongoing tradition, extending and transforming an inherited comic form, so do the learned navigate a landscape of historical precedent and contemporary circumstance, creating a language that is both erudite and adequate to the conditions of everyday life.[22]

In spite of his aversion to custom, Asper himself provides evidence of comedy's conventional nature. Asper promises to "oppose a mirror" to the spectators' "courteous eyes," confronting them with a reflection of their own vices in order to shame them into repentance. As we have seen, the figure of the mirror represents the conjunction of the mimetic and the didactic: it presents images that are drawn from life and endowed with normative authority. In this case, the images are cautionary, to be shunned rather than imitated. If Xenophon's Cyrus made many Cyruses, Jonson's gulls, braggarts, and bad poets are designed to prevent such figures from appearing on the world's stage. But in spite of this negative character, Asper's satire nevertheless functions through embodied example, exhibiting for his audience in material form the affectation, social climbing, and greed that they should shun. The rules it presents are not absolute laws founded in nature or reason: they are drawn from the conduct and practices of early modern London, native to the social world they are intended to govern.

A later discussion between Mitis and Cordatus echoes Asper's language, affirming the conception of comedy as a normative mode of representation. In an interlude about halfway through the action, Mitis questions whether it might have been better for Asper to write a play more in line with the romantic comedies popular in the 1590s. He suggests that "the argument of his comedy might have been of some other nature, as of a duke to be in love with a countess, and that countess to be in love with the duke's son, and the son to love the lady's waiting-maid: some such cross-wooing, with a clown to their servingman, better than to be thus near and familiarly allied to the time" (3.1.516–20). Cordatus responds to this travesty of the romance genre by defending Asper's realism, citing "Cicero's definition ... who would have a comedy be *imitatio vitae, speculum consuetudinis, imago veritatis*: a thing throughout pleasant and ridiculous, and accommodated to the correction of manners" (3.1.524–9).[23] Comedy is the "imitation of life, mirror of manners, image of truth": it reflects the world as it is, representing the manners and practices of the society in which it is written. Although the play seeks to restore ancient virtue, its means of doing so is to represent the practices and customs of the present day: Jonson insists that comedy be "allied to the time," presenting realistic depictions of contemporary behaviour. In doing so, he embraces a model of satire that is immanent and situated, its values embodied in everyday social practice.

The Rule of Humour

Every Man Out's Induction shows that the play is conceived as an exercise in exemplary instruction. Humours are both the instruments and the objects of its satire: the play presents images of distempered and affected behaviour in order to chasten the same practices in its audience. Within the narratives of the humour plays themselves, we find a similar dynamic. In both *Every Man In* and *Every Man Out*, those who act to correct the humours are themselves conspicuously humorous, suggesting the continuity between the rules and the world upon which they are imposed.

Like *Every Man Out*, *Every Man In* parades a group of humorous and ridiculous characters before the audience, among them the jealous husband Thorello, the choleric brawler Giuliano, the braggart Bobadilla, and the hapless gulls Stephano and Matheo, who affect courtly fashions and poetic sensibilities. The schemes of the protagonists Lorenzo Junior and Prospero and the clever servant Musco eventually lead to a confrontation with the justice Doctor Clement, who sentences the worst of the offenders to public shaming and presides over a ritual in which each character is disburdened of his or her humours. He burns Matheo's plagiarized poems in a bonfire and invites the assembled cast to consign their cares to the flames: "I conjure you all here to put off all discontentment. First you, Senior Lorenzo, your cares; [*To Thorello and*

Bianca] you and you, your jealousy; [*To Giuliano*] you, your anger; [*To Prospero*] and you, your wit, sir" (5.3.450–4). Clement is identified in the Folio version of the play as a "merry magistrate," placing him in a theatrical tradition that also includes Henry V in Dekker's *Shoemaker's Holiday* and the title character in Munday and Chettle's *Sir Thomas More*, authorities who govern with wit and charity and show particular sympathy to the poor and vulnerable. His name may recall Seneca's *De clementia*, a defence of mercy in princes that Jonson cites in the *Discoveries*. As a "merry" figure, Clement does not apply the law in a rational or consistent manner, governing instead by whim and caprice. He threatens those under his power with immoderate punishment – at one point brandishing a sword over Musco and promising to behead him for his treachery – yet ultimately relents, displaying the merciful nature that gives him his name. In short, he is humorous: apart from his charitable motivations, it is difficult to distinguish him from the rest of the idiosyncratic figures that populate the play.

In *Every Man Out*, those who act to discipline the humours are similarly afflicted with what they seek to heal. Asper's fanaticism, his consuming hatred of vice, is clearly a humour by his own definition: a "peculiar quality" that "Doth so possess a man that it doth draw / All his affect, his spirits, and his powers / ... all to run one way." Cordatus considers Asper's zeal a kind of madness: "Why this is right *furor poeticus*! ... a madman speaks" (Induction 146–8). The scholar Macilente – the protagonist of the main action, played by the same actor as Asper – is a stirring critic of the abuses of the age.[24] It is his plots that lead the other characters out of their humours, revealing to them the vanity of their various passions and obsessions. Yet the play makes it clear that he is motivated not by ethical considerations, but by his envy of the wealth and preferment of those around him, a jealous disposition that the chorus refers to as "his humour" (1.3.159). After Macilente occasions the dishumouring of the rest of the cast, he himself must be cured by a *deus ex machina*: a chance encounter with Queen Elizabeth, whose majesty inspires him to renounce his envy and reform his life.

Even the most apparently reasonable characters in the plays are not free from humour's influence. In *Every Man In*, the gallants Lorenzo Junior and Prospero, who seem to represent an urbane sophistication opposed to the foolishness of the other characters, are implicated in humorousness. Lorenzo Senior complains that his son "affects" a "vain course of study," recalling that in his own youth he was "Fed with the self-same humour he is now / Dreaming on naught but idle poetry" (1.1.9, 16–17). And as we have seen, Prospero's "wit" is counted alongside anger and jealousy as a "discontentment" in the dishumouring scene. Even the judiciousness of the chorus in *Every Man Out*, precisely the kind of critical discrimination that Jonson so values, becomes a humour at the end of the play. Mitis and Cordatus decline to offer a final judgment on the performance, abandoning their critical "humours" in imitation of the play's characters: "Nay, we ha' done censuring now ... we'll imitate your actors and be out of our humours" (5.4.43–7). That none of the characters escape the charge of humorousness suggests that humour is as much a pervasive affective atmosphere in the plays as it is a particular distemper or disposition.

This ubiquity of humour has implications for the generic classification of the plays. There has been a long-standing debate on whether Jonson's humours plays should be considered Juvenalian or Horatian satire, the former characterized by moral indignation and an uncompromising condemnation of vice, the latter by moderation and tolerance, wry irony, and an element of self-parody.[25] The leniency of Doctor Clement is consistent with the Horatian mode, but Asper's righteous anger and Macilente's acerbic critique of hypocrisy are clear cases of Juvenalian vitriol. Helen Ostovich argues persuasively that the definition of comedy provided by Cordatus in *Every Man Out* – "a thing throughout pleasant and ridiculous, and accommodated to the correction of manners" – suggests that Jonson favours Horatian satire: "The combination of 'pleasant' and 'ridiculous' suggests a comical tone that is tolerant, wry, and informal – a far cry from Juvenal's *saeva indignatio*" (Introduction to *Every Man Out* 13). As the Juvenalian characters are themselves revealed to be humorous, it might be said that the two styles of satire are folded together in Jonson's plays. Consistent with the Horatian tendency toward self-parody, the plays rebuke their own often vituperative style: they are in part Horatian satires on the Juvenalian mode, self-conscious critiques of the satirist's moralistic fervour.

More significant than these generic considerations, however, is what the ubiquity of humour suggests about Jonson's understanding of the nature of social norms and the didactic function of the theatre. Humour's universal rule suggests that embodiment is a condition of social existence. All of the characters, even those distinguished by their discernment, fall under the sway of folly and distemper: there is no "outside" of humour from which the wise can offer definitive judgments on the actions of the foolish. As I have shown, the plays seek to educate through exemplary instruction, representing characters and actions drawn from the world of contemporary London in an effort to influence their audience. The moral reformations that they stage operate in an analogous way: the humorous characters are confronted with behaviour much like their own, prompting them to recognize their folly and amend their conduct. By acknowledging the kinship between the satirist and the object of satire, Jonson's plays assume an immanent understanding of ethical and aesthetic principles consistent with humanist conventionalism and the pragmatic approach to rules we find in Wittgenstein. We see once again that the rules the plays enforce are not ideal moral principles, but situated and provisional judgments that take place within the social world they critique.

In this book, I have argued that the passions and affects appear in Renaissance literature as rule-guided practices, actions and performances rendered coherent by conventional standards, just as language is made meaningful by grammatical rules. Like Sidney and Shakespeare, Jonson represents humour as a practice, a characteristic pattern of behaviour that abides by social convention. Prospero gives voice this perspective in wryly observing that Giuliano's choleric nature is only realized in its performance: "a tall man is never his own man till he be angry. To keep his valour in obscurity is to keep himself, as it were, in a cloak-bag. What's a musician unless he play? What's a tall man unless he fight?" (*Every Man In* 4.3.8–11). Moreover, Jonson's self-conscious satire helps to elucidate the nature of rules that define such affective practices. By presenting images of humoral action as rules to govern the actions of his audience, the plays suggest that the rules are nothing other than actions that have acquired the force of example over time. In Wittgenstein's terms, they are practices that have "hardened" into rules through regularity and repetition (*Remarks on the Foundations of Mathematics* VI-23). The passions are thus situated within an ongoing sequence of affective practices, defined and judged according to established precedent, suggesting their irreducibly social and historical nature. Though humoralism is rooted in physiological theory, Jonson's humours, intimately connected with the culture of early modern London, demand the attention not of the physician, but of the historian and the critic.

Conclusion

In the foregoing chapters, I have sought to show that humanist ped-agogy's emphasis on the priority of linguistic practice over gram-matical rules had a profound influence on the writing of its students, especially in their representations of emotional life. Writers trained in the humanist program bring together the idioms of the grammar school and the discourse of the passions, representing love, grief, and envy as practices guided by conventional standards. In *Astrophil and Stella*, Sidney locates the love affair in the schoolroom, depicting Astrophil as a student and Stella as his beloved "schoole-mistresse" (46.10). The poems thus suggest that love is a kind of pedagogical activity, a performance like the rehearsal of a schoolboy's lessons. In *Love's Labour's Lost*, we saw the mockery of rhetorical excess become so pervasive that it threatened to empty out language altogether, suggesting that words are fundamentally meaningless. But when the lovers are parted in its final act, they are forced to prove their devo-tion through a series of vows, establishing explicit criteria by which their love is defined and rooting the sense of their words in social practice. *Hamlet* shows the beginnings of a turn away from human-ism in Hamlet's insistence that his interiority exceeds the representa-tional capacities of language and rhetoric. Yet the descriptions of this affective interior rely upon concepts of substance, activity, and pas-sivity that derive from the structures of language, showing that even deeply felt and hidden passions are fundamentally social. In Jon-son's comedies of humour, we encounter explicitly didactic works that borrow from the exemplary teaching practices of the grammar school. The plays present images of vain and foolish behaviour in order to discipline the affections of their spectators. In so doing, they suggest that the rules governing social behaviour are the relics of past practices, actions that have acquired a normative force through repeated performance. Emerging from these texts is a view of emotion as malleable and social, an embodied practice conditioned by cultural norms.

This book appears in the wake of several others that have offered a qualified rehabilitation of the institutions of early modern education. Earlier scholarship had emphasized the coercive and repressive aspects of humanist pedagogy. The work of Anthony Grafton and Lisa Jardine was perhaps the most critical, arguing that, in spite of humanist calls for reform, early modern education was defined by corporal punishment and the rigid and stultifying imposition of the Ciceronian style. Without denying that the grammar school remained an institution pervaded by sexism, elitism, and disciplinary violence, more recent studies have been less antagonistic. Lynn Enterline, for instance, shows how the pedagogical techniques of the grammar school cultivated empathy for women even as the institution sought to foster a distinctly masculine identity in its students.[1] If I were to speculate, I would suggest that this turn – which corresponds with a more general shift from suspicion to sympathy in literary studies – may be a response to the diminished position of the humanities in recent decades, which may better dispose us to the humanistic enterprises of the past. Writing this book during what many have described as a crisis in the humanities, I found the refusal to subordinate the use of language to the rules of grammar valuable both for the emphasis it placed on the autonomy of humanistic practice and for the political possibilities of its critique of metaphysical foundations. For this reason, I would like to conclude with a brief discussion of Michel de Montaigne, the figure who, I believe, carries the critical potential of humanism further than any other in the period.

Montaigne was himself the product of an experimental education: in accordance with a program designed by his father and his humanist associates, the infant Montaigne was entrusted to the care of a Latin scholar who was without French and thereby raised in an environment in which Latin was the only language spoken.[2] By this method, Montaigne recalls, "without art, without books, without grammar or rule [*sans grammaire ou precepte*], without whips and without tears, I ... learned Latin as pure as that which my schoolteacher knew" (158).[3] He argues that Latin instruction should be consistent with the program developed by his father, eschewing the rote learning of grammatical rules and integrated with the practices and routines of daily life. This position is consistent with the humanist advocacy of an education that prepared students for an active, engaged life, though it goes further in this direction than is typical, questioning the value of classical literature and preferring conversation, travel, and exercise as means of cultivating virtue and ability.

Montaigne's childhood experience did not simply serve in his writings as an ideal pedagogical model, however. More significantly, it emphasized for him the foundational role of custom in human life and the malleability of human nature. Montaigne's most extensive examination of the power of custom and habit appears in the essay "On Custom" (*De la Coustume*). Likely composed in the early 1570s around the same time as his writings on education, the essay surveys the vast variety of human practices and traditions, adducing numerous examples of extraordinary behaviour from the ancient and modern worlds: children who nurse until the age of twelve, fathers who lie with their daughters and mothers with their sons, people who mix the ashes of the dead into their wine, cultures that venerate patricide as an act of piety. While these practices may seem strange, according to Montaigne this is only because his readers are unaccustomed to them, as there is nothing other than their unfamiliarity that differentiates these cultural traditions from those of sixteenth-century Europe. Other cultures, he writes, "are in no wise more of a wonder to us than we are to them" (126). Custom establishes the horizons of our understanding and judgment, and we have no other standard by which to determine whether an action is right or proper: "The laws of conscience which we say are born of Nature are born of custom."[4] Moreover, the influence of custom is so pervasive that we fail to realize that we are entirely within its grasp. "[T]he principal activity of custom is so to seize us in her claws that it is hardly in our power to struggle free and to come back into ourselves, where we can reason and argue about her ordinances. Since we suck them in with our mothers' milk and since the face of the world is presented thus to our infant gaze, it seems to us that we are born with the property of continuing to act that way" (130). The reference to "our mothers' milk" (*le laicte de nostre naissance*) suggests the importance of early childhood education and experience for Montaigne. It is thus unsurprising that he begins the essay with a pedagogical metaphor: "Custom," he writes, "is a violent and treacherous schoolmistress [*une violente et traistresse maistresse d'escole*]" (122).

In "On Experience" (*De l'Experience*), the last and perhaps most celebrated of the *Essays*, the connections between humanist views on language and pedagogy and Montaigne's philosophy are even clearer. The essay's well-known argument on the arbitrariness of the law recalls the humanist claim that the rules of grammar are only post-hoc approximations of the practice of language. Consider Colet's comments on Latin grammar, which I have already discussed in some detail in chapter 1:

> But howe and in what maner, and with what constructyon of wordes, and all the varietees, and dyuersitees, and chaunges in latyn speche, whiche be innumerable, if any man wyll knowe, and by that knowledge attayne to vnderstande latyn bokes, and to speke & to wryte the clene latyn. Let hym aboue all besyly lerne and rede good latyn auctors of chosen poetes and oratours, and note wysely howe they wrote, and spake, and study alway to folowe them, desiryng none other rules but their example. For in the beginning men spake not latyn bycause suche rules were made but contrary wyse, bycause men spake suche latyn, vpon that folowed the rules were made. That is to saye latyn speche was before the rules, not the rules before the latyn speche. (*Aeditio* D6)

Montaigne's critique of the foundations of the law echoes Colet's account with striking precision:

> The number [of our laws] bears no relationship to the infinite diversity of human actions. The multiplicity of our human inventions will never attain to the variety of our cases ... There is hardly any relation between our actions (which are perpetually changing) and fixed unchanging laws ... Now laws remain respected not because they are just but because they are laws. That is the mystical basis of their authority. They have no other. (1208)

Both passages emphasize the infinite variations of practice and the impossibility of addressing this variety with a set of explicit rules. Just as the strictures of grammar fail to comprehend the numberless varieties and vicissitudes of linguistic usage, so are laws unable to account for the unlimited diversity of human action. As the grammar book is incapable of adapting to the constant innovations in linguistic usage, so is the fixed canon of legal statutes inadequate to the ever-changing flux of human behaviour. The means by which Colet and Montaigne propose to address this discontinuity between practice and rule are also similar: both insist upon sustained engagement with practice as it exists in the world. Colet recommends that students become familiar with Latin as it is actually spoken and written, reading widely in the poetry and rhetoric of ancient Rome. Montaigne contends that the laws should be general and few, allowing the judge to examine the facts of the individual case at hand and to arrive at a decision through the exercise of practical intuition.

Montaigne's essays suggest the radical potential of humanism's emphasis on the priority of practice. If the rules directing the fundamentally human institution of language are merely conventional, then the laws that govern human action may be similarly unfounded. Even the laws of nature cannot be absolute: God's creation, as Montaigne describes it, is made up of an "infinite number of forms" (*l'infinité des formes*) that are impossible to reduce to observable regularities (806). There are certainly limits to this perspective: without unchanging rational or moral principles upon which to found its critique, it risks becoming an acquiescent relativism, a charge to which Montaigne's own fideism is vulnerable. But I nevertheless see value in its capacity to enable a thorough critique of existing institutions.

Notes

Introduction

1 When Falstaff reflexively recurs to a grammatical vocabulary to describe his engagement with Mistress Ford, he suggests the degree to which Latin grammar became second nature to those educated in exhaustive methods of the schools. According to the schoolmaster John Brinsley, those trained in the rigours of early modern Latin instruction would become so "exquisite in the Grammar" that it would serve "as a Dictionary in their minds," ready to be applied to any situation (*Ludus literarius, or the Grammar Schoole* 86). I discuss the way that Renaissance writers internalized grammatical principles at greater length in chapter 1.

2 England's educational reforms began under Henry VIII, who made his court into a centre of humanist learning in an attempt to compete with the cultural prestige of Italy and France, attracting such figures as Erasmus and Juan Luis Vives to England. Alongside English humanists like Thomas More, John Colet, and Thomas Linacre, these scholars developed a new pedagogical program focused on Latin grammar and literature. When Henry broke with Rome and declared his supremacy over the Church, he also asserted control over the educational system, mandating the use of standard teaching materials and curricular models in schools across England. Edward VI continued these efforts after his father's death, establishing a system of new or reformed grammar schools through a combination of royal patronage and private donation. These schools would help put into practice the curricular and pedagogical reforms developed by Erasmus and his circle. See Jewell, *Education in Early Modern England*; Orme, *English Schools in the Middle Ages* and *Education and Society in Medieval and Renaissance England*. On the education of women in the period, see Jewell, *Education*, especially 11–13 and 58–60. On the educational background of prominent Renaissance writers, see Williams, *The Long Revolution*, 269–85.

3 Baldwin, *William Shakespere's Smal Latine and Lesse Greke* and *William Shakespere's Petty School*; Clark, *John Milton at St. Paul's School*.

4 Ong, "Latin Language Study as a Renaissance Puberty Rite"; Halpern, *The Poetics of Primitive Accumulation*; see especially chapter 1, "A Mint of Phrases: Ideology and Style Production in Tudor England" 19–60.

5 My use of the term "grammar" in this book is intended to bring together two critical movements that have assumed prominence in recent years. The first is the historiography of early modern grammar and pedagogy as practised by Lynn Enterline, Lynne Magnusson, Brian Cummings, Jeff Dolven, and others. See Enterline, *Shakespeare's Schoolroom*; Magnusson, "A Play of Modals"; Cummings, *The Literary Culture of the Reformation*; Dolven, *Scenes of Instruction in Renaissance Romance*; Wallace, *Virgil's Schoolboys*. For important earlier work on the subject, see Altman, *The Tudor Play of Mind*; Kinney, *Humanist Poetics*; Bushnell, *A Culture of Teaching*; Stewart, *Close Readers*. These scholars have shown the crucial role that humanist pedagogy had in the Renaissance, not only by introducing students to classical literature but in cultivating characteristic modes of writing and habits of thoughts. The second is literary scholarship influenced by Wittgenstein and ordinary language philosophy, a critical program that Toril Moi describes in her 2018 book *Revolution of the Ordinary*. In Shakespeare studies, Sarah Beckwith and David Schalkwyk have been perhaps the most prominent critics working in this mode. See Moi, *Revolution of the Ordinary*; Beckwith, *Shakespeare and the Grammar of Forgiveness*; Schalkwyk, *Speech and Performance in Shakespeare's Sonnets and Plays* and *Shakespeare, Love and Language*. In bringing together these two areas, I hope to synthesize historicist and theoretical modes of literary analysis, grounding philosophical readings of Renaissance texts in the period's institutions and discourses. I should note, however, that my interpretation of Wittgenstein is somewhat different from the one usually adopted by literary critics. Most Wittgensteinian scholarship of literature is heavily indebted to Stanley Cavell, whose brilliant readings of Shakespeare represent the most impactful and influential encounter between ordinary language philosophy and literary criticism. Moi calls the line of descent that runs from Wittgenstein through J.L. Austin and Cavell the "ordinary reading," a tradition she defines by its resistance to systematic theorizing. According to Moi, critics in the Cavellian mode are distinguished by an attitude or "spirit" rather than a theoretical method. In spite of his aphoristic and fragmentary style, I understand Wittgenstein to offer an elliptical but ultimately coherent account of language, social practice, mental events, and other related concepts. My reading of Wittgenstein is less in the tradition of Cavell and more influenced by figures like Robert Brandom and Theodore Schatzki who have developed his remarks into comparatively systematic accounts of social life and practice.

6 Hans-Johann Glock describes Wittgenstein's philosophy as "schoolmasterly" in "Necessity and Normativity" 223. On Wittgenstein's experience
  as a schoolteacher, see Monk, *Ludwig Wittgenstein* 193–223.

7 Spencer Robins has suggested the degree to which Wittgenstein's experience as a teacher informed his late philosophy. Writing in the *Paris Review*,
  Robins observes that Wittgenstein's "later work is full of references to
  teaching and children. His *Philosophical Investigations* opens with a long
  discussion of how children learn language, in order to investigate what
  the essence of language is. And Wittgenstein is sometimes explicit about
  the connection; he once said that in considering the meaning of a word,
  it's helpful to ask, 'How would one set about teaching a child to use this
  word?' If nothing else, the style of his later work is absolutely teacherly;
  his post-return writings are so full of thought experiments phrased in the
  imperative that they can feel like exercises in a textbook or transcripts of
  a class discussion" ("Wittgenstein, Schoolteacher," *Paris Review*, 5 March
  2015).

8 Kahn and Saccamano, Introduction to Kahn, Saccamano, and Coli, eds.,
  Politics and the Passions 1500–1800 1; Bruce Smith, *The Key of Green* 5.

9 See Arikha, *Passions and Tempers*.

10 Paster, *The Body Embarrassed* 3. For other important examples of work on
   humoralism and early modern literature and culture, see Schoenfeldt, *Bodies and Selves in Early Modern England*; Floyd-Wilson, *English Ethnicity and
   Race in Early Modern Drama*; Trevor, *The Poetics of Melancholy in Early Modern England*; Paster, Rowe, and Floyd-Wilson, eds. *Reading the Early Modern
   Passions*. For recent work on emotion in early modern literature, which
   tends to be more engaged with sources and discourses outside of the Ga-
   lenic tradition, see Cummings and Sierhuis, eds. *Passions and Subjectivity in
   Early Modern Culture*; Sullivan and Meek, eds., *The Renaissance of Emotion*;
   Sullivan, *Beyond Melancholy*; Mukherji and Stuart-Buttle, eds., *Literature,
   Belief and Knowledge in Early Modern England*; Craik, ed., *Shakespeare and
   Emotion*.

11 Bruce R. Smith, Introduction to "Forum: Body Work," 19. See also Paster,
   Humoring the Body.

12 See Bruce Smith, *Acoustic World* and *Key of Green*, and Paster, *Humoring the
   Body*.

13 Dympna Callaghan was among the first to question the focus on the body
   in early modern literary studies, offering a prescient critique in *Shakespeare
   without Women*. Callaghan cites Lucy Gent and Nigel Llewellyn's contention that the body is "the solidly central unrepresented fact of existence, a
   materiality that is itself inarticulate. It is the mute substance of which 'figure' is a more nervous and expressive shadow." She counters by arguing
   that "this appearance of substance occurs only because this is how, within

the transactions of discourse, the body is rendered intelligible in our culture. When Gent and Llewellyn refer to the body's sheer physicality, the mute facticity of its materiality, they reduce the material to the elemental" (28). For the quotation from Gent and Llewellyn, see Gent and Llewellyn, eds., *Renaissance Bodies*.

14 Massumi, "Notes on the Translation and Acknowledgements," in Deleuze and Guattari, *A Thousand Plateaus* xvii; Massumi, "The Autonomy of Affect" 88. For more on the distinction between affect and emotion, see Shouse, "Affect, Feeling, Emotion."

15 See Bailey and DiGangi, eds., *Affect Theory and Early Modern Texts*; Daniel, *The Melancholy Assemblage*; Hobgood, *Passionate Playgoing in Early Modern England*; Arab, Dowd, and Zucker, eds., *Historical Affects and the Early Modern Theater*.

16 For perhaps the most prominent and polemical critique of the affect studies program, see Leys, "The Turn to Affect" and *The Ascent of Affect*. Affect theorists have defended the program against the charges brought by Leys and others. Massumi, for instance, argues that that affects are social insofar as they result from the influences of exterior forces upon the body. Political relations are thus fundamentally affective, developing from the corporeal intensities and agitations produced by the interactions of bodies rather than from rational decisions or conscious calculations. See *The Politics of Affect*. In early modern studies, Mario DiGangi has offered a persuasive account of the way literary texts "might formally or stylistically encode a distinction between emotion (or passion) and affect." Examining the work of dramatist Samuel Rowley, DiGangi argues that early modern drama can record the affective dynamics of politics by foregrounding the happenstance encounters of bodies over the conscious designs of authoritative actors, emphasizing "trivial, improvisational, and ahistorical episodes" in order to reveal "political agencies that are … spontaneous, provisional, and collective, and that take their occasions from unexpected and ephemeral bodily encounters." See "Affective Entanglements and Alternative Histories," 48–9. DiGangi's reading suggests that while pre-conscious affects may fail to register in the linguistic expression of those who experience them, they may nevertheless be recorded in a text that stages the kinds of bodily encounters and collectivities by which they are engendered, thus entering into the historical and textual record. While DiGangi's persuasive account of the affective dynamics of early modern drama goes a long way toward dispelling the claim that affect is beyond the reach of language, the charge of dualism remains.

17 See Scheer, "Are Emotions a Kind of Practice (And Is That What Makes Them Have a History?)."

18 The cognitive scientist Antonio Damasio is perhaps the foremost contemporary advocate of the view that emotion is a form of bodily alteration that precedes the conscious recognition and verbal expression of feeling, a position that follows the influential work of the philosopher William James. The neo-Jamesian distinction between emotion and feeling is roughly equivalent to the division of affect and emotion in affect theory. See Damasio, *Looking for Spinoza*, and James, "What Is an Emotion?"

19 For a representative account of this position, see Solomon, *The Passions*.

20 Scheer supports this point with recent work in phenomenology and the philosophy of psychology and neurology. See in particular Noë, *Out of Our Heads*. Evelyn Tribble and John Sutton have employed models of distributed cognition that emphasize the continuities between mind and world to analyse early modern texts and theatrical practices in "Cognitive Ecology as a Framework for Shakespearean Studies." See also Tribble, *Cognition in the Globe*, and Floyd-Wilson and Sullivan, eds. *Environment and Embodiment in Early Modern England*.

21 See Schatzki, *Social Practices* and *The Site of the Social*. The key works of Bourdieu are *Outline of a Theory of Practice* and *The Logic of Practice*. For more on practice theory, see Ortner, "Theory in Anthropology since the Sixties."

22 Wittgenstein was preoccupied with the philosophy of psychology from the completion of the *Philosophical Investigations* in 1945 to his death in 1949. The scholars collected in Danièle Moyal-Sharrock's volume *The Third Wittgenstein* consider this period to represent a distinct phase in his thought, a "third" Wittgenstein similar in importance to the usually recognized "early" and "late" Wittgensteins that we find, respectively, in the *Tractatus Logico-Philosophicus* and the *Philosophical Investigations*.

23 Schatzki's account of mental events is more complex than the one I have offered here: his reading of Wittgenstein leads him to describe mental events as "conditions of life" expressed by bodily activity. I have found it slightly more parsimonious to identify emotions and other mental events *as* embodied practices.

24 I am thinking here of terms like *wabi-sabi*, the aesthetic of the Japanese tea ceremony. There can be no equivalent to this word in English, for there is no place within the Western form of life for it to fit.

25 On Wittgenstein's notion of "patterns," see ter Hark, "'Patterns of Life.'"

26 The term "thick description" has of course been of crucial importance to Shakespeare scholarship since the new historicists imported it from the anthropology of Clifford Geertz. But it is worth pointing out that Geertz himself borrowed the phrase from Gilbert Ryle, a key figure in ordinary language philosophy.

27 The celebrated thought experiment with which the *Philosophical Investigations* begins may help to explain the amalgamation of the verbal and the physical in emotional practice. Wittgenstein imagines a builder directing an assistant to bring him certain items and pieces of equipment. In order to identify what he requires, the builder calls out terms like "block" and "pillar," points to places on the building site, and at times gestures toward a sample of a particular colour in order to a distinguish between similar objects (§§2–16). The description of this scenario is the prototypical example of what Wittgenstein calls a "language game," a linguistic activity conducted according to a particular set of rules and interwoven with other forms of worldly action. Wittgenstein's discussion of the builder's language shows that a word like "block" is not simply the sign of an object, but an expression with a particular purpose: in this case, it is an order directing the assistant to perform a physical action. The builder's language is one of actions and commands rather than names. According to Wittgenstein, the colour sample functions as part of the builder's language, performing the same role as his verbal utterances in directing the assistant to a particular object. The sample, a material thing, has been conscripted into linguistic service, demonstrating the thorough interpenetration of language and the world. As David Schalkwyk puts it, the sample shows that "the world is always already 'in' language in the form of the instruments of representation" ("Fiction as 'Grammatical' Investigation" 288–9). I would like to suggest that the practice of emotion involves a similar integration of physical objects and verbal expressions. In a love affair, a lover may draw attention to her racing heart or flushed cheek. When called upon in this way, such phenomena become part of an emotional practice: to point to one's heartbeat or reddened face is a gesture interwoven in the practice of the lover, and the physical phenomena part of the means by which one manifests love. Blood speaks on behalf of love, testifying to the truth of one's feeling or disclosing one's desire. In such cases, Wittgenstein writes, the physical object "is not something that is represented, but is a means of representation" (§50). Thus, while the language of emotion may not be separated from our embodied engagement with the world, neither can emotion simply be reduced to the phenomena of the body. Words, bodies, and actions all have an equally important place in the practices that make up our affective lives.

28 P.M.S. Hacker explains that, for Wittgenstein, there is a "fundamental epistemological asymmetry" between first-person statements such as "I am frightened" and third-person statements such as "she is frightened." The latter is typically a description based on observations of a person's appearance and behaviour, while the former is an expression of one's own fear: it manifests fear and makes a claim for reassurance or sympathy. Unlike

the report, it cannot be mistaken, though it may be deceptive. See Hacker, *Wittgenstein* 181.

29 On the various senses of *pathos*, see Peters, *Greek Philosophical Terms* 152–5. See also Auerbach's work on passion: "In antiquity and long afterwards, *passio* (*pathos*), in accordance with its origins, has a purely 'passive' meaning … the characteristic mark of *pathos-passio*, 'suffering,' is passivity … *Pathos* signifies a state of being afflicted, a state of being affected, a reception or suffering" ("*Passio* as Passion" 288–9). This general sense of the term has disappeared from our vocabulary almost entirely, though it remains distantly familiar through the theological concept of Christ's Passion. As late a source as Johnson's *Dictionary* privileged the broad sense of the term as passive affection, defining passion as "Any effect caused by external agency" before listing the more familiar modern senses.

30 See Aristotle, *On the Soul, Parva Naturalia, On Breath*.

31 Vives, *The Passions of the Soul* 5. See also Thomas Wright's Galenized model of passion as passive affection in *The Passions of the Minde in General*: "The motions of the soul, called by the Greekes *pathe*, some Latines, as *Cicero*, called them perturbations, others affections, others affects, others more expressly name them passions. They are called passions … because when these affections are stirring in our minds, they alter the humours of our bodies, causing some passion or alteration in them" (7–8).

32 Aristotle, *Categories* 10a. In the anatomies of the *pathe* that appear in the *Rhetoric* and the *Ethics*, Aristotle continues this grammatical investigation of the nature of the passions, delineating their characteristically passive structure. Writing of the *Ethics*, L.A. Kosman observes that "Insofar as Aristotle sees fear, anger, desire, pleasure, and pain as *pathe*, as passions, he views what we would call these feelings or emotions as modes of a subject being acted upon … The majority of items on this list are described by passive verbs; in thinking of fear, anger, pleasure, or pain, Aristotle is thinking of being frightened, being angered, being pleased, being pained. When I am afraid, something is frightening me; when I am angry, something is angering me" ("Being Properly Affected" 104–5).

33 For another important account of the language of the *pathe*, see Aristotle, *The Art of Rhetoric*. As the *Rhetoric* is concerned with the use of the *pathe* in public debate, the text is especially attentive to the way they arise through linguistic encounters. For a recent account of the affective dimension of the *Rhetoric*, see Konstan, *The Emotions of the Ancient Greeks*.

34 On the distinction between passion and emotion, see Dixon, *From Passions to Emotions*.

35 The idea of affective language as performative has been usefully developed by William M. Reddy in his book *The Navigation of Feeling*. According to Reddy, affective expressions are neither purely referential nor

performative; affective language has "a descriptive appearance" (that is, it seems to describe some state or feeling), "relational intent" (it "occur[s] most frequently as part of ... specific scenarios, relationships, or action orientations"), and "self-exploring or self-altering effec." (10). Another important account of the affect and performative is Stanley Cavell's concept of "passionate utterances," which I discuss further in chapter 3. See also Cavell, "Passionate and Performative Utterances."

36 See Knecht, "Invaded by the World."

37 Twyne, "Corpus Christi College, Oxford, MS 263," 162. Among the many other expressions of love's paradoxical activity and passivity, see the exchange between Beatrice and Benedick in *Much Ado about Nothing*:

> BEATRICE
>> But for which of my good parts did you first suffer love for me?
>
> BENEDICK
>> "Suffer love"! a good epithet! I do suffer love indeed, for I love thee against my will. (5.2.60–3)

38 Cummings, *Literary Culture* 21. "Grammar" in this broader sense might be usefully compared to the way we use the word "letters" to refer to accomplishment in language and literature, as in the phrase "a person of letters." Indeed, as "grammar" is derived from the Greek *gramma*, "letter," the two terms are closely related.

39 Thomas of Erfurt, *Grammatica speculativa*, 216–17. Translation slightly altered.

40 The word "passion" might refer to an impassioned speech in the early modern period – as in Hamlet's "tear a passion to tatters" (*OED*, "passion") – suggesting a close association between passion and affective language.

41 Harvey, *Schola cordis* 192. Bernard F. Scholz observes that in Harvey's poem, grammar, rhetoric, and logic, the subjects of the trivium, "are no longer viewed as disciplines which gather *knowledge about the heart*. Instead, they are presented as the *artes* – in the sense of skills – which should govern the very speaking of the heart" ("Religious Meditations on the Heart" 113).

42 Francis Bacon would echo this sentiment in *The Advancement of Learning*: "For the expressing of affections, passions, corruptions, and customs we are beholding to poets more than to the philosophers' works" (188).

43 Sidney's insightful description of the relation between passion and poetry informs the critical approach I adopt in this book. As Sidney suggests, literature and emotional practice are intimately entwined: literary texts routinely represent emotional practices, and emotional practices often incorporate literary elements. An elegy like Milton's "Lycidas," for instance, is a representation of mourning: it tells the story of an "uncouth swain"

who laments the untimely death of his companion Lycidas. But it is also a key element within a particular historical practice of mourning, having been written as part of a collection commemorating the death of Milton's Cambridge colleague Edward King. The love lyric has a similar relation to the practice of courtship, typically depicting the relations of lovers within its fictions and serving as a token of exchange or instrument of persuasion in the context of an actual love affair. For this reason, I approach poems and plays both as literary texts and as examples of emotional expression, opportunities to analyse the characteristic forms that affective practice takes within a particular social context and historical period.

44 In his analysis and critique of the anthropology of his day, Bourdieu writes that the "informants" who explain unfamiliar practices to anthropologists act as teachers or instructors: "The relationship between informant and anthropologist is somewhat analogous to a pedagogical relationship, in which the master must bring to the state of explicitness, for the purpose of transmission, the unconscious schemes of his practice." In doing so, informants draw upon "the highly ambiguous vocabulary of *rules*, the language of grammar," an abstract vocabulary that results from "a quasi theoretical reflection on their practice." This reflection may misleadingly intellectualize the practice in question, for to engage in a practice is typically to act immediately and unreflectively, to be guided by "practical knowledge not comprising knowledge of its own principles," rather than to recur to an explicit set of rules or procedures. Yet it is nevertheless necessary to articulate the unspoken principles of a practice in order to explain it to outsiders, even if this explicit account can never capture the intuitive actions and subtle improvisations that distinguish practical expertise. In this book, I consider the Renaissance writers who use "the language of grammar" to depict passionate experience as analogous to Bourdieu's cultural informants. While they may not provide us with direct access to the unreflective mastery that enables active participation in cultures of courtship, devotion, honour, or mourning, they do give us a glimpse of this mastery through the "quasi theoretical reflection" prompted by their own educational experience (Bourdieu, *Outline of a Theory of Practice* 18–19).

1. "Precept and Practice": Grammar and Pedagogy from the Medieval Period to the Renaissance

1 Writing exists at a yet more distant remove, for "written words are the signs of words spoken" (Aristotle, *On Interpretation* 16a).

2 On Aristotle's claim and its influence over Western thinking on language, see Heller-Roazen. The classic critique of the idea of the mind as a reflection of the natural world is Rorty, *Philosophy and the Mirror of Nature*.

3 See Burckhardt, *The Civilization of the Renaissance in Italy*, and Cassirer, *The Individual and the Cosmos in Renaissance Philosophy*.

4 Heidegger, *Being and Time* 165; Erasmus, *De pueris insituendis* 345.

5 Quoted in Hunt, *The History of Grammar in the Middle Ages* 1.

6 On the connections between the grammatical theories of Thomas and Chomsky, see Godfrey, "Late Mediaeval Linguistic Meta-Theory and Chomsky's Syntactic Structures."

7 Thomas of Erfurt, *Grammatica speculativa* 153. Thomas's specific terms are *modus entis* and *modus esse*, "mode of an entity" and "mode of being," but these are generally equivalent to the more familiar Platonic categories. *Esse* or "being" in Thomas refers somewhat confusingly to "change and succession."

8 Thomas of Erfurt, *Grammatica speculativa* 224–5. Translation slightly altered (I have substituted "affections" for Bursill-Hall's "effects" in translating *affectus*). Thomas cites Peter Helias in making this claim. The ultimate source is a well-known dictum of Priscian's: "The moods are the different inclinations of the mind and show its various affections" (*modi sunt diuersae inclinationes animi, uarios eius affectus demonstrantes*). See Priscian, *Excerptiones de Prisciano* 188–92.

9 Translation slightly altered (I have translated Thomas's *passionem* as "passion" in lieu of Bursill-Hall's "being acted upon").

10 Bursill-Hall, Introduction to *Grammatica speculativa* 74.

11 Plato's *Cratylus* is typically thought to be the *locus classicus* of the naturalist perspective, though that text, which I discuss further in chapter 3, is ambiguous on this point. Proponents of naturalism often point to onomatopoeia as evidence of the intrinsic relation between words and things. For more on the debate between nature and convention in the history of grammar, see Robins, *Ancient and Medieval Grammatical Theory in Europe*.

12 An exemplary epistle included in *De conscribendis epistolis*, a text on the composition of letters, offers a kind of allegory of Erasmus's rejection of the medieval theory of grammar. In it, Erasmus outlines a four-stage program for mastering passages from Latin texts. First, the reader engages with the text in a naïve and unsystematic way, seeking only to arrive at a general understanding of the passage. At this primary stage, the reader explores the text, so to speak, by feel, engaging with it as one would with a partner in dialogue. Once this initial exploration is complete and the reader has achieved a basic familiarity with the passage, he or she maps out the grammatical structure of the text, "examining individual words and observing only points of grammar in the process." The reader then assesses the rhetorical and ornamental qualities of the passage in a third reading, noting "any phrasing [that] seems to have a special charm, elegance, or neatness." Finally, the reader considers the philosophical implications of the passage,

"seeking out what seems to relate to philosophy, especially ethics, to discover any example that may be applicable to morals. What is there from which either a model of life, or some illustration or advantage can be drawn?" It is only after a basic engagement with the text and an analysis of its formal properties that the reader may derive from it some moral or philosophical meaning. The order of this procedure upends the hierarchy established by Thomas, in which the tenets of philosophy determine the rules of grammar, which in turn govern the use of language. In Erasmus, language itself is primary: the rules of grammar are derived from the use of language, and the systems of philosophy emerge only after the establishment of grammatical rules. By prioritizing an immediate encounter with language over grammar and philosophy, Erasmus suggests that both the structures of grammar and the "model[s] of life" outlined in philosophy are abstractions derived from linguistic use (*De conscribendis epistolis* 192–3).

13 On the influence of *De ratione studii*, see Baldwin, *William Shakespere's Smal Latine and Lesse Greke*.

14 Of this inversion, Terence Cave writes: "In some contexts, it is true, *res* could be defined as the extra-linguistic reality apprehended by the mind and reproduced in the form of *verba*; in this sense, according to the classic mimetic model, words copy or represent the objects of thought. But in the *De copia* … this reassuring hierarchy is disturbed, if not inverted. *Res* do not emerge from the mind as spontaneous 'ideas'; they are already there, embedded in language, forming the materials of the writing exercise" (*The Cornucopian Text* 19).

15 Erasmus, *De ratione studii*, 164. As Richard Halpern writes in his political analysis of the culture of the Tudor grammar school, Erasmus rejects a "juridical" model of language in favour of social and discursive model, moving from a conception of language based on "the legal apparatuses of the state" to one rooted in "the practices of civil society." This shift, according to Halpern, prefigures the broader political upheavals of the early modern period, in which the power of the sovereign gives way to bourgeois hegemony. See *The Poetics of Primitive Accumulation* 31.

16 See Baldwin, *William Shakespere's Smal Latine*, especially 75–93.

17 John Brinsley echoes this emphasis on affective engagement with the child, writing that "the masters must not be ashamed, nor weary, to do as the nurse with the child, as it were stammering and playing with them, to seeke by all meanes to breede in the little ones a loue of their masters, with delight in their bookes, and a ioy that they can vnderstand; and also to the end to nourish in them that emulation mentioned, to striue who shall doe best" (*Ludus Literarius* 55).

18 The humanist program bears striking similarities to what José Medina has described as the "enculturation view" of language learning that one finds

in Wittgenstein. See Medina, "Wittgenstein's Social Naturalism." Also relevant are some comments of Wittgenstein's on how one learns to judge the genuineness of expressions: "Can one learn this knowledge? Yes; some can learn it. Not, however, by taking a course of study in it, but through *'experience'*. – Can someone else be a man's teacher in this? Certainly. From time to time he gives him the right *tip*. – This is what 'learning' and 'teaching' are like here. – What one acquires here is not a technique; one learns correct judgements. There are also rules, but they do not form a system, and only experienced people can apply them rightly. Unlike calculating rules" (Wittgenstein, *Philosophical Investigations* 227).

19 The line adapts Lily's entry on the interjection: "An Interiection is a part of speache which betokeneth a sodaine passion of the minde, vnder an vnperfect voice. Some are of … Laughing: as Ha ha he" (*A Short Introduction* Ciiii).

2. "Heart-Ravishing Knowledge": Love and Learning in Sidney's *Astrophil and Stella*

1 Philip Sidney, *Astrophil and Stella*, *The Poems of Sir Philip Sidney*, ed. W.A. Ringler (Oxford: Oxford University Press, 1962), 79.8; 73.2; 46.10. All citations refer to line numbers in this edition.

2 See Ong, "Latin Language Study."

3 It should be noted that Enterline challenges Ong's claim that the grammar school cultivated a strictly masculine ethos.

4 Ann Rosalind Jones and Peter Stallybrass offer a sophisticated treatment of this opposition, arguing that although Astrophil opposes the private world of love to the public world of poetry and the court, the private realm is nevertheless structured and defined by poetic and courtly values: "Astrophil responds to external expectations by setting up a deceptively simple antithesis: public ambition versus the privacy of love … As lover, as private man, he defines himself as non-poet, non-courtier; he justifies himself toward a public whose claim on his attention consists precisely in their indifference to love. The privileged realm of love, in the economy of the poem, occupied an area defined by the *subtraction* of the worldly activities of poetry-writing and courtiership. Both nonetheless determine the structure and phrasing of the poem, and they are powerfully present, precisely, in Astrophil's denial of them" ("The Politics of *Astrophil and Stella*" 57).

5 See Dolven, *Scenes of Instruction*; for more on the heart as the seat of memory, see Bound Alberti, *This Mortal Coil*.

6 Green, *The Christian's ABC* 232. Also quoted in Dolven, *Scenes of Instruction* 7. Green's analysis of the catechism is especially relevant to *Astrophil and Stella*, as the thirty-fourth sonnet takes the form of a child's catechism:

> Come let me write, "And to what end?" To ease
> A burthned hart. "How can words ease, which are
> The glasses of thy dayly vexing care?"
> Oft cruell fights well pictured forth do please. (34.1–4)

7 For an early treatment of the paradox of the poems' artifice and their claims of spontaneity, see Hallett Smith, *Elizabethan Poetry* 142–57.

8 "Spell" here is used with its archaic sense of speaking or reciting aloud. Christopher Harvey expresses a similar sentiment: "My Rhetorick is not so much an Art, / As an infused habit in mine Heart" (*Schola cordis* 193).

9 On invention and the canons of rhetoric, see Mack, *Elizabethan Rhetoric* 9.

10 See Seneca, *Epistles 66–92* 276–83.

11 We should note that Wittgenstein argues that a truly private language is impossible. I discuss Wittgenstein's comments on private language in greater depth in chapter 5.

12 See in particular the cycle's fourth song, which concludes each stanza with a refrain in Stella's voice denying Astrophil's entreaties: "*No, no, no, no, my Deare, let bee*" (6). In the final stanza, the despondent Astrophil expresses his intent to abandon his appeals and kill himself. The same refrain answers him, but the different context alters its meaning: Stella's denial of his suit becomes a request that he spare himself and, perhaps, continue to court her. This ambiguous moment may be read as a cynical attempt by Astrophil to manipulate Stella by changing the context of her words or by provoking her guilt through histrionic self-pity.

13 For a more recent perspective on Renaissance poetry and potentiality, see Rosenfeld, "Poetry and the Potential Mood."

14 Modern linguists distinguish between Latin mood (a form of inflection) and the English modal verb. But as F.R. Palmer writes, the two forms are closely related and serve a similar semantic function. In order to show this, Palmer cites a verse from Virgil's *Aeneid* in the subjunctive mood and an English translation using the modal "should": "At tu dictis, Albane, maneres," "But thou, Alban, shouldst have kept they word" (*Mood and Modality* 1). As early modern grammarians lacked the vocabulary for describing modal verbs, they used the term "mood" to describe Latin moods such as the optative and English verbs such as "would" and "should."

15 Linacre, we might note, counted among his students Erasmus, More, Colet, and Lily, making him a central figure in the development of English education by virtue of his mentorship alone.

16 Here we may recall *Coriolanus*, in which it is the tribune's "peremptory 'shall'" that announces his seditious intent: it is "the horn and noise o'the'monster's" (3.1.95–6).

17 See Duncan-Jones, footnote to sonnet 33 in *The Major Works*.

18 Alysia Kolentsis has suggested that this self-conscious usage is in part an attempt to make a case for the distinct versatility of English as opposed to Latin. As Latin lacks modal auxiliaries, their ostentatious use in English poetry suggests the advantages of Sidney's native tongue. See "'Grammar Rules' in the Sonnets."

19 The quotation is from Alan Sinfield, *Literature in Protestant England, 1560–1660* 47, but Sinfield first advanced this line of argument in "Astrophil's Self-Deception." There he claims that "the speaker of *Astrophil and Stella* is meant to illustrate the errors of unregulated passion," and that in "the battle between right reason and Christian virtue on the one side, and sense and will on the other," Sidney is aligned with the former and Astrophil with the latter (1).

20 Palmer explains that "The interrogative in English belongs ... to a formal system that is not part of the modal system, but interacts with it." In other languages, questions may be expressed via the modal system (*Mood and Modality* 30–1).

21 Sidney's comparison of philosophy's discrete facts (the shape, colour, and size of the elephant) with the holistic picture proffered by the arts mirrors later discourse on science and the humanities. Compare, for instance, Sidney's discussion to Wilhelm Dilthey's influential distinction between explanation and understanding: "The human studies differ from the sciences because the latter deal with facts which present themselves to consciousness as external and separate phenomena, while the former deal with the living connections of reality experienced in the mind" (*Ideas about a Descriptive and Analytic Psychology* 89).

22 It was a commonplace of rhetorical theory that art may move an audience indifferent to real events. In *De Anima et Vita*, Juan Luis Vives explains, "There are still some people who are moved by a story but would hardly be touched if the event had taken place in their very presence. Quintilian says: 'The same words and the same sound draw our emotions more when expressed by a stage character.' While we listen to them the emotion is reinforced by our fantasy and thought. The same disaster rouses our emotions more with the help of the actor's artistry. The likelihood of our being touched by the story is increased by the emphasis upon the gravity of the suffering, by realizing how undeserving the victim is, how much more entitled to good than evil things" (*The Passions of the Soul* 49). For the quotation from Quintilian, see *Institutio Oratoria* 5.1.26.

23 Christopher Warley sees the sonnet as privileging the power of narrative over that of lyric; see *Sonnet Sequences and Social Distinction in Renaissance England*.

24 "[P]ure subjectivity and individuality" is a phrase the Romantic critic Jochen Schmidt used to describe the genius of Shakespeare (quoted in

Höfele, *No Hamlets* 5). The classic accounts of the Renaissance as the beginning of modern subjectivity and individualism are Burckhardt, *The Civilization of the Renaissance in Italy*, and Cassirer, *The Individual and the Cosmos
in Renaissance Philosophy*.

3. The Ablative Heart: Love as Rule-Guided Action in Shakespeare's *Love's Labour's Lost*

1 For a review of the play's reception, see Carroll, *The Great Feast of Language
in "Love's Labour's Lost"* 3–8. William Hazlitt's dismissive and frequently
quoted judgment of the play is representative: "If we were to part with
any of the author's comedies, it should be this" (quoted in Carroll, *The
Great Feast of Language* 6).
2 The relationship between Berowne and Rosaline, characterized by rivalry
and witty exchanges, has been read as an early version of *Much Ado's* Benedick and Beatrice, for instance. See Garber, *Shakespeare after All* 176.
3 Elam, *Shakespeare's Universe of Discourse* 10–11. I should note that Elam's
use of Wittgenstein is different from mine. Elam uses the concept of the
language-game directly as a means of advancing a pragmatic reading of
Shakespeare's plays. He approaches the plays themselves as linguistic activities governed by particular rules and directed toward particular ends.
My approach is comparatively less formal and more symptomatic: I am
more interested in the ways that early modern literature is engaged with
such affective practices and languages as courtship and mourning and
helps to clarify their nature.
4 In his *Odes*, Horace writes that his poetry represents "a monument more
lasting than bronze and loftier than the Pyramid's royal pile," by virtue of
which he "shall not altogether die, but a mighty part of [him] shall escape
the death-goddess" (*Odes and Epodes* 3.30.1–2). Shakespeare's engagement
of the theme is best represented by the famous couplet from his eighteenth
sonnet: "So long as men can breathe or eyes can see, / So long lives this,
and this gives life to thee" (*Shakespeare's Sonnets* 18.13–14).
5 Malcolm Evans sees the discrepancy between form and content as a central conflict in the play, addressing it in two different studies. In his book
Signifying Nothing, he argues that the distinction invokes that between oral
and print culture, a difference emphasized by the play's concluding line
of dialogue: "The words of Mercury are harsh after the songs of Apollo"
(5.2.918–19). The reading is influenced by the work of Malcolm McLuhan
and Terence Hawkes on orality and print. In "Deconstructing Shakespeare's Comedies," he pursues a more post-structuralist line of analysis,
suggesting that the moments of divorce between signifier and signified
provide a key to understanding Shakespeare's comedies. When the pedant

Holofernes claims that "*Imitari* is nothing" (4.2.125), he suggests the way that the comedies problematize the mimetic model of theatrical representation and even the function of signification itself.

6   Ralph Berry makes a similar claim about the attitude to language found in the play's clowns and dandies in "The Words of Mercury."

7   The description of Rosaline as "beauteous as ink" invokes early modern discourse on race. In an earlier scene, the courtiers discuss her appearance in more explicitly racialized terms, comparing her complexion to that of the "Ethiops" (4.3.264). The line exemplifies a motif Miles P. Grier has identified in an important recent essay. Grier shows that early modern writers tended to represent "black skin as the product of a permanent, overlaid ink – in other words, as a tattoo." Imagining blackness as inked onto the skin serves a crucial function in facilitating England's imperial ambitions, stigmatizing Africans and displacing anxieties about England's own history as a Roman colony (the English were themselves tattooed during the Roman period). It also casts light on the relation between the early English empire and the rise of print technology. See "Inkface" 195. On Shakespeare and the idealization of a racialized "fairness," see Hall, "These Bastard Signs of Fair" and *Things of Darkness*. On national and ethnic difference in *Love's Labour's Lost*, see Archer, *Citizen Shakespeare* 31–9.

8   Costard, who is relatively unusual in Shakespeare for his combination of wit and ignorance, offers a similar sequence of puns on the terms "form" and "matter": "The matter is to me, sir, as concerning Jaquenetta. The manner of it is, I was taken with the manner … In manner and form following, sir, all those three. I was seen with her in the manor-house, sitting with her upon the form, and taken following her into the park, which, put together, is 'in manner and form following'. Now, sir, for the manner: it is the manner of a man to speak to a woman; for the form: in some form" (1.1.197–207).

9   Quoted in Halpern, *The Poetics of Primitive Accumulation* 47. Sidney makes a similar claim in *Astrophil and Stella*: "Oft cruell fights well pictured forth do please" (34.4).

10   Quoted in Halpern, *The Poetics of Primitive Accumulation* 24.

11   See also Navarre's sardonic description of Berowne's learned opposition to learning: "How well he's read, to reason against reading" (1.1.94). Elam comments on this paradox in the conclusion of *Shakespeare's Universe of Discourse*, writing that the rejection of poetic language "proves to be the most powerful of tropes or fictions" (308).

12   Thomas M. Greene has argued that the play's critique of rhetorical inflation did not amount to a rejection of ornament or an embrace of plain-speaking. Instead, he contends that Shakespeare pursued a paradoxical ideal of "authentic artifice," something similar to what I have

discussed in Sidney. Greene writes: "There could be no greater mistake than to conclude from this judgment that Shakespeare disliked rhetorics and forms, patterns of words and of experience. He was not, needless to say, in favor of the crude expression of raw passion. He knew that society, the happiness of life, depends on configurations and rituals. He represented the Muscovite masquing to be silly not because it was artificial but because, in his sense of the word, it was not artificial enough; it was 'shallow' and 'rough' and 'vilely penned'. That being so, one may ask whether Shakespeare did not provide within the play an instance of authentic artifice, and the answer is that he did provide it, in the form of the two concluding songs" ("*Love's Labour's Lost*" 325).

13 Austin, *How to Do Things with Words*. The prominence of Austin in literary criticism is largely owing to influence of Jacques Derrida and Judith Butler, who have employed Austin's speech act theory in advancing arguments on the nature of language and the contingency of gender identity, respectively.

14 See Elam, *Shakespeare's Universe of Discourse*; Maus, "Transfer of Title"; Schalkwyk, *Speech and Performance*; Kerrigan, *Shakespeare's Promises*. Though they touch on *Love's Labour's Lost* only briefly, James Loxley and Mark Ronson offer an extensive account of promises and other speech acts in Shakespeare in *Shakespeare, Jonson, and the Claims of the Performative*. For a more general discussion of oath-taking in *Love's Labour's Lost*, see Dash, *Wooing, Wedding, and Power*. James L. Calderwood describes a different sense of linguistic agency in the play, arguing that the play's lack of dramatic intrigue makes language into the main source of the play's action: "action and plot" in the play are "reduced to a series of verbal events … the play seems almost an experiment in seeing how well language, spun into intricate, ornate, but static patterns, can substitute for the kinetic thrust of action in drama" ("*Love's Labour's Lost*" 329).

15 Maclean, *Meaning and Interpretation in the Renaissance* 168–70. Austin himself looked to the law for existing versions of his understanding of performative speech, finding in the concept of "operative" language something like his own theory: "One technical term that comes nearest to what we need is perhaps 'operative', as it is used strictly by lawyers in referring to that part, i.e. those clauses, of an instrument which serves to effect the transaction (conveyance or what not) which is its main object, whereas the rest of the document merely 'recites' the circumstances in which the transaction is to be effected" (*How to Do Things with Words* 7).

16 Beyond the basic comparison of the concept of *vis* and the modern sense of linguistic agency, Maclean offers a detailed analysis of Renaissance philosophy of law and its relation to speech act theory, discovering in the writings of the jurist Alessandro Turamini "a tripartite theory of speech acts … worthy of comparison with Austin" (*Meaning and Interpretation in the*

Renaissance 168). Turamini compares the language of law to a fire, which is composed of the wood that is burnt, the fire that burns, and the heat that the fire generates. These three elements are equivalent to *verba*, the words of the law; *vis*, the force by which it governs people's actions; and *potestas*, the more general power it holds in setting precedents and contributing to lawful governance. Maclean observes that this taxonomy is strikingly similar to Austin's distinction between locutionary, illocutionary, and perlocutionary speech acts, which I will discuss later in the chapter.

17 This sense of language's agency appears throughout the play. In the opening scene, both the oath and the debate provide evidence of it. As we have seen, Berowne adopts a playful and poetic style of language in taking up the cause of love against the moral philosophy of the other courtiers, forsaking argumentative content in favour of poetic form. This is precisely the kind of language – stylized, teasing, and nonsensical – that the historian Alan Macfarlane has identified with the practice of early modern courtship. In adopting this style, then, Berowne does not simply advocate on behalf of love: he also performs the role of the lover, transforming the dialogue from an academic debate into a lover's game. His nonsense is not without purpose: it plays a part of the language game of courtship. See Macfarlane, *Marriage and Love in England* 303.

18 Cavell, "Passionate and Performative Utterances." Cavell and Eve Sedgwick stand at the outset of traditions on language and affect that are in many ways opposed to one another. Yet it bears mentioning that both make the case for expanding the concept of performativity into the affective realm. Against the strict taxonomies of analytic philosophy, in which performativity was only associated with certain ritualistic utterances, Sedgwick proposes a spectrum within which many kinds of affects, objects, and expressions may have a performative dimension, citing Wittgenstein as an inspiration for a more capacious understanding of meaningful action: "With Wittgenstein … I have an inclination to deprecate the assignment of a very special value, mystique, or thingness to meaning and language. Many kinds of objects and events *mean*, in many heterogeneous ways and contexts, and I see some value in not reifying or mystifying the linguistic kinds of meaning unnecessarily" (*Touching Feeling* 6).

19 Elam notes that the lines draw attention to "the signifying power of the body" (*Shakespeare's Universe of Discourse* 114).

20 Also quoted in Daniel, *The Melancholy Assemblage* 6.

21 For more on Wittgenstein's concepts of "natural history" and "second nature," see Medina, "Wittgenstein's Social Naturalism."

22 This is something of an extreme case, but it is easy to imagine other situations in which love may involve expectations of deferred desire and self-examination.

23 Katie Barclay has noted that Butler's version of performativity has signifi-
cant implications for the study of affect, comparing her work on gender to
Monique Scheer's pragmatic approach to emotion. See "Performance and
Performativity."

4. "Shapes of Grief": The Ineffable and the Grammatical in Shakespeare's *Hamlet*

1 Paterson, "The Word in *Hamlet*" 47.
2 The phrase is from Shakespeare's *Troilus and Cressida* 5.3.108.
3 See Waswo, *Language and Meaning* 154–6; Weimann, "Mimesis in *Hamlet*";
Danner, "Speaking Daggers."
4 This is Gabriel Harvey's well-known description of *Hamlet* (and *The Rape
of Lucrece*), which appears in a manuscript note in his copy of Chaucer's
Works. The note is reproduced in an appendix to Jenkins's edition of *Hamlet*, 573–4. See also Guillory, "'To Please the Wiser Sort.'"
5 Joel B. Altman makes this point in *The Tudor Play of Mind*: "Standing on
the edge of Elizabethan Humanism," he writes, "[Hamlet] gives eloquent
testimony to the failure of deep-searching wit to extricate itself from the
limitations of its own condition" (10–11).
6 Ferry, *The "Inward" Language* 66. See also Miller, "The Passion Signified."
7 See *Richard III* 3.7.188 and *King Henry IV, Part Two* 2.3.166 (the line in the
Folio appears as "From a god to a bull? A heavy declension!" while the
Quarto has "descension"). See also the use of "decline" in *Richard III*
4.4.97, which "connotes a scholastic exercise," according to Russ McDonald, *Shakespeare and the Arts of Language* 38.
8 See Lily, *A Short Introduction* B4.
9 Wittgenstein, *Remarks on the Philosophy of Psychology* vol. 2, §570. Emphasis
in original.
10 *Venus and Adonis* similarly uses "passion" as a verb to describe Venus's
mourning for Adonis: "This solemn sympathy poor Venus noteth; / Over
one shoulder doth she hang her head. / Dumbly she passions, frantically
she doteth; / She thinks he could not die, he is not dead" (*Shakespeare's Poems* 1057–60).
11 Lavinia's thoroughly corporealized mode of expression typifies what Lynn
Enterline has called the "rhetoric of the body" in classical and Renaissance
literature. The Ovidian tradition presents us with a succession of bodies
marked by violence and freighted with ethical and cultural significance.
From Daphne and Philomel in *Metamorphoses* to Shakespeare's Lucrece
and Lavinia, representations of women's violated and transfigured forms
insist "that the body is both a bearer of meaning as well as a linguistic
agent, a place where representation, materiality, and action collide." Ovid,

we should recall, was central to the curriculum of the grammar schools (Enterline, *The Rhetoric of the Body from Ovid to Shakespeare* 6).

12 Peter Mack suggests that the rhetorical tradition may have begun to wane at the end of the sixteenth century, citing a decline in the production of rhetorical manuals beginning around this time. See *A History of Renaissance Rhetoric* 32. On Pauline discourse, see Ferguson, "*Hamlet*: Letters and Spirits."

13 Scholars have proposed that the phrase indicates a hidden Oedipal desire for his mother, a groping anticipation of Cartesian interiority, and resentment over his political disenfranchisement. For the classic statement of the Oedipal complex in *Hamlet*, see Ernest Jones, who writes that Hamlet's "emotions are inexpressible ... because there are thoughts and wishes that no one dares to express even to himself. We plumb here the darkest depths" (*Hamlet and Oedipus* 100). On Hamlet's gestures toward Cartesian metaphysics, see Barker, *The Tremulous Private Body*; for the political reading of Hamlet's "that within," see de Grazia, "*Hamlet*" *without Hamlet*.

14 On the motive capacity of passion in *Hamlet*, see Tilmouth, *Passion's Triumph over Reason*.

15 For accounts of passion and action in ancient, medieval, and early modern discourse, see Crampton, *The Condition of Creatures*, and James, *Passion and Action*.

16 Paster, *Humoring the Body* 30. See also Tilmouth, *Passion's Triumph*. The question of passion and action has a long held a central place in the literature on *Hamlet*. It appears as early as 1765 in the edition of Samuel Johnson, in which Johnson argued that "Hamlet is, through the whole play, rather an instrument than an agent," a vessel through which external agency operates rather than a self-motivated actor. Unconstrained by the post-Romantic pieties regarding Shakespeare, Johnson attributed this passivity to faulty composition, the failure to properly cast the play's hero as the prime mover of the action (*Johnson on Shakespeare* 1011). Goethe's seminal discussion of the play in *Wilhelm Meister's Apprenticeship* also addresses Hamlet's apparent lack of agency, suggesting that the tragedy in the play follows from the fact that the hero is "passive" like a character in a novel, and thus unable to rise to the requirements of the dramatic genre. Hamlet, according to Goethe, is a "sentimental" figure whose character is defined by feeling and impression rather than the active revenger that the drama demands: he is a poet thrust into the role of a butcher, the task imposed upon him "an oak tree planted in a precious pot that should only have held delicate flowers" (*Wilhelm Meister's Apprenticeship* 146). Coleridge, following the criticism of Schlegel, differs from Goethe in his lectures on Shakespeare by considering Hamlet's fatal flaw to be not a passive mind, but conversely a mind lacking in passivity and consequently overactive.

According to Coleridge, a "healthy" mind strikes "a balance between the
passive impression received from outward things, and the internal activity
of the mind in reflecting and generalizing" (quoted in de Grazia, *"Hamlet"*
without Hamlet 16). In Hamlet, "this balance is disturbed … Hence we see
a great, an almost enormous intellectual activity, and a proportionate aversion to real action consequent upon it" (Coleridge, *Lectures and Notes* 344).
The opposition of passion and action also informs the dramatic theory of
A.C. Bradley, who writes that Shakespearean tragedy as a whole is composed of "the characteristic deeds, and the sufferings and circumstances,
of the persons" (*Shakespearean Tragedy* 7). The particular situation of
Hamlet, according to Bradley, is not simply determined by either a pliant
passivity or a restive mental activity. Instead, it is the result of succession
of extraordinary "catastrophes" – first the death of his father, then the betrayal of his mother, then the revelation of his father's murder by his uncle –
that fall upon Hamlet with such force and at such moments of vulnerabil-
ity that his melancholic, but otherwise brave and capable, temperament is
reduced to a state of apathy and loathing of the world, a misanthropic dis-
gust which prevents him from acting upon the ghost's command. For an
in-depth survey of the critical and philosophical tradition on *Hamlet*, see
de Grazia, *"Hamlet" without Hamlet.*

17 Aristotle, *Categories* 2a. Translation slightly altered (I have replaced "Affection" with "Passion" as the translation of *paschein*). On the various senses
   of *paschein* and *pathos*, see Peters, *Greek Philosophical Terms.*

18 Aristotle, *Categories* 10a. Translation slightly altered.

19 On this relationship, see Agamben, "Philosophy and Linguistics." Agamben writes that "The history of the relations between philosophy and the
   science of language … is so rich in exchanges, crossings, and accidents that
   any attempt to distinguish the two with precision appears both necessary
   and impossible. Not only does the ancient tradition attribute to Plato and
   Aristotle the origin of grammar, but further, from the beginning, logical
   categories and grammatical categories have been so tightly interlaced as to
   appear inseparable" (62).

20 Jenkins suggests that the phrase "sounds like a conjuration formula." See
   Hamlet LN to 1.5.157. Nevill Coghill observes that the property of being
   "here and everywhere" traditionally belonged solely to God or the devil,
   suggesting that Hamlet may be ruminating on the question of the ghost's
   divine or diabolical nature. See *Shakespeare's Professional Skills.*

21 Quoted and translated in Greenblatt, *Hamlet in Purgatory* 255.

22 William Empson's reading of the metatheatrical scenes offers a formal and
   contextual rather than a psychological solution to the traditional problem of
   Hamlet's delay, freeing the critic from the task of assembling a fully coherent
   psychology from the often inconsistent language of the play. Empson begins

by observing that *Hamlet* came to the stage at a time when revenge drama was falling out of fashion, a period between the vogue for Senecan drama like Kyd's *Spanish Tragedy*, the lost ur-*Hamlet*, and Shakespeare's own *Titus Andronicus* and the later appearance in the Jacobean period of a satirical and self-consciously gratuitous revenge theatre. To justify a return to a mode which was at the time considered clumsy and old-fashioned, but not yet rehabilitated by revelry in its own excesses, Shakespeare had two options. He could aspire to psychological realism, bringing to a genre defined by declamatory rhetoric the subtle characterization that was beginning to appear on the stage in comedy and history. Or he could take the opposite path, drawing attention to the well-worn conventions of the genre with a knowing wink. Presented with these opposed routes, Shakespeare took them both: he crafted in Hamlet a character of immense complexity and interest, yet at every opportunity emphasized the conventions and demands of the genre in which he operated. In Empson's jocular paraphrase, Hamlet says to his audience: "You think this is an absurd old play, and so it is, *but I'm in it*, and what can I do?" (*Essays on Shakespeare* 104). The enduring mystery and delight of the character are in part attributable to this restless vacillation between richly defined psychology and playful, knowing self-consciousness. What is more, the latter method is made the instrument of the former: "What is technically so clever," writes Empson, "is to turn this calculated collapse of dramatic illusion into an illustration of the central theme" (86). As Hamlet uses the business with the players both to explore his own role as revenger and to advance the action of the play, the metatheatrical material "has been turned into an exposition of the character of the hero and the central dramatic theme," thus serving "the central task ... of making the old play seem real by making the hero life-like" (87). "Life-like" psychological realism is paradoxically achieved by a self-conscious emphasis on dramatic and literary convention. I would like to suggest that both modes observed by Empson are informed by the discourse of the grammar school. In the scenes that deliberately ironize the play's naturalism, Hamlet's "antic disposition" refers to schoolboy drama like *Ralph Roister Doister*, and generally resembles the satiric and self-conscious wit of the early comedies. And in the scenes that aspire toward naturalism, the language of ineffability relies upon certain basic metaphysical structures, such as the opposition of passion and action, that Shakespeare would have encountered in the grammar school.

23 Quoted in Jenkins's edition of *Hamlet*, LN to 3.1.56–88. For Augustine's full discussion, see *The Free Choice of Will*. Augustine imagines a debate with one who "says he would rather not exist than be unhappy" (181), arguing against this interlocutor that any existence is better than none at all.

24 See Petronella, "Hamlet's 'To Be or Not to Be' Soliloquy" and Bruster, *To Be or Not To Be*.

25 See McElroy, "'To Be or Not to Be' – Is That the Question?"

26 Jenkins's edition of *Hamlet*, LN to 3.1.56–88.

27 For an account of these influences, see Anders, *Shakespeare's Books* 275. The resemblance to a passage in Florio's Montaigne – "If it be a consummation of ones being, it is also an amendment and entrance into a long and quiet night. Wee finde, nothing so sweete in life, as a quiet rest and gentle sleepe, and without dreams" – is striking, but Florio's translation appeared after *Hamlet* and it is impossible to establish that Shakespeare had encountered Montaigne at this point.

28 See, for instance, Bruster, *To Be or Not to Be* 17–18. For the text from Marlowe, see *Doctor Faustus* 1.1.12, in *The Complete Plays*.

29 Lily, *Short Introduction* B3. Given the immense volume of *Hamlet* criticism, it is impossible be sure that the resemblance of these passages has entirely passed notice, but it does not form part of the standard literature on the speech. Despite listing many citations of Lily in Shakespeare as well as several sources for Hamlet's soliloquy, Anders's comprehensive source study *Shakespeare's Books* does not connect the two.

30 Jenkins's edition of *Hamlet*, LN to 3.1.57–60.

31 Wittgenstein, *Philosophical Investigations* §371. Emphasis in original.

32 Wittgenstein's lukewarm description of Shakespeare's drama, which he personally found artificial. See *Culture and Value* 36–7.

5. "Drunken Custom": Rules, Embodiment, and Exemplarity in Jonson's Humours Plays

1 Jonson was imprisoned and nearly executed for killing a fellow actor in a duel in 1598, escaping the gallows only by claiming benefit of clergy. While awaiting trial in Newgate, he was visited by a priest and converted to Catholicism, a faith he would profess for more than a decade before returning to the Church of England in 1610. There is reason to believe that the priest was Wright, an English Jesuit who was under house arrest at the time but permitted to minister to prisoners in Newgate. See Donaldson, *Ben Jonson* 138–44.

2 Wright follows tradition in positioning the passions between reason and sense but associating them more closely with the latter. The passions are "certaine internall acts or operations of the soule, bordering vpon reason and sense … yet they keep not equall friendship with both." Because of the "amitie betwixt the passions and sense," there is "greater conformitie and likenesse betwixt them, then there is betwixt Passions and reason" (*The Passions of the Minde* 8).

3 Robert Miola cites Chapman's *Blind Beggar of Alexandria* (1595–6) and *An Humorous Day's Mirth* (1597) as the earliest examples of the genre (Introduction to *Every Man in His Humour* 13–14).

4 Shylock uses this sense of the term in *The Merchant of Venice* when he explains his apparently irrational pursuit of revenge by saying "it is my humour" (4.1.42).

5 The envious husband Thorello is perhaps the best example in the two plays of a character who suffers from a "legitimate" distemper. His account of the anguish of jealousy, which draws heavily on Galenic descriptions of melancholy, is plaintive enough that scholars have identified him as a source for Shakespeare's *Othello*.

6 Edmund Wilson, in an influential Freudian reading that diagnosed Jonson as an anal-erotic type, went so far as to claim that he is "sometimes disgusting to such a degree that he makes one sympathetic with the Puritans in their efforts to clean up the theater" (*The Triple Thinkers* 216).

7 Koslow, "Humanist Schooling and Jonson's 'Poetaster'" 120. On Jonson's stoic ethics, see Robert C. Evans, *Jonson, Lipsius, and the Politics of Renaissance Stoicism*, and Maus, *Ben Jonson and the Roman Frame of Mind*.

8 Koslow, "Humanist Schooling" 123. For materialist interpretations of Jonson, see Paster, *The Body Embarrassed*, especially 34–9 and 143–62; Patricia Fumerton, *Cultural Aesthetics*, especially 111–67; Boehrer, *The Fury of Men's Gullets*.

9 For more on Jonson's education and his connections to humanism, see McCanles, *Jonsonian Discriminations*, and Young, "Ben Jonson and Learning."

10 On the gendering of the humours, see Paster, *The Body Embarrassed*.

11 Gender was primarily a grammatical term in the Renaissance, and only began to refer to men or women as a group in the sixteenth century. Jonson's most significant engagement with grammatical gender is the 1609 comedy *Epicoene*. The title character, a cross-dressed boy, is named for the "epicene" gender, one of seven Latin genders typically enumerated in early modern grammar (the others are the masculine, the feminine, the neuter, the commune of two, the commune of three, and the doubtful). Epicene nouns have a fixed gender but may be used to refer to males or females: *aquila*, a feminine noun that can be applied to both male and female eagles, is a commonly cited example. The use of the term contributes to the tension in the play between sexual licence and misogyny. On the one hand, the deployment of the grammatical term "epicene" in a play that so ostentatiously dramatizes the vicissitudes of gendered identity suggests that gender is a matter of convention in grammar and society alike, an implication consistent with the play's frequent gender inversion and anarchic representation of sexuality. On the other hand, however, the play engages extensively in the misogynistic traditions of the medieval and early modern period, representing learned and vocal women as unnatural. For more on grammar and gender in *Epicoene*, see Mann, *Outlaw Rhetoric* 161–8.

12 This account of poetry may seem narrowly didactic to modern readers, but it resembles Robert Pippin's claim that literary texts "provide the best

example of what Hegel called the 'concrete universal'" (*The Persistence of Subjectivity* 266), that which straddles the line between the general and the particular. For Pippin, it is the special role of literature to narrate events and offer images which have appeal both for their irreducible particularity and for their larger significance. Citing the example of *Madame Bovary*, Pippin explains that we are enthralled by the individual details of Emma Bovary's life, which we do not take as simply symptomatic of some general state of affairs. But at the same time, we are convinced that this life has some significance beyond itself, that it speaks to our own lives, or the dawn of modernism, or the state of nineteenth-century France, or some other larger theme.

13 Shakespeare, *Hamlet* 3.1.155. For more on mirrors as objects and metaphors in the Renaissance, see Shuger, "The 'I' of the Beholder."

14 For the debate on the nature of rules in Wittgenstein, see Kripke, *Wittgenstein on Rules and Private Language*; McDowell, "Wittgenstein on Following a Rule"; Brandom, *Making It Explicit*, especially 3–66. My own perspective is indebted to Brandom.

15 On Wittgenstein's understanding of pedagogy and its importance to his larger philosophy, see Medina, "Wittgenstein's Social Naturalism."

16 Stephen Orgel discusses *Every Man Out*'s induction and Jonsonian metatheatre in his classic work *The Jonsonian Masque* 199.

17 *Every Man In His Humour* offers a simpler definition of humour in an exchange between the water-bearer Cob and the clerk Piso, focusing on the contemporary use of the term to describe affectation:

COB

> Humour? Mack, I think it be so, indeed. What is this humour? It's some rare thing, I warrant.

PISO

> Marry, I'll tell you what it is, as 'tis generally received in these days: it is a monster bred in a man by self-love and affectation, and fed by folly.
> (3.1.147–51)

18 Critics have long associated Asper and Jonson. C.H. Herford, for instance, writes in his Introduction to the play that "Asper bears an unmistakable resemblance to Jonson himself" ("Introduction to *Every Man Out of His Humour*" 92).

19 For the "art vs nature" comparison, see Jonson, "To the Memory of My Beloved." Jonson's harsher critics have dismissed him as a mere pedant. George Bernard Shaw called him a "brutish pedant" in an 1896 review of a performance of *Doctor Faustus* that savaged Elizabethan drama ("The Spacious Times" 39). In diagnosing Jonson as an "anal erotic type," Wilson quotes from a psychoanalytic textbook to claim that Jonson was primarily

defined by "orderliness … in an over-accentuated form, pedantry." See Wilson, *The Triple Thinkers* 218.

20 For more on Jonson's perspective on custom and currency, see Hedley, *Power in Verse* 158–9.

21 Jonson's meritocratic vision of an assembly of the learned recalls Navarre's academy in the way it shifts authority from a martial aristocracy to a scholarly community. Yet for Jonson, a former soldier, the field of letters was very much like the field of battle: contentious, combative, and demanding of discipline.

22 This reconciliation of custom and learning may help explain why Jonson has been accused by hostile critics of pedantry and vulgarity in nearly equal measure.

23 The critique is a bold one in this context, as *Every Man Out* was first performed by the Lord Chamberlain's Men, who had recently performed plays like *A Midsummer Night's Dream* that closely resemble Jonson's parody. Early commentators believed the reference to the duke, the countess, and the clown indicated that Jonson had *Twelfth Night* specifically in mind, but more recent scholarship places Shakespeare's play a few years after Jonson's. The phrase *"imitatio vitae, speculum consuetudinis, imago veritatis"* is actually found in the grammarian Donatus, who attributes it to Cicero. Sidney quotes the line in the *Defence* as well.

24 Macilente's condemnation of the power of wealth to cover iniquity provides evidence of his insight and eloquence as a critic:

> Be a man ne'er so vile
> In wit, judgement, manners, or what else,
> If he can purchase but a silken cover,
> He shall not pass, but pass regarded;
> Whereas, let him be poor and meanly clad,
> Though ne'er so richly parted, you shall have
> A fellow that knows nothing but his beef,
> Or how to rinse his clammy guts in beer,
> Will take him by the shoulders or the throat
> And kick him down the stairs. Such is the state
> Of virtue in bad clothes.   (3.3.11–21)

His words anticipate a celebrated speech in *King Lear*:

> Through tattered clothes small vices do appear;
> Robes and furred gowns hide all. Plate sin with gold,
> And the strong lance of justice hurtless breaks:
> Arm it in rags, a pigmy's straw does pierce it.   (4.6.160–3)

25 On the Horatian and Juvenalian modes in Jonson, see Moul, *Jonson, Horace, and the Classical Tradition*, especially 94–134, and Dutton, "Jonson's Satiric Style."

Conclusion

1 Here I would also like to mention Judith Owens's book *Emotional Settings*, which similarly stages a recuperative reading of early modern pedagogy. I thank Judith Owens for granting me permission to cite this forthcoming book.
2 For more on Montaigne's early life and education, see Frame, *Montaigne*.
3 All quotations in English are from Screech's translation, *The Complete Essays*, to which I have made a few very minor amendments. Quotations of Montaigne's French are from *Les Essais*.
4 Montaigne, *Essays* 130. Jonathan Dollimore has compared this understanding of custom to the modern concept of ideology. See *Radical Tragedy*.

Works Cited

Agamben, Giorgio. "Philosophy and Linguistics." Translated by Daniel Heller-Roazen. In *Potentialities: Collected Essays in Philosophy*, 62–76. Stanford: Stanford University Press, 1999.

Altman, Joel B. *The Tudor Play of Mind: Rhetorical Inquiry and the Development of Elizabethan Drama*. Berkeley: University of California Press, 1978.

Anders, Heinrich. *Shakespeare's Books: A Dissertation on Shakespeare's Reading and the Immediate Sources of His Works*. Berlin: Georg Keimer, 1904.

Arab, Ronda, Michelle Dowd, and Adam Zucker, editors. *Historical Affect and the Early Modern Theater*. New York: Routledge, 2015.

Archer, John Michael. *Citizen Shakespeare: Freemen and Aliens in the Language of the Plays*. New York: Palgrave, 2004.

Arikha, Noga. *Passions and Tempers: A History of the Humours*. New York: HarperCollins, 2007.

Aristotle. *The Art of Rhetoric*. Translated by John Henry Freese. Cambridge, MA: Harvard University Press, 1994.

– *Categories, on Interpretation, Prior Analytics*. Translated by H.P. Cooke and Hugh Tredennick. Cambridge, MA: Harvard University Press, 1938.

– *On the Soul, Parva Naturalia, on Breath*. Translated by W.S. Hett. Cambridge, MA: Harvard University Press, 1957.

Ascham, Roger. *The Scholemaster*. London, 1571.

Auerbach, Erich. "*Passio* as Passion." Translated by Martin Elsky. *Criticism* 43 (2001): 288–308.

Augustine. *The Free Choice of Will*. Translated by Robert P. Russell. In *The Fathers of the Church*, vol. 59, 181–7. Washington, DC: Catholic University of America Press, 1968.

Austin, J.L. *How to Do Things with Words*. Edited by J.O. Urmson and Marina Sbisà. Cambridge, MA: Harvard University Press, 1975.

Bacon, Francis. *The Advancement of Learning*. In *The Major Works*, edited by Brian Vickers, 120–299. Oxford: Oxford University Press, 2002.

Bailey, Amanda, and Mario DiGangi, editors. *Affect Theory and Early Modern Texts: Politics, Ecologies, and Form*. New York: Palgrave, 2017.

Baldwin, T.W. *William Shakespere's Petty School*. Urbana: University of Illinois Press, 1943.

– *William Shakespere's Smal Latine and Lesse Greke*. Urbana: University of Illinois Press, 1944.

Barber, C.L. *Shakespeare's Festive Comedy: A Study of Dramatic Form and Its Relation to Social Custom*. Princeton: Princeton University Press, 1959.

Barclay, Katie. "Performance and Performativity." In *Early Modern Emotions: An Introduction*, edited by Susan Broomhall, 14–17. New York: Routledge, 2017.

Barker, Francis. *The Tremulous Private Body*. London: Methuen, 1984.

Beckwith, Sarah. *Shakespeare and the Grammar of Forgiveness*. Ithaca: Cornell University Press, 2012.

Bellucci, Francesco. "Wittgenstein's Grammar of Emotions." *RIFL* 7 (2013): 3–17.

Berry, Ralph. "The Words of Mercury." *Shakespeare Survey* 22 (1969): 69–77.

Boehrer, Bruce. *The Fury of Men's Gullets: Ben Jonson and the Digestive Canal*. Philadelphia: University of Pennsylvania Press, 1997.

Bound Alberti, Fay. *This Mortal Coil: The Human Body in History and Culture*. Oxford: Oxford University Press, 2016.

Bourdieu, Pierre. *The Logic of Practice*. Translated by Richard Nice. Stanford: Stanford University Press, 1990.

– *Outline of a Theory of Practice*. Translated by Richard Nice. Cambridge: Cambridge University Press, 2017.

Bradley, A.C. *Shakespearean Tragedy: Lectures on "Hamlet," "Othello," "King Lear," and "Macbeth."* New York: Palgrave Macmillan, 2007.

Brandom, Robert. *Making It Explicit: Reasoning, Representing, and Discursive Commitment*. Cambridge, MA: Harvard University Press, 1998.

Brinkema, Eugenie. *The Forms of the Affects*. Durham, NC: Duke University Press, 2014.

Brinsley, John. *Ludus Literarius, or the Grammar Schoole*. London, 1612.

– *The Posing of the Parts*. London, 1615.

Bruster, Douglas. *To Be or Not to Be*. New York: Continuum, 2007.

Burckhardt, Jacob. *The Civilization of the Renaissance in Italy*. Translated by S.G.C. Middlemore. New York: Penguin, 1990.

Burton, Robert. *The Anatomy of Melancholy*. Vol. 1. Edited by Thomas C. Faulkner, Nicolas K. Kiessling, and Rhonda L. Blair. Oxford: Clarendon Press, 1989.

Bushnell, Rebecca. *A Culture of Teaching: Early Modern Humanism in Theory and Practice*. Ithaca: Cornell University Press, 1996.

Calderwood, James L. "*Love's Labour's Lost*: A Wantoning with Words." *SEL: Studies in English Literature, 1500–1900* 5 (1965): 317–32.

Callaghan, Dympna. *Shakespeare without Women: Representing Gender and Race on the Early Modern Stage*. New York: Routledge, 2000.

Carroll, William C. *The Great Feast of Language in "Love's Labour's Lost."* Princeton: Princeton University Press, 1976.

Cassirer, Ernst. *The Individual and the Cosmos in Renaissance Philosophy*. Translated by Mario Domandi. Chicago: University of Chicago Press, 2010.

Castiglione, Baldassare. *The Book of the Courtier*. Translated by George Bull. New York: Penguin, 2003.

Cave, Terence. *The Cornucopian Text: Problems in Writing in the French Renaissance*. Oxford: Clarendon Press, 1979.

Cavell, Stanley. "Passionate and Performative Utterances: Morals of Encounter." In *Contending with Stanley Cavell*, edited by Russell B. Goodman, 177–98. Oxford: Oxford University Press, 2005.

Chomsky, Noam. *Language and Mind*. New York: Harcourt Brace, 1972.

Clark, Donald Lemen. *John Milton at St. Paul's School: A Study of Ancient Rhetoric in English Renaissance Education*. New York: Columbia University Press, 1948.

Coghill, Nevill. *Shakespeare's Professional Skills*. Cambridge: Cambridge University Press, 1964.

Coleridge, Samuel Taylor. *Lectures and Notes on Shakespeare and Other English Poets*. London: George Bell and Sons, 1907.

Colet, John. *Aeditio*. London, 1534.

Corderius. *A Select Century of Corderius' Colloquies*. Translated by John Clarke. London, 1759.

Craik, Katharine, editor. *Shakespeare and Emotion*. Cambridge: Cambridge University Press, 2020.

Crampton, Georgia Ronan. *The Condition of Creatures: Suffering and Action in Chaucer and Spenser*. New Haven: Yale University Press, 1974.

Cummings, Brian. *The Literary Culture of the Reformation: Grammar and Grace*. Oxford: Oxford University Press, 2002.

Cummings, Brian, and Freya Sierhuis, editors. *Passions and Subjectivity in Early Modern Culture*. Farnham: Ashgate, 2013.

Damasio, Antonio. *Looking for Spinoza: Joy, Sorrow, and the Feeling Brain*. Orlando: Harcourt, 2003.

Daniel, Drew. *The Melancholy Assemblage: Affect and Epistemology in the English Renaissance*. New York: Fordham University Press, 2013.

Danner, Bruce. "Speaking Daggers." *Shakespeare Quarterly* 54 (2003): 29–62.

Dash, Irene G. *Wooing, Wedding, and Power: Women in Shakespeare's Plays*. New York: Columbia University Press, 1981.

de Grazia, Margreta. *"Hamlet" without Hamlet*. Cambridge: Cambridge University Press, 2007.

– "Lost Potential in Grammar and Nature: Sidney's *Astrophil and Stella.*" *SEL: Studies in English Literature, 1500–1900* 21 (1981): 21–35.

Deleuze, Gilles, and Félix Guattari. *A Thousand Plateaus.* Translated by Brian Massumi. New York: Continuum, 2004.

DiGangi, Mario. "Affective Entanglements and Alternative Histories." In *Affect Theory and Early Modern Texts: Politics, Ecologies, and Form,* edited by Amanda Bailey and Mario DiGangi, 47–66. New York: Palgrave, 2017.

Dilthey, Wilhelm. *Ideas about a Descriptive and Analytic Psychology.* In *Selected Writings,* edited by H.P. Rickman. Cambridge: Cambridge University Press, 1976.

Dixon, Thomas. *From Passions to Emotions: The Creation of a Secular Psychological Category.* Cambridge: Cambridge University Press, 2006.

Dollimore, Jonathan. *Radical Tragedy: Religion, Ideology and Power in the Drama of Shakespeare and His Contemporaries.* Durham, NC: Duke University Press, 2003.

Dolven, Jeff. *Scenes of Instruction in Renaissance Romance.* Chicago: University of Chicago Press, 2007.

Donaldson, Ian. *Ben Jonson: A Life.* Oxford: Oxford University Press, 2012.

Dutton, Richard. "Jonson's Satiric Style." In *The Cambridge Companion to Ben Jonson,* edited by Richard Harp and Stanley Stewart, 58–71. Cambridge: Cambridge University Press, 2000.

Elam, Keir. *Shakespeare's Universe of Discourse: Language-Games in the Comedies.* Cambridge: Cambridge University Press, 1984.

Empson, William. *Essays on Shakespeare.* Edited by David B. Pirie. Cambridge: Cambridge University Press, 1986.

Enterline, Lynn. "Rhetoric, Discipline, and the Theatricality of Everyday Life in Elizabethan Grammar Schools." In *From Performance to Print in Shakespeare's England,* edited by Peter Holland and Stephen Orgel, 173–90. New York: Palgrave, 2006.

– *The Rhetoric of the Body from Ovid to Shakespeare.* Cambridge: Cambridge University Press, 2000.

– *Shakespeare's Schoolroom: Rhetoric, Discipline, Emotion.* Philadelphia: University of Pennsylvania Press, 2012.

Erasmus, Desiderius. *De conscribendis epistolis.* Translated by Charles Fantazzi. In *The Collected Works of Erasmus,* edited by J.K. Sowards. Toronto: University of Toronto Press, 1985.

– *De pueris insituendis.* Translated by Beert C. Verstraete. In *The Collected Works of Erasmus,* edited by J.K. Sowards, 291–347. Toronto: University of Toronto Press, 1985.

– *De ratione studii.* Translated by William Harrison Woodward. In William Harrison Woodward, *Desiderius Erasmus Concerning the Aim and Method of Education,* 161–78. Cambridge: Cambridge University Press, 1904.

– *The Epistles of Erasmus: From His Earliest Letters to His Fifty-First Year.* Translated by Francis Morgan Nichols. New York: Longmans, Green, and Co., 1901.

Evans, Malcolm. "Deconstructing Shakespeare's Comedies." In *Alternative Shakespeares,* edited by John Drakakis, 67–94. London: Routledge, 1985.

– *Signifying Nothing: Truth's True Contents in Shakespeare's Text.* Brighton: Harvester Press, 1986.

Evans, Robert C. *Jonson, Lipsius, and the Politics of Renaissance Stoicism.* Wakefield: Longwood, 1992.

Ferguson, Margaret. "*Hamlet*: Letters and Spirits." In *Shakespeare and the Question of Theory,* edited by Patricia Parker and Geoffrey Hartman, 292–309. New York: Methuen, 1985.

Ferry, Anne. *The "Inward" Language: Sonnets of Wyatt, Sidney, Shakespeare, Donne.* Chicago: University of Chicago Press, 1983.

Floyd-Wilson, Mary. *English Ethnicity and Race in Early Modern Drama.* Cambridge: Cambridge University Press, 2003.

Floyd-Wilson, Mary, and Garrett A. Sullivan, Jr, editors. *Environment and Embodiment in Early Modern England.* New York: Palgrave, 2007.

Frame, Donald. *Montaigne: A Biography.* San Francisco: North Point Press, 1984.

Fumerton, Patricia. *Cultural Aesthetics: Renaissance Literature and the Practice of Social Ornament.* Chicago: University of Chicago Press, 1991.

Garber, Marjorie. *Shakespeare after All.* New York: Random House, 2004.

Gent, Lucy, and Nigel Llewellyn, editors. *Renaissance Bodies: The Human Figure in English Culture c. 1540–1660.* London: Reaktion, 1990.

Gil, Daniel Juan. *Before Intimacy: Asocial Sexuality in Early Modern England.* Minneapolis: University of Minnesota Press, 2005.

Glock, Hans-Johann. "Necessity and Normativity." In *The Cambridge Companion to Wittgenstein,* edited by Hans D. Sluga and David G. Stern, 198–225. Cambridge: Cambridge University Press, 1996.

– *A Wittgenstein Dictionary.* Oxford: Blackwell, 1996.

Godfrey, Robert G. "Late Mediaeval Linguistic Meta-Theory and Chomsky's Syntactic Structures." *Word* 21 (1965): 251–6.

Goethe, Johann Wolfgang von. *Wilhelm Meister's Apprenticeship.* Translated by Eric A. Blackall. Princeton: Princeton University Press, 1989.

Green, Ian. *The Christian's ABC: Catchism and Catechizing in England c. 1530–1740.* Oxford: Clarendon Press, 1996.

Greenblatt, Stephen. *Hamlet in Purgatory.* Princeton: Princeton University Press, 2001.

– "Introduction to *Hamlet*." In *The Norton Shakespeare,* edited by Walter Cohen, Stephen Greenblatt, Jean E. Howard, and Katharine Eisaman Maus. New York: Norton, 2008.

Greene, Thomas M. *"Love's Labour's Lost*: The Grace of Society." *Shakespeare Quarterly* 22 (1971): 315–28.

Grier, Miles P. "Inkface: The Slave Stigma in England's Early Imperial Imagination." In *Scripturalizing the Human: The Written as Political*, edited by Vincent Wimbush, 193–220. New York: Routledge, 2015.

Guillory, John. "'To Please the Wiser Sort': Violence and Philosophy in *Hamlet*." In *Historicism, Psychoanalysis, and Early Modern Culture*, edited by Carla Mazzio and Douglas Trevor, 82–109. New York: Routledge, 2000.

Hacker, P.M.S. *Wittgenstein: Connections and Controversies*. Oxford: Clarendon Press, 2001.

– *Wittgenstein: Meaning and Mind*. Oxford: Blackwell, 1997.

Hall, Kim F. "These Bastard Signs of Fair: Literary Whiteness in Shakespeare's Sonnets." In *Post-Colonial Shakespeares*, edited by Ania Loomba and Martin Orkin, 64–83. New York: Routledge, 1998.

– *Things of Darkness: Economies of Race and Gender in Early Modern England*. Ithaca: Cornell University Press, 1996.

Halpern, Richard. *The Poetics of Primitive Accumulation: English Renaissance Culture and the Genealogy of Capital*. Ithaca: Cornell University Press, 1991.

Harvey, Christopher. *Schola cordis*. London, 1647.

Hedley, Jane. *Power in Verse: Metaphor and Metonymy in the Renaissance Lyric*. University Park: Pennsylvania State University Press, 1988.

Heidegger, Martin. *Being and Time*. Translated by John Macquarrie and Edward Robinson. New York: Harper and Row, 1962.

– "Duns Scotus' Theory of the Categories and of Meaning." Translation by Harold Robbins. PhD Dissertation, DePaul University, 1978.

Heller-Roazen, Daniel. "Language or No Language." *Diacritics* 29 (1999): 22–39.

Herford, C.H. "Introduction to *Every Man Out of His Humour*." In *Ben Jonson: A Collection of Critical Essays*, edited by Jonas Barish, 82–93. Englewood Cliffs, NJ: Prentice Hall, 1963.

Hobgood, Allison P. *Passionate Playgoing in Early Modern England*. Cambridge: Cambridge University Press, 2014.

Höfele, Andreas. *No Hamlets: German Shakespeare from Nietzsche to Carl Schmitt*. Oxford: Oxford University Press, 2016.

Horace. *Odes and Epodes*. Translated by C.E. Bennett. Cambridge, MA: Harvard University Press, 1927.

Hunt, Richard William. *The History of Grammar in the Middle Ages: Collected Papers*. Amsterdam: John Benjamins, 1980.

James, Susan. *Passion and Action: The Emotions in Seventeenth Century Philosophy*. Oxford: Oxford University Press, 2007.

James, William. "What Is an Emotion?" *Mind* 9 (1884): 188–205.

Jewell, Helen M. *Education in Early Modern England*. New York: St Martin's Press, 1998.

Johnson, Samuel. *A Dictionary of the English Language*. Vol. 2. London, 1810.

– *Johnson on Shakespeare*. In *The Yale Edition of the Works of Samuel Johnson*, vol. 8, edited by Arthur Sherbo. New Haven: Yale University Press, 1968.

Jones, Ann Rosalind, and Peter Stallybrass. "The Politics of *Astrophil and Stella*." *SEL: Studies in English Literature, 1500–1900* 24 (1984): 53–68.

Jones, Ernest. *Hamlet and Oedipus*. London: Victor Gollancz, 1949.

Jonson, Ben. *The Cambridge Edition of the Works of Ben Jonson*. Edited by David Bevington, Martin Butler, and Ian Donaldson. Cambridge: Cambridge University Press, 2012.

– *Discoveries*. Edited by Lorna Hutson. In *The Cambridge Edition of the Works of Ben Jonson*, vol. 7, 481–596.

– "Epistle to Katherine, Lady Aubigny." *The Cambridge Edition of the Works of Ben Jonson*, vol. 5, 239–43.

– *Every Man In His Humour*. Edited by Robert Miola. Manchester: Manchester University Press, 2008.

– *Every Man Out of His Humour*. Edited by Helen Ostovich. Manchester: Manchester University Press, 2008.

– *The Forest*. Edited by Colin Burrow. In *The Cambridge Edition of the Works of Ben Jonson*, vol. 5, 199–248.

– *Hymenaei*. In *The Cambridge Edition of the Works of Ben Jonson*, vol. 2, 657–712.

– *Poetaster*. In *The Cambridge Edition of the Works of Ben Jonson*, vol. 2, 1–181.

– "To the Author." In *The Cambridge Edition of the Works of Ben Jonson*, vol. 2, 501.

– "To the Memory of My Beloved." In *The Cambridge Edition of the Works of Ben Jonson*, vol. 5, 638–42.

Kahn, Victoria, Neil Saccamano, and Daniela Coli, editors. *Politics and the Passions 1500–1800*. Princeton: Princeton University Press, 2006.

Kant, Immanuel. *The Critique of Pure Reason*. Translated by Marcus Weigelt. New York: Penguin, 2007.

Kerrigan, William. *Shakespeare's Promises*. Baltimore: Johns Hopkins University Press, 1999.

Kinney, Arthur. *Humanist Poetics: Thought, Rhetoric, and Fiction in Sixteenth-Century England*. Amherst: University of Massachusetts Press, 1986.

Knecht, Ross. "'Invaded by the World': Passion, Passivity, and the Object of Desire in Petrarch's *Rime sparse*." *Comparative Literature* 63 (2011): 235–52.

Kolentsis, Alysia. "'Grammar Rules' in the Sonnets: Sidney and Shakespeare." In *The Oxford Handbook of Shakespeare's Poetry*, edited by Jonathan Post, 168–84. Oxford: Oxford University Press, 2013.

Konstan, David. *The Emotions of the Ancient Greeks: Studies in Aristotle and Classical Literature*. Toronto: University of Toronto Press, 2006.

Koslow, Julian. "Humanist Schooling and Jonson's 'Poetaster.'" *ELH* 73 (2006): 119–59.

Kosman, L.A. "Being Properly Affected: Virtues and Feelings in Aristotle's Ethics." In *Essays on Aristotle's Ethics*, edited by Amélie Oksenberg Rorty, 103–16. Berkeley: University of California Press, 1980.

Kripke, Saul. *Wittgenstein on Rules and Private Language: An Elementary Exposition*. Cambridge, MA: Harvard University Press, 1982.

Landreth, David. "Once More into the Preech: The Merry Wives' English Pedagogy." *Shakespeare Quarterly* 55 (2004): 420–49.

Leroy, Louis. *Of the Interchangeable Course or Variety of Things*. Translated by R.A. London, 1594.

Leys, Ruth. *The Ascent of Affect: Genealogy and Critique*. Chicago: University of Chicago Press, 2017.

– "The Turn to Affect: A Critique." *Critical Inquiry* 37 (2011): 434–72.

Lily, William. *A Short Introduction of Grammar*. London, 1567.

Loxley, James, and Mark Ronson. *Shakespeare, Jonson, and the Claims of the Performative*. New York: Routledge, 2013.

Macfarlane, Alan. *Marriage and Love in England: Modes of Reproduction 1300–1840*. Oxford: Blackwell, 1986.

Mack, Maynard. "The World of *Hamlet*." *Yale Review* 41 (1952): 502–23.

Mack, Peter. *Elizabethan Rhetoric: Theory and Practice*. Cambridge: Cambridge University Press, 2002.

– *A History of Renaissance Rhetoric: 1380–1620*. Oxford: Oxford University Press, 2011.

Maclean, Ian. *Meaning and Interpretation in the Renaissance: The Case of Law*. Cambridge: Cambridge University Press, 1992.

Magnusson, Lynne. "A Play of Modals: Grammar and Potential Action in Early Shakespeare." *Shakespeare Survey* 62 (2009): 69–80.

Mann, Jenny C. *Outlaw Rhetoric: Figuring Vernacular Eloquence in Shakespeare's England*. Ithaca: Cornell University Press, 2012.

Marlowe, Christopher. *The Complete Plays*. Edited by J.B. Steane. New York: Penguin, 1986.

Massumi, Brian. "The Autonomy of Affect." *Cultural Critique* 31 (1995): 83–109.

– *The Politics of Affect*. Cambridge: Polity, 2015.

Maus, Katharine Eisaman. *Ben Jonson and the Roman Frame of Mind*. Princeton: Princeton University Press, 1984.

– *Inwardness and Theater in the English Renaissance*. Chicago: University of Chicago Press, 1995.

– "Transfer of Title in *Love's Labor's Lost*: Language, Individualism, Gender." In *Shakespeare Left and Right*, edited by Ivo Kamps, 205–23. New York: Routledge, 1991.

Mazzio, Carla. *The Inarticulate Renaissance: Language Trouble in an Age of Eloquence*. Philadelphia: University of Pennsylvania Press, 2009.

McCanles, Michael. *Jonsonian Discriminations: The Humanist Poet and the Praise of True Nobility*. Toronto: University of Toronto Press, 1992.

McDonald, Russ. *Shakespeare and the Arts of Language*. Oxford: Oxford University Press, 2002.

McDowell, John. "Wittgenstein on Following a Rule." *Synthese* 58 (1984): 325–64.

McElroy, Davis D. "'To Be or Not to Be' – Is That the Question?" *College English* 25 (1964): 543–5.

Medina, José. "Wittgenstein's Social Naturalism: The Idea of '*Second Nature*' after the *Philosophical Investigations*." In *The Third Wittgenstein*, edited by Danièle Moyal-Sharrock. Farnham: Ashgate, 2004.

Miller, Jacqueline T. "The Passion Signified: Imitation and the Construction of Emotions in Sidney and Wroth." *Criticism* 43 (2001): 407–21.

Moi, Toril. *Revolution of the Ordinary: Literary Studies after Wittgenstein, Austin, and Cavell*. Chicago: University of Chicago Press, 2017.

Moncrief, Kathryn M. "'Teach us, sweet madam': Masculinity, Femininity, and Gendered Instruction in *Love's Labor's Lost*." In *Performing Pedagogy in Early Modern England: Gender, Instruction, and Performance*, edited by Kathryn M. Moncrief and Kathryn R. McPherson, 113–30. Farnham: Ashgate, 2011.

Monfasani, John. "Was Lorenzo Valla an Ordinary Language Philosopher?" *Journal of the History of Ideas* 50 (1989): 309–23.

Monk, Ray. *Ludwig Wittgenstein: The Duty of Genius*. New York: Macmillan, 1990.

Montaigne, Michel de. *The Complete Essays*. Translated by M.A. Screech. New York: Penguin, 2003.

– *Les Essais*. Edited by Pierre Villey and V.L. Saulnier. Paris: Presses Universitaires de France, 1924.

Moul, Victoria. *Jonson, Horace, and the Classical Tradition*. Cambridge: Cambridge University Press, 2000.

Moyal-Sharrock, Danièle. *The Third Wittgenstein*. Farnham: Ashgate, 2004.

Mukherji, Subha, and Tim Stuart-Buttle, editors. *Literature, Belief and Knowledge in Early Modern England: Knowing Faith*. New York: Palgrave, 2018.

Mulcaster, Richard. *First Part of the Elementarie*. London, 1582.

Nauta, Lodi. *In Defense of Common Sense: Lorenzo Valla's Humanist Critique of Scholastic Philosophy*. Cambridge, MA: Harvard University Press, 2009.

Noë, Alva. *Out of Our Heads: Why You Are Not Your Brain, and Other Lessons from the Biology of Consciousness*. New York: Hill and Wang, 2009.

Ong, Walter J. "Latin Language Study as a Renaissance Puberty Rite." *Studies in Philology* 56 (1959): 103–24.

Orgel, Stephen. *The Jonsonian Masque*. Cambridge, MA: Harvard University Press, 1967.

Orme, Nicholas. *Education and Society in Renaissance England*. London: Hambledon Press, 1989.

– *English Schools in the Middle Ages*. London: Methuen, 1973.

Ortner, Sherry B. "Theory in Anthropology since the Sixties." *Comparative Studies in Society and History* 26 (1984): 126–66.

Owens, Judith. *Emotional Settings: "Hamlet," "The Faerie Queene," "Arcadia," and Early-Modern Pedagogical Culture*. New York: Palgrave, forthcoming 2021.

Palmer, F.R. *Mood and Modality*. Cambridge: Cambridge University Press, 1986.

Parker, Patricia. *Shakespeare from the Margins*. Chicago: University of Chicago Press, 1996.

Paster, Gail Kern. "The Body and Its Passions." *Shakespeare Studies* 29 (2001): 44–50.

– *The Body Embarrassed: Drama and the Disciplines of Shame in Early Modern England*. Ithaca: Cornell University Press, 1993.

– *Humoring the Body: Emotions and the Shakespearean Stage*. Chicago: University of Chicago Press, 2004.

Paster, Gail Kern, Katherine Rowe, and Mary Floyd-Wilson, editors. *Reading the Early Modern Passions: Essays in the Cultural History of Emotion*. Philadelphia: University of Pennsylvania Press, 2004.

Paterson, John. "The Word in *Hamlet*." *Shakespeare Quarterly* 2 (1951): 47–55.

Peters, F.E. *Greek Philosophical Terms: A Historical Lexicon*. New York: New York University Press, 1967.

Petrarch. *The Tryumphes of Fraunces Petrarcke*. Translated by Henry Parker, Lord Morley. London, 1555.

Petronella, Vincent F. "Hamlet's 'To Be or Not to Be' Soliloquy: Once More into the Breach." *Studies in Philology* 71 (1974): 72–88.

Pinborg, Jan. "Speculative Grammar." In *The Cambridge History of Later Medieval Philosophy: From the Rediscovery of Aristotle to the Disintegration of Scholasticism 1100–1600*, edited by Anthony Kenny, Norman Kretzmann, Jan Pinborg, and Eleonore Stump, 254–70. Cambridge: Cambridge University Press, 1982.

Pippin, Robert. *The Persistence of Subjectivity: On the Kantian Aftermath*. Cambridge: Cambridge University Press, 2005.

Plato. *Cratylus, Parmenides, Greater Hippias, Lesser Hippias*. Translated by H.N. Fowler. Cambridge, MA: Harvard University Press, 1939.

Priscian. *Excerptiones de Prisciano*. Edited by David W. Porter. Cambridge: D.S. Brewer, 2002.

Reddy, William M. *The Navigation of Feeling: A Framework for the History of Emotions*. Cambridge: Cambridge University Press, 2001.

Robins, R.H. *Ancient and Medieval Grammatical Theory in Europe*. London: Bell, 1951.

Robins, Spencer. "Wittgenstein, Schoolteacher." *Paris Review*, 5 March 2015.

Ronson, Mark, and James Loxley. *Shakespeare, Jonson, and the Claims of the Performative*. New York: Routledge, 2013.

Rorty, Richard. *Philosophy and the Mirror of Nature*. Princeton: Princeton University Press, 1979.

Rosenfeld, Colleen Ruth. "Poetry and the Potential Mood: The Counterfactual Form of Ben Jonson's 'To Fine Lady Would-Be.'" *Modern Philology* 112 (2014): 336–57.

Ruck, Carl A.P. *Latin: A Concise Structural Course*. Lanham, MD: University Press of America, 1987.

Sanchez, Melissa E. "'In my Selfe the Smart I Try': Female Promiscuity in *Astrophil and Stella*." *ELH* 80 (2013): 1–27.

Schalkwyk, David. "Fiction as 'Grammatical' Investigation: A Wittgensteinian Account." *Journal of Aesthetics and Art Criticism* 53 (1995): 287–98.

– *Shakespeare, Love and Language*. Cambridge: Cambridge University Press, 2018.

– *Speech and Performance in Shakespeare's Sonnets and Plays*. Cambridge: Cambridge University Press, 2002.

Schatzki, Theodore R. *The Site of the Social: A Philosophical Account of the Constitution of Social Life and Change*. University Park: Pennsylvania State University Press, 2002.

– *Social Practices: A Wittgensteinian Approach to Human Activity and the Social*. Cambridge: Cambridge University Press, 1996.

– "Wittgenstein + Heidegger on the Stream of Life." *Inquiry* 36 (2008): 307–28.

Scheer, Monique. "Are Emotions a Kind of Practice (And Is That What Makes Them Have a History?): A Bourdieuian Approach to Understanding Emotion." *History and Theory* 51 (2012): 193–220.

Scherer, Klaus R., Angela Schorr, and Tom Johnstone, editors. *Appraisal Processes in Emotion: Theory, Methods, Research*. Oxford: Oxford University Press, 2001.

Schoenfeldt, Michael C. *Bodies and Selves in Early Modern England: Physiology and Inwardness in Spenser, Shakespeare, Herbert, and Milton*. Cambridge: Cambridge University Press, 1999.

Scholz, Bernard F. "Religious Meditations on the Heart: Three Seventeenth Century Variations." In *The Arts and the Cultural Heritage of Martin Luther*. Copenhagen: Museum Tusculanum Press, 2003.

Sedgwick, Eve Kosofsky. *Touching Feeling: Affect, Pedagogy, Performativity*. Durham, NC: Duke University Press, 2003.

Seneca. *Epistles 66–92*. Translated by Richard M. Gummere. Cambridge, MA: Harvard University Press, 1920.

Shakespeare, William. *As You Like It*. Edited by Juliet Dusinberre. London: Bloomsbury, 2013.

– *Coriolanus*. Edited by Peter Holland. London: Bloomsbury, 2013.
– *Hamlet*. Edited by Harold Jenkins. New York: Methuen, 1982.
– *King Henry IV, Part Two*. Edited by A.R. Humphreys. London: Methuen, 1966.
– *King Lear*. Edited by R.A. Foakes. London: Methuen, 1997.
– *Love's Labour's Lost*. Edited by H.R. Woudhuysen. London: Methuen, 1998.
– *The Merchant of Venice*. Edited by John Drakakis. London: Bloomsbury, 2014.
– *The Merry Wives of Windsor*. Edited by H.J. Oliver. London: Methuen, 1971.
– *Much Ado about Nothing*. Edited by Claire McEachern. London: Cengage, 2006.
– *Richard III*. Edited by James R. Siemon. London: Methuen, 2009.
– *Romeo and Juliet*. Edited by René Weis. London: Methuen, 2012.
– *Shakespeare's Poems*. Edited by Katherine Duncan-Jones and H.R. Woudhuysen. London: Thomson, 2007.
– *Shakespeare's Sonnets*. Edited by Katherine Duncan-Jones. London: Methuen, 2010.
– *Titus Andronicus*. Edited by Jonathan Bate. London: Thomson, 2006.
– *Troilus and Cressida*. Edited by Kenneth Palmer. London: Methuen, 1982.
Shaw, George Bernard. "The Spacious Times." In *Dramatic Opinions and Essays*, 36–43. New York: Brentano's, 1906.
Shouse, Eric. "Affect, Feeling, Emotion." *M/C Journal* 8 (2005).
Shuger, Debora. "The 'I' of the Beholder: Renaissance Mirrors and the Reflexive Mind." In *Renaissance Culture and the Everyday*, edited by Patricia Fumerton and Simon Hunt, 21–41. Philadelphia: University of Pennsylvania Press, 1999.
Sidney, Philip. *The Countess of Pembroke's Arcadia*. New York: Penguin, 1987.
– *The Defence of Poesy*. In *The Major Works*, 212–50.
– "The Lady of May." In *The Major Works*, 5–13.
– *The Major Works*. Edited by Katherine Duncan-Jones. Oxford: Oxford University Press, 2008.
– *The Poems of Sir Philip Sidney*. Edited by W.A. Ringler. Oxford: Oxford University Press, 1962.
Sinfield, Alan. "Astrophil's Self-Deception." *Essays in Criticism* 28 (1978): 1–18.
– *Literature in Protestant England, 1560–1660*. New York: Routledge, 2009.
Smith, Bruce R. *The Acoustic World of Early Modern England: Attending to the "O" Factor*. Chicago: University of Chicago Press, 1999.
– "Introduction to 'Forum: Body Work.'" *Shakespeare Studies* 29 (2001): 19–26.
– *The Key of Green: Passion and Perception in Renaissance Culture*. Chicago: University of Chicago Press, 2009.
Smith, Hallett. *Elizabethan Poetry: A Study in Conventions, Meaning, and Expression*. Cambridge, MA: Harvard University Press, 1952.

Solomon, Robert C. *The Passions: Emotions and the Meaning of Life*. New York: Doubleday, 1976.

Stallybrass, Peter, Roger Chartier, J. Franklin Mowery, and Heather Wolfe. "Hamlet's Tables and the Technologies of Writing in Renaissance England." *Shakespeare Quarterly* 55 (2004): 379–419.

Stewart, Alan. *Close Readers: Humanism and Sodomy in Early Modern England*. Princeton: Princeton University Press, 1997.

Strycharski, Andrew. "Literacy, Education, and Affect in *Astrophil and Stella*." *SEL: Studies in English Literature, 1500–1900* 48 (2008): 45–63.

Sullivan, Erin. *Beyond Melancholy: Sadness and Selfhood in Renaissance England*. Oxford: Oxford University Press, 2016.

Sullivan, Erin, and Richard Meek, editors. *The Renaissance of Emotion: Understanding Affect in Shakespeare and His Contemporaries*. Manchester: Manchester University Press, 2015.

ter Hark, Michael. "'Patterns of Life': A Third Wittgensteinian Concept." In *The Third Wittgenstein*, edited by Danièle Moyal-Sharrock, 125–44. Farnham: Ashgate, 2004.

Thomas of Erfurt. *Grammatica speculativa*. Translated by G.L. Bursill-Hall. London: Longman, 1972.

Thrax, Dionysios. *The Grammar of Dionysios Thrax*. Translated by Thomas Davidson. St Louis: R.P. Studley Co., 1874.

Tilmouth, Christopher. *Passion's Triumph over Reason: A History of the Moral Imagination from Spenser to Rochester*. Oxford: Oxford University Press, 2007.

Trevor, Douglas. *The Poetics of Melancholy in Early Modern England*. Cambridge: Cambridge University Press, 2004.

Tribble, Evelyn. *Cognition in the Globe: Attention and Memory in Shakespeare's Theatre*. New York: Palgrave, 2011.

Tribble, Evelyn, and John Sutton. "Cognitive Ecology as a Framework for Shakespearean Studies." *Shakespeare Studies* 39 (2011): 94–103.

Trigg, Stephanie. "Affect Theory." In *Early Modern Emotions: An Introduction*, edited by Susan Broomhall, 10–13. New York: Routledge, 2017.

Twyne, Brian. "Corpus Christi College, Oxford, Ms 263." In *Sidney: The Critical Heritage*, edited by Martin Garrett, 158–65. New York: Routledge, 1996.

Udall, Nicholas. *Ralph Roister Doister*. In *Five Pre-Shakespearean Comedies*, edited by Frederick S. Boas, 113–206. Oxford: Oxford University Press, 1934.

Valla, Lorenzo. *Dialectical Disputations*. Translated by Brian P. Copenhaver and Lodi Nauta. Cambridge, MA: Harvard University Press, 2012.

– "In Praise of St. Thomas Aquinas." Translated by M. Esther Hanley. In *Renaissance Philosophy: New Translations*, edited by Leonard A. Kennedy, 17–27. Paris: Mouton, 1973.

Vives, Juan Luis. *The Passions of the Soul in General: The Third Book of De Anima et Vita*. Translated by Carlos G. Noreña. Lewiston: Edwin Mellen Press, 1990.

Wallace, Andrew. *Virgil's Schoolboys: The Poetics of Pedagogy in Early Modern England*. Oxford: Oxford University Press, 2010.

Warley, Christopher. *Sonnet Sequences and Social Distinction in Renaissance England*. Cambridge: Cambridge University Press, 2005.

Waswo, Richard. *Language and Meaning in the Renaissance*. Princeton: Princeton University Press, 1987.

Weimann, Robert. "Mimesis in *Hamlet*." In *Shakespeare and the Question of Theory*, edited by Patricia Parker and Geoffrey Hartman, 275–91. New York: Methuen, 1985.

Williams, Raymond. *The Long Revolution*. Cardigan: Parthian Books, 1961.

Wilson, Edmund. *The Triple Thinkers: Twelve Essays on Literary Subjects*. Oxford: Oxford University Press, 1948.

Wittgenstein, Ludwig. *Culture and Value*. Translated by Peter Winch. Oxford: Blackwell, 1980.

– *Last Writings on the Philosophy of Psychology*. Vol. 1. Translated by C.G. Luckhardt and Maximilian A.E. Aue. Oxford: Blackwell, 1982.

– *Philosophical Grammar*. Translated by Anthony Kenny. Oxford: Blackwell, 1974.

– *Philosophical Investigations*. Translated by P.M.S. Hacker, G.E.M. Anscombe, and Joachim Schulte. West Sussex: Wiley-Blackwell, 2009.

– *Remarks on the Foundations of Mathematics*. Translated by G.E.M. Anscombe. Oxford: Blackwell, 1978.

– *Remarks on the Philosophy of Psychology*. Vol. 1. Translated by G.E.M. Anscombe. Oxford: Blackwell, 1980.

– *Remarks on the Philosophy of Psychology*. Vol. 2. Edited by G.H. Von Wright and Heikki Nyman, translated by C.G. Luckhardt and M.A.E. Aue. Oxford: Blackwell, 1980.

– *Tractatus Logico-Philosophicus*. Translated by C.K. Ogden. In *Major Works*, 1–84. New York: HarperCollins, 2009.

– *Zettel*. Translated by G.E.M. Anscombe. Berkeley: University of California Press, 2007.

Wright, Thomas. *The Passions of the Minde in General*. London, 1604.

Young, R.V. "Ben Jonson and Learning." In *The Cambridge Companion to Ben Jonson*, edited by Richard Harp and Stanley Stewart, 43–57. Cambridge: Cambridge University Press, 2000.

Index